'*Why Read Ogden?* is a compilation of papers that offers a scholarly assessment of Thomas Ogden's contributions to psychoanalysis in many aspects and through different angles. It is written and edited by leading Brazilian academics and psychoanalysts and addresses not only Ogden's work, but also the way through which he reads classic authors of psychoanalysis such as Freud, Klein, Bion and Winnicott. Ogden's writing never tries to merely explain a concept and never seeks to be revered: he invites the reader to think alongside him and reinvent psychoanalysis as a whole for him or herself. I was going to say that Ogden's work is vast, but it would be more accurate to say that the experience of being in the world with someone else, of living a shared story in a consulting room, is vast. Ogden is an explorer of this vastness.'

Elias Mallet da Rocha Barros *is a training and supervising analyst and docent at the Brazilian Psychoanalytic Society of São Paulo (SBPSP) and a fellow of the British Psychoanalytic Society and Institute.*

I0094964

Why Read Ogden? The Importance of Thomas Ogden's Work for Contemporary Psychoanalysis

Why Read Ogden? explores the importance of Thomas Ogden's work to contemporary psychoanalysis, both as an interpreter of classic psychoanalytic thinkers and as a new and original theorist and clinician in his own right.

Ogden writes about the literary genre of psychoanalytic writing, emphasising the amalgamation of theoretical and clinical writing with the author's personality. Ogden also considers psychoanalytic writing a form of thinking: We do not write what we think, but we are thinking something unprecedented in writing. Inspired by Ogden's proposal of a transitive and creative reading, which the authors show him to demonstrate in his own writing about Freud, Klein, Bion and Winnicott, this book takes as its organising principle the question of how Ogden's texts resonate with them personally. Ogden is regarded as one of the most important and influential living psychoanalysts, and this book addresses the lack of attention given to summarising and examining his key contributions.

This book will be essential reading for psychoanalysts and psychotherapists, in practice and in training, who wish to gain a comprehensive understanding of Ogden's work.

Marina F. R. Ribeiro, PhD, is a psychoanalyst, associate professor and research supervisor and advisor for Master's and PhD students in the Clinical Psychology Postgraduate Program at the University of São Paulo (USP). She is also the author of several books and papers and most recently co-authored *Reading Bion's Transformation* (2024).

Why Read Ogden? The Importance of Thomas Ogden's Work for Contemporary Psychoanalysis

Edited by Marina F. R. Ribeiro

Routledge
Taylor & Francis Group

LONDON AND NEW YORK

Designed cover image: © Sandra Ogden

First English edition published 2025
by Routledge
4 Park Square, Milton Park, Abingdon, Oxon OX14 4RN

and by Routledge
605 Third Avenue, New York, NY 10158

Routledge is an imprint of the Taylor & Francis Group, an informa business

© 2025 selection and editorial matter, Marina F. R. Ribeiro; individual chapters, the contributors

The right of Marina F. R. Ribeiro to be identified as the author of the editorial material, and of the authors for their individual chapters, has been asserted in accordance with sections 77 and 78 of the Copyright, Designs and Patents Act 1988.

Authorised translation from the Portuguese language edition, *Por que Ogden?*, published by Zagodoni Editora.

Trademark notice: Product or corporate names may be trademarks or registered trademarks, and are used only for identification and explanation without intent to infringe.

British Library Cataloguing-in-Publication Data
A catalogue record for this book is available from the British Library

ISBN: 9781032729480 (hbk)
ISBN: 9781032729466 (pbk)
ISBN: 9781003423188 (ebk)

DOI: 10.4324/9781003423188

Typeset in Optima
by Newgen Publishing UK

We are grateful to Thomas H. Ogden for his profoundly inspiring writings, which resonate with countless others.

Contents

Contributors

Ana Fátima Aguiar is a psychologist and psychoanalyst, with a master's degree in Clinical Psychology from the Institute of Psychology at the University of São Paulo (IPUSP). She is a researcher/collaborator at LIPSIC (Interinstitutional Laboratory for Studies of Intersubjectivity and Contemporary Psychoanalysis), and organizer editor of the book *Psychology on the Scene: Cinema, life and subjectivity* (2021), an author of chapters in the books (in press) *Why Read Ogden?* (Zagadoni, 2023), *Vast Emotions and Imperfect Thoughts: Bionian dialogues* (Blucher, 2023) and *Presences and Virtualities: Psychoanalytic perspectives* (Pedro and João, 2023).

Alberto Rocha Barros holds a bachelor's degree and a PhD in Philosophy from the University of São Paulo (USP) Brazil and is an affiliated member of the Brazilian Psychoanalytic Society of São Paulo (SBPSP). He is co-director of the collection "Kultur" of Escuta Publishing House, where he has edited several books by international authors within the field of Contemporary Psychoanalysis, especially the work of Thomas H. Ogden.

Idete Zimerman Bizzi is a psychiatrist, psychoanalyst, full member of the Porto Alegre Psychoanalytic Society (SPPA), and professor of the Institute of Psychoanalysis, SPPA; International Psychoanalytical Association (IPA) member. She is professor and supervisor of the Analytically Oriented Psychotherapy Program of Centro de Estudos Luis Guedes, Department of Psychiatry and Legal Medicine, Federal University of Rio Grande do Sul; guest supervisor of Analytically Oriented Psychotherapy at the Psychiatry Residency Program of Hospital Materno Infantil Presidente Vargas, Federal University of Health Sciences of Porto Alegre; guest supervisor of Psychiatry Residency Program in Psychotherapy of Hospital de Clínicas de Porto Alegre, Federal University of Rio Grande do Sul.

Érico Bruno Viana Campos is a psychologist, with master's and doctoral degrees in Psychology from the Institute of Psychology at the University of São Paulo (IPUSP), where he also had a post-doctoral internship at the Department of Learning, Development, and Personality Psychology. He is currently assistant professor at the Department of Psychology from the

Faculty of Sciences (FC) of São Paulo State University (UNESP) in Bauru. He is accredited as an effective collaborator in the Postgraduate Program in Developmental and Personality Psychology at the FC-UNESP, and a member of Working Groups on National Postgraduate and Research Associations: Psychoanalysis and Expanded Clinical, at ANPEPP (Psychology), and Philosophy and Psychoanalysis, at ANPOF (Philosophy). He is also the recipient of a CNPq Research Productivity Scholarship Grant.

Fátima Flórido Cesar is a psychoanalyst, with PhD and post-doctoral degrees from Pontifícia Universidade Católica de São Paulo (PUCSP) (2018) and the Institute of Psychology at the University of São Paulo (IPUSP) (2024). She is the author of several books and papers in Portuguese, free translation of the books: *Of those who dwelling in the moving sea: Elasticity of psychoanalytic technique* (2003), *Wings trapped in the attic: Psychoanalysis of difficult cases* (2009), *Of the people of the fog* (2019) and *Rain in the soul. The vitalizing function of the analyst* (2023). The original titles: *Dos que moram em móvel-mar: elasticidade da técnica psicanalítica* (2003), *Asas presas no sótão: psicanálise dos casos intratáveis* (2009), *Do povo do nevoeiro* (2019), and *Chuva n'alma. A função vitalizadora do analista* (2023).

Elisa Maria de Ulhôa Cintra is a psychoanalyst, with a doctorate in Clinical Psychology from Pontifícia Universidade Católica de São Paulo (PUCSP). She is a professor in the Clinical Psychology Post-Graduate Studies Program at PUCSP and the Faculty of Human and Health Sciences at PUCSP. Coordinator of the Inter-Institutional Laboratory for Studies on Intersubjectivity and Contemporary Psychoanalysis (LIPSIC), she is also the author of the books *Why Klein?/Por que Klein?* (co-authored with Marina F. R. Ribeiro), *Melanie Klein: Style and thinking/Melanie Klein: estilo e pensamento*, and *Folha Explain Melanie Klein/Folha Explica Melanie Klein* (co-authored with Luís Claudio Figueiredo).

Nelson Ernesto Coelho Junior is a psychoanalyst, PhD in Clinical Psychology, professor and researcher at the Instituto de Psicologia - Universidade de São Paulo (IPUSP). He is the author, among other books, of Psychic Illness and Healing Strategies. Matrices and models in psychoanalysis/Adoecimentos psíquicos e estratégias de cura. Matrizes e modelos em psicanálise" (Blucher, 2018) and Ethics and Technique in Psychoanalysis/Ética e técnica em psicanálise (Escuta, 2008, 2nd ed.), both written with Luís Claudio Figueiredo, and, with Adriana Barbosa, Dreaming: representing terror, sustaining desire/Sonhar: figurar o terror, sustentar o desejo (Zagodoni, 2021).

Davi Berciano Flores is a psychologist and psychoanalyst. With a master's degree and ongoing doctoral studies in Clinical Psychology at the Institute of Psychology, University of São Paulo (IPUSP), he is also a collaborator at LIPSIC (Interinstitutional Laboratory of Intersubjectivity Studies and Contemporary Psychoanalysis) and a member of GBPSF (Sándor Ferenczi

Brazilian Research Group). He is currently a professor at the Center for Psychoanalytic Studies (CEP) and an invited professor in postgraduate studies in psychoanalytic therapy at Presbyterian Mackenzie University, São Paulo. Davi has also authored chapters in Vast Emotions and Imperfect Thoughts: Bionian Dialogues (Blucher, 2023) and Voices of Psychoanalysis (Blucher, 2023), among other publications.

Daniel Kupermann is a psychoanalyst and a professor at the Institute of Psychology at University of São Paulo (IPUSP). He is currently the president of the Sándor Ferenczi Brazilian Research Group and a member of the board of the International Sándor Ferenczi Network. He has authored articles published in French, English, Spanish, Italian and Portuguese, and books published in Brazil and France, with emphasis on *Porquoi Ferenczi? Le style empathique dans la clinique psychanalytique* (Les éditions d'Ithaque, 2022) and *Why Ferenczi?* (Blucher, 2024).

Pedro Hikiji Neves is a psychologist, and master's degree student in the Department of Clinical Psychology at the University of São Paulo (USP). He is the author of chapters in the books *Vast Emotions and Imperfect Thoughts: Bionian dialogues* (Blucher, 2023) and *Presences and Virtualities: Psychoanalytic perspectives* (Pedro and João, 2023). This chapter is the product of his research project "Thomas Ogden reading Winnicott: A bibliographical survey", funded by the National Council for Scientific and Technological Development (CNPQ).

Janderson Farias Silvestre Ramos is a psychoanalyst, with a master's and PhD degrees in Clinical Psychology from the Institute of Psychology at the University of São Paulo (IPUSP). He is a member of the Inter-Institutional Laboratory for Studies on Intersubjectivity and Contemporary Psychoanalysis (LIPSIC) (IPUSP/ PUCSP). He is a psychologist at the University Hospital of the University of São Paulo, and author of chapters in the books *Why Bollas?* (Zagodoni, 2024), *Melanie Klein in Contemporary Psychoanalysis: Theory, Clinic and Culture* (Zagodoni, 2019) and *Academic Research in Psychoanalysis: Theoretical Reflections and Clinical Illustrations* (Pedro & João Editores, 2022).

Marina F. R. Ribeiro (Editor) is a Psychoanalyst, PhD, Associate Professor, and research supervisor and advisor for master's and PhD students in the Clinical Psychology Postgraduate Program at the University of São Paulo. Coordinator of LiPSic (Interinstitutional Laboratory for the Study of Intersubjectivity and Contemporary Psychoanalysis). Editor of Serie in Blucher Publisher (Brazil): Psychoanalysis Academy. Author of several books and papers in Portuguese, free translation: From Mother 'into' Daughter. Transmission of Femininity, 2011; Bion in nine lessons. Reading Transformation (2011, co-author); Balint in Seven Lessons (2012, co-author); Why Read Klein? (2018, co-author); Beyond countertransference – the implied psychoanalyst (Editor and author, 2017); Melanie Klein in Contemporary Psychoanalysis. Theory, Clinic, and Culture (Editor and author, 2019); Vast Emotions and Imperfect Thoughts: Bionian Dialogues (Editor and author, 2023) and Rain in the Soul. The vitalizing function of the analyst (2023, co-author). Currently in press is Dreamy Talk. The Psychoanalytic Function of Personality (In Portuguese, 2025) and Reading Bion's Transformation (co-author, Routledge, 2024).

Gina Tamburrino is a psychoanalyst, with a PhD in Clinical Psychology from Pontifícia Universidade Católica de São Paulo (PUCSP). She is effective member of the Department of Psychoanalysis at the Sedes Sapientiae Institute, and professor and coordinator of the improvement course "Beyond countertransference: The involved analyst" and of the specialization course "Training in Psychoanalysis", at the same institute. She is the author of the books *Escutando com imagens: clínica psicanalítica* (2007) and *Enactments e transformações no campo analisante* (2016), co-author of the books *Bion in Nine Lessons* (2011) and *Balint em sete lições* (2012). Currently in press is *Reading Bion's Transformation* (Routledge, 2024), of which she is co-author.

Acknowledgments

I would like to thank the texts by Thomas H. Ogden, which have become a living presence in my career as a psychoanalyst, ever since my first encounter with these "black marks" on paper in 1996. I would like to thank Ogden himself for his receptiveness to this book project and for his promptness in replying to my emails, which were always vital for the work's realization.

Thank you for my colleagues in University of São Paulo (USP), Nelson Coelho and Daniel Kupermann, the last coordinator of the Great Psychoanalysts series, to inviting me to organize this collection.

To the Rocha Barros – Elias, Elisabeth and Alberto – for their encouragement and generosity in various situations that were fundamental to the book's existence.

To Idete Zimerman Bizzi, for her receptiveness to the book project.

To Adriano Zago, for immediately accepting the translation project.

To all the authors, for their dedication and care in writing the chapters and translating them into English.

I would also like to thank my students and supervisees who have collaborated directly or indirectly with this project.

Finally, thanks for the Department of Clinical Psychology – Institute of Psychology at the University of São Paulo (IPUSP), for the budget to do part of the translation.

Introduction

Reading Thomas H. Ogden

Marina F. R. Ribeiro

Inspired in Bion[1] and Thomas Ogden, I propose some guiding questions for this book: is it possible to know an author through his texts? When we read their texts, can we "read" people?[2] Can a text generate resonances in its readers which become presences? Can a psychoanalytic text generate a transformative emotional experience in its reader? Can psychoanalytic writing be a transforming experience? Is writing a way of thinking? Is there an analytic third emerging in between reader and writer? Could writing be favored by a reverie state of mind? Is writing to be in a favoring state of reverie?

Ogden (2004, 2005) writes[3] about the literary genre of the psychoanalytic writing, emphasizing the amalgamation between theoretical and clinical writing and the author's personality. Ogden considers psychoanalytic writing a form of thinking, that is, we do not write what we think, but in writing, we are thinking something unprecedented:

> ...This 'state of writing' is very similar to my experience of reverie in the analytic setting. When in a 'state of writing', I am in a heightened state of receptivity to unconscious experience while, at the same time, bringing to bear on the experience an ear for how I may be able to make literary use of what I am thinking and feeling.
>
> (Ogden, 2004, p. 23)

The presented book starts from the idea that we are writing about the resonances in us from reading Ogden's texts. The group of authors was inspired by the methodological proposal of a transitive and creative reading, described in several texts by Thomas Ogden. Colleagues who study Ogden's work were invited, as well as some post-graduate[4] students of whom I have been a supervisor and advisor.

Recently, in a text on psychoanalytic research methodology, I proposed the expression "intersubjective fragment", which would be a selected fact, or a set of selected facts, that emerge in the mind of the psychoanalyst-researcher in a state of negative capacity (without memory, without desire and without previous comprehension). This methodological proposal comes from the reading of several texts by Thomas Ogden, among other authors. I will resume what we wrote in this text, because it clearly presents the reading proposal of Ogden's texts in this book:

> In the articles in the book *Creative Readings,* and in numerous other publications, Thomas Ogden (2012) shares with his readers his experiences with reading the works of other authors, the multiple crossings that come from them which enrich his daily life as a psychoanalyst. Thus, he weaves a lively relationship between the productions that circulate in the field of Psychoanalysis and the reports of emblematic cases of his clinic. Ogden (2012) calls this experience in which new meanings are produced 'transitive reading', in the sense of interpreting the text in such a way as to recognize in it something that was not explicitly found before. For the author, reading can never be an impartial or passive experience. He mentions that the text, 'black marks on the page' (p. 22), would carry possibilities of otherness in this blurred border between the end of the reader's voice and the beginning of the text's voice, referring to this indiscrimination in his mind. It applies terms of his own thinking and the knowledge, he has about Bion, for example. Furthermore, we can add to the interpretation of the texts the concept that, in a single reading, multiple voices are involved. Ogden (2003) already said that he could no longer read *Mourning and Melancholy* (Freud, 1917/1969) in the same way after becoming familiar with Melanie Klein's theory of object relations. The author's voice appears in the Freudian text, as well as in a research process whose methodology carries this polyphonic quality, in which seriality is replaced by a set of voices capable of illuminating a concept or a clinical phenomenon.
>
> (Ribeiro et al., p. 37)

It is from this singular place of reading that we are composing this book: how Thomas Ogden's texts cross us, inhabit us, collaborate with our theoretical and clinical thinking, creating a kind of fertile personal archive for clinical listening and psychoanalytic writing. We consider that reading a text can be a transformative emotional experience, and psychoanalytic writing can be a way to think and dream our emotional experiences as analysts:

> Thomas Ogden is an author who repeatedly presents a writing format that circumscribes a point of psychoanalytic theory and his creative and transitive reading of it, subsequently bringing the theoretical web closer to clinical narratives.
>
> (Ribeiro et al., 2022, p. 38)

In other words, the "intersubjective fragment" is an amalgam; it unifies the clinical experience, the reading, the training and the life trajectory of each of the authors; a chimera of unique experiences. The text is framed by ethics in the care with concepts, and there are points of undecidability in the text in which we no longer know whose idea it is. Following Bion's (1977/2014) provocation: thoughts have no owners, yet they can and should be ethically referenced in their authorship. Our effort in this book moves in the direction of free creative thought framed by conceptual ethics and the transformative potentiality of a psychoanalytic text. These are implicated, singular, authorial texts, and we may ask: could it be different when writing about how we have been inhabited by the work of Thomas H. Ogden?

In sequence, I describe my history with Ogden's texts, how this book was dreamed up and realized, and I briefly present the chapters based on the writing of the authors of this collection.

The first contact I had with Ogden's texts was in 1996, when the book *Subjects of Analysis* was published in Portuguese; I was in a study group with Ignácio Gerber. Over the years, I have followed Ogden's vast production. In the early 2000s, I began to systematically study his texts and those of Antonino Ferro in an activity coordinated by me at Institute *Sedes Sapientiae*, called "Open Dialogues". We held scientific meetings to study authors still little known and invited colleagues to talk about the texts.

In 2006, I began to teach post-graduation classes (at Institute *Sedes Sapientiae* – São Paulo) using texts by Ogden and Antonino Ferro. The specialization course, "Beyond the countertransference, the implicated analyst", remains ongoing, and is currently taught by a colleague, Gina Tamburrino, who is also a contributor to thisvolume.

In 2016, at the Institute of Psychology of the University of São Paulo (IPUSP), I began to teach in post-graduate course "Thomas Ogden's contributions to contemporary psychoanalytic clinical thought and its origins in the work of Melanie Klein and W. R. Bion". Throughout the semesters in which the course was taught, I had the collaboration of my colleagues Daniel Kupermann[5] and Nelson Coelho Junior, also contributors to this volume. The course increased the interest in Ogden's texts and attracted psychoanalytic researchers to dedicate themselves to a study of Ogden's work.

Because I have taught a considerable number of classes on Ogden's texts, the way I present the work and the design of the book was something I did not know I knew (Ogden, 2002). It emerged naturally, as a reverie originating from the experience of the analytical third, which also happens in reading texts, creating its own authorial intertextuality, as well as analytic relationships:

> The analytic relationship is unique. (The invention of a new form of human relatedness may be Freud's most remarkable contribution to humankind. Being alive in the context of the analytic relationship is different from the experience of being alive in any other form of human relatedness.)
>
> (Ogden, 2004, p. 866)

The following is a brief presentation of the chapters. Therefore, in the following lines, it is the voice and writing of the contributors to this collection that will resonate with the readers.

Opening the collection, Alberto da Rocha Barros gives us a consistent and panoramic view of Ogden's life and work, besides informing us about his biographical data. Alberto also closes the book with a proposal for an Ogdenian metapsychology, an authorial reading based on five pillars:

1. The notion of deep psychological structure;
2. The revision of Kleinian metapsychology to include the autistic-contiguous position;
3. The defense of an intersubjective scheme for the psychoanalytic model of mind (Ogden's psychology is a "two-person-psychology");
4. The insistence on the dialectic nature of psychic dynamism;
5. "Dreaming" as a paradigm of the prosperous, full and creative functioning of the mind.

At the end of the volume, we have a detailed timeline of his life and publications, as well as unpublished and reference material for future researchers, the result of interviews between Alberto Rocha Barros and Thomas Ogden.

The chapter "Tradition and Innovation: The Style of Thomas Ogden", by Nelson Coelho Junior, presents the central ideas of Ogden's psychoanalytic theorization through two of his main concepts, the autistic-contiguous position and the analytic third, and also through two clinical vignettes of the author. The aim of the chapter is to highlight the psychoanalytic style of the American author, based on a permanent tension between tradition and innovation, both in theory and in the psychoanalytic clinic.

Nelson considers that Ogden demonstrates, without being eclectic, how fertile can be a way of thinking and working the ideas of the psychoanalytic field beyond the rigid boundaries that marked the period of the great schools in psychoanalysis. Finally, the chapter seeks to establish that Ogden is "far from being only a continuator, a protector of tradition, but also far from being a creator who produces an acute break with tradition, [and who thus] indicates a path that simultaneously values tradition and takes risks in the necessary and vitalizing innovations of a theoretical and clinical field".

Moving on to the theoretical texts, we have the chapter by Érico Bruno Viana Campos, which discusses the Freudian legacy presented as a reference in Ogden's work. Besides, the author presents a consistent methodological discussion for psychoanalytic researchers:

Few are the authors who approach Freud in a freer way, without the mark of deference, but mainly, from an effectively more dialogical position, that is, in a more horizontal debate in which differences are put to work in the contradictions of meaning within the theoretical-conceptual discourse, but also in its clinical and literary strata. Thomas Ogden is an author of this sort, and he does it in a distinctive style. He is effectively an author of contemporary psychoanalysis, which, therefore, transcends the scholastic matrices of the field and dialogues with different traditions in an original perspective. His work is relatively extensive in time and in the weight of contributions, being multifaceted, although marked by some axes of questions and interests.

Janderson Farias Silvestre Ramos and Elisa Maria Ulhôa Cintra, in the chapter "Ogden, Reader of Melanie Klein: Understanding Klein to Transcend Her", consider that much of the dialogue underlying the development of the theory of object relations were reactions to Kleinian ideas. In a way, this statement extends to Ogden himself. Some of his work can be thought of as a reaction and a creative appropriation of certain Kleinian ideas. He claims that one must understand Kleinian theory in order to transcend it. Ogden's readings of the concepts of unconscious fantasy, projective identification, paranoid-schizoid and depressive position, point to this path of transcendence. At the same time, he pays tribute to the Kleinian tradition and appropriates it in a creative way for the construction of his own ideas.

The chapter "Ogden, Reader of Bion: From the Theory of Thinking to the Intuitive Thinking", written by me with Davi Berciano Flores, presents some of the main resonances of Bion's work in Ogden's theory and clinic. In it, the four principles of mental functioning presented by Ogden are traced and detailed, in one of the Bionian-inspired texts in the author's work. From each principle, it is possible to derive aspects of Bion's theory that resonate directly or subliminally in Ogden's work (from the contributors' point of view), traversing a path from epistemological psychoanalysis to ontological psycho-analysis, demonstrating that there is, in Ogden's work, an authorial consideration of Bion's work.

The writing of the chapter draws ontological inspiration from both authors. They share the quality of considering the reading of a text as a transitive capture of the truth between reader and author, that is, a text cannot be read without taking into account the authorial bias of the reader. At the end of the chapter, besides having presented evident and possible articulations between the authors, it is possible to identify a research methodology, presented by Bion and embodied in Ogden's work. This development was done in another text, already mentioned above, "Fishing for the Intersubjective Fragment in Psychoanalytic Research" (Ribeiro et al., 2022).

Pedro Hikiji Neves and Daniel Kupermann explore the relationship between Ogden and Winnicott, in "Ogden, Reader of Winnicott: Epistemological, Clinical, Theoretical and Aesthetic Dialogues", contextualizing the manner in which the former transforms the work of the latter, in a process of creating/encountering. Taking the notion of subject as a foundation and relying on terms outside the original text, such as dialectics, intersubjectivity, reverie and the analytic third, Ogden suggests another scenario for reading Winnicott's texts. The authors propose to understand Ogden and Winnicott's dialogues in three axes: firstly, an epistemological one, related to the understanding that the subject is intersubjectively constituted;

secondly, a theoretical-clinical one, related to the conceptual description of what happens between analysand and analyst in the psychoanalytic setting, and finally, a third, an aesthetic one, in which the emphasis is on the phenomenological description of how the analyst is affected by the clinical encounter. These three axes are directly related to each other, since the notion of intersubjective subject (epistemological axis) engenders an understanding of the theory of the clinic (theoretical-clinical axis) which, in turn, is used to interpret the specific experiences of the analyst in the session (aesthetic axis).

In the chapter "From Projective Identification to Thomas Ogden's Concept of the Analytic Third Party: Psychoanalytic Thinking in Search of an Author", I present the passage and transformation of the concept of projective identification (Klein, 1946) to that of the analytic third (Ogden, 1994) by means of the analysis and discussion of the author's publications, in which he makes articulations with concepts by both Winnicott and Bion. For Ogden, the concepts are metaphors that name different aspects of mental functioning, and the conceptual transformations would be, then, in the small slips of meaning, in the subtleties of the text and in the diverse use of expressions. I highlight some ideas:

> Ogden (2004) writes that not only do earlier contributions affect later ones, following a chronological order, but that reading contemporary authors alters our reading of classic texts of psychoanalysis.
>
> ...
>
> If we understand the unconscious, our field of observation, as immanence and not as oracle (Ogden, 2004), we can think that theories are ways to capture a meaning, a conceptual metaphor, as expressed by Ogden (2016).
>
> ...
>
> Considering the idea that thoughts have no owner, but arise precisely from the continuous interaction between people, and are referred to from their authors, we can conjecture that concepts are created, discovered and named by different authors, at different times, and *a posteriori* of several texts, in complex intertextuality (Paz, 1984). An author, in the field of psychoanalysis, may be the one who has the ability to capture, to conceptualize and to narrate clinical phenomena and, furthermore, to articulate them with the existing theoretical paradigms, creating new conceptual wefts, new paradigm crossings.
>
> ...
>
> Ogden (2004, 1997 , 2016) writes at various times that psychoanalysis needs to be invented with each patient, that is, as analysts, we are vividly reconstructing in each session our theoretical weft, our Ariadne's thread. As scholars and researchers of psychoanalysis, it is up to us to historicize and articulate the concepts, crossing paradigms with rigor and ethics, in this creative transmatricial universe of contemporary psychoanalysis.

Following the horizon broadened by the concept of the analytic third, we have the next two chapters. The first, entitled "An Encounter with Thomas Ogden in the Analytic Third", by Gina Tamburrino, with whom I have partnered in the studies of Ogden's work since the early 2000s, approaches the concept through a clinical experience that reveals the singular and unique way in which the third is born in the analytic setting, and clinical and theoretical writing implicated.

Following the concept of the analytical third party, we have the chapter "Supervising with Thomas H. Ogden: Narratives from the Analytic Third", in which Idete Zimerman Bizzi narrates the analytical experience within the supervision bond with Thomas H. Ogden. Idete writes that the trajectory of seven years of coexistence, in its unique richness and fullness of meanings, can be synthesized through the description of two remarkable moments of the work in supervision. The author narrates a circumstance of change of the supervision setting, on the occasion of her visit to San Francisco, where a few face-to-face work meetings took place, in Dr. Ogden's office, allowing a deepening in the emotional density of this collaboration and bringing a unique vivacity to the bond of analytical supervision.

The second moment reported in the chapter describes the elaboration of a clinical case of analysis based on the concept of the analytic third, which allows glimpses of both the content and the form of Dr. Ogden's analytical thinking, in full and vivid construction. Both circumstances prioritized in the writing of this text, attempt to portray the dialectical interplay between the epistemological and ontological dimensions of psychoanalysis, present in the analytic supervision relationship with Thomas Ogden. Idete illustrates the richness of this experience, especially regarding the coherence that is perceived, in the supervision meetings, between the theoretical frame of this great thinker and his genuine way of doing analytical work.

In "From Limbo to Light: Reverie in Ogden", written jointly by Ana Fátima Aguiar and Pedro Hikiji Neves, the reader is introduced to the notion of reverie. Reverie is an experience that emerges from sensorial and imagery elements in the intersubjective relationship. Its use demands tolerance from the part of the analyst to the feeling of being adrift, in contact with the unknown, with the incognizable of the experience. Although it may cause such unsettling sensations, Ogden compares reverie to an emotional compass, from which the analyst is led to experience a multitude of sensations that are simultaneously his, the analysand's, and the analytic third's. Through a vivid and fluid psychoanalysis, the author places us before an implicated clinic, which is structured in the presence and in the receptive listening to the human and to the vitality of the analytic experience. Imbricated in the perspective that analysis needs to be a living experience, intersubjectivity is a central theme of Ogdenian thought. From this understanding, in an open and receptive listening to the other, it is possible to capture the sonority between notes, the echoes between words, to dream the ineffable and unthinkable present in the clinic. When one can dream, one can live one's own emotional experience and, thus, transform it.

At the end of the book, we have two chapters about the language and the processes of vitality and devitalization, both written by Fátima Flórido Cesar and myself. In the first, "The Winged Words of Thomas Ogden":

> ... let us discuss the thought of Thomas Ogden in what regards the understanding of the ideas of vitality and devitalization in the analytic process, but, primordially, about the importance of the analyst's language; of what we call here winged words. We introduce a first sense for such words with wings: the imprecision and uncertainty installed in what we several times call winged words make it possible to keep the phenomenon alive, with tears and slips, that is, the experience of the analytic encounter. Life-giving words and silences by releasing the chains of the desire to know everything. The verb that flies and escapes and that only in the refusal of certainties sustains the living experience.

In the second chapter, "Some Thoughts on Ogden's Direct, Tangential, and Non Sequitur Discourses and the Search for the Unlived Life. Visitation: When Words Come to Meet Us":

> We witness words of sensitive affectation that occur in the human encounter and emerge from unconscious dimensions: this is what we have termed "visitation". They are ways of being or words that overwhelmingly visit us, when then we are captured by states of wonder that, if we make ourselves available to the condition of hospitality (being hospitable so that the feast of novelty can happen), we become inhabited, pregnant with infinite possibilities.
>
> We use the metaphorical image of the visitation to explain how, through words between the analytic duo, an emotional truth emerges, as it appears in several of Thomas Ogden's clinical vignettes. We initially chose one of these vignettes, which are presented in the text *The Fear of Breakdown and the Unlived Life* ... We will emphasize the transforming force of the words that are directed to what the author points out as proper of human existence and of psychic illness: portions of life that have not been lived and that need to be integrated for the individual to become what they are. We will also present clinical vignettes of our own, hoping that between their lines will emerge both what we here call "visitation" and the duo's joint search for the unlived life. We will try to align Ogden's ideas involving language, truth, and unlived life ... .

When organizing and writing this book, I had, as an aim, a horizon, the desire that this small community of authors' writing would take place in a creative, ethical and rigorous way in their presentations and conceptual articulations. The contributors to this collection were inhabited by the presence that emanates from Thomas Ogden's texts, as he did with several seminal authors of psychoanalysis.

We hope that our readers will also make themselves available for a creative reading that will be lived as a transforming experience, so that it becomes part of each analyst's own collection.

The annunciation of winged words leaves vestiges in us and composes our being with every analytic experience lived and dreamed. Is it possible to find living and vitalizing presences in the black marks of a blank page?

We leave it up to the reader to answer this!

São Paulo, February 2023

Notes

1 "But the book will have failed for the reader if it does not become an object of study, and the reading of it an emotional experience itself. My hope is that it will be an experience leading to an increased ability on the part of the analyst to mobilize his own resources of knowledge, clinical observation, theory construction ... " (Bion, 1992/2014, p. 251).

2 "A philosopher is concerned with understanding and misunderstanding, but he cannot do what a psychoanalyst can do: that is, observe and listen to a person while he is understanding and while the person is misunderstanding. This is one of the reasons why I am not very interested in psychoanalytic theories. If one is trained, one can look them up in a book, but the practice of analysis is the only place where one can read people, not books. It is therefore a shame to spend time that could be spent in reading a person, reading a book" (Bion, 1973/2014, p. 63). Bion addresses, in the epigraph cited at the beginning of this text, a different version of the sentence above in which he makes a criticism of the excess of psychoanalytic theories that function as protection from the emotional turbulences generated by the encounter between two personalities.

3 NT: Dear reader, translating from Portuguese, a language rich in vocabulary, to the more concise English can be challenging. We've aimed to make the text palatable, but some nuances may be lost. Thank you for understanding. Eduardo Jefferson de Oliveira (cmo.edu@gmail.com) is the translator for the introduction and chapters 5, 7, 8, 11, and 12. Laís Maria Busatto Bestetti, (laisbestetti@gmail.com), was tasked with the revision of the Introduction and the chapters mentioned earlier.

4 Ana Fátima Aguiar, Davi Berciano Flores, Janderson Silvestre, and Pedro Hikiji Neves are my advisees. Fátima Flórido Cesar is a postdoctoral student under my supervision. They are psychoanalyst-researchers who have dedicated their master's, doctoral, and postdoctoral research to an in-depth study of the work of Thomas H. Ogden.

5 I appreciate Daniel Kupermann's invitation and encouragement to organize this collection.

References

BION, W. R. (1973/2014). Brazilian Lectures. In: *The Complete Works of W. R. Bion* (v. VII, pp. 1–197). London: Karnac Books.

BION, W. R. (1977/2014). Taming wild thoughts [II]: Untitled. In: *The Complete Works of W. R. Bion* (v. X, pp. 165–199). London: Karnac Books.

BION, W. R. (1992/2014). *Cogitations*. London; New York: Karnac Books.

FIGUEIREDO, L. C., RIBEIRO, M. F. R. & TAMBURRINO, G. (2024). *Reading Bion's Transformation*. London; New York: Routledge.

FREUD, S. (1917/1969). Luto e Melancolia. In: *Obras psicológicas completas de Sigmund Freud: edição standard brasileira*. *Rio de Janeiro: Imago* (v. 14. pp. 271–296).

KLEIN, M. (1946/1977). Notes on some schizoid mechanisms. In: *Envy and Gratitude and Other Works*. New York: Dell Publishing.

OGDEN, T. H. (1994). *Subjects of Analysis*. Northvale, NJ & London: Jason Aronson Inc.

OGDEN, T. H. (2002). What's true and whose idea was it? *International Journal of Psychoanalysis* v. 84, pp. 593–606, London.

OGDEN, T. H. (2004). On holding and containing, being and dreaming. In: *This art of psychoanalysis: Dreaming undreamt dreams and interrupted cries*. London: International Journal of Psychoanalysis.

OGDEN, T. H. (2005). *This Art of Psychoanalysis: Dreaming Undreamt Dreams and Interrupted Cries*. (New Library of Psychoanalysis). London and New York: Routledge.

OGDEN, T. H. (2012). *Creative Readings: Essays on Seminal Analytic Works*. London & New York: Routledge.

OGDEN, T. H. (2016). *Reclaiming Unlived Life: Experiences in psychoanalysis*. London; New York: Routledge.

PAZ, O. (1984). *Os filhos de barro*. Rio de Janeiro: Nova Fronteira.

RIBEIRO, M. F. R. & CINTRA, E. M. (org.) (2023). *Vastas Emoções e Pensamentos Imperfeitos. Diálogos Bionianos*. São Paulo: Blucher.

RIBEIRO, M. F. R., FLORES, D. B. & RAMOS, J. F. (2022). A pesca do fragmento intersubjetivo na pesquisa psicanalítica [Fishing for the intersubjective fragment in psychoanalytic research]. In: *Pesquisas acadêmicas em psicanálise: reflexões teóricas e ilustrações práticas*. São Carlos: Pedro & João Editores, https://pedroejoaoeditores.com.br/2022/wp-content/uploads/2022/05/Pesquisas-academicas-em-Psicanalise.pdf (Último acesso 14 de janeiro de 2023)

1 An Experience in Language

A General Overview of the Work of Thomas H. Ogden[1]

Alberto Rocha Barros

Introduction

The purpose of this chapter is merely to offer a general overview of Thomas Ogden's work, intertwining his scientific production with aspects of his training as a psychoanalyst and his main intellectual interests. It is a broad review of his general lines of thought and temperament as a writer. For this reason, many of his conceptual innovations will not be accompanied by detailed explanations. Throughout this book, colleagues will delve deeper into these themes. If this chapter, therefore, lacks the finishing touches of fine brushstrokes on the one hand, I think on the other hand it reaps the benefits that a bird's-eye view provides, especially as the opening chapter to a book dedicated to Ogden's body of work. A great deal of my efforts throughout these pages has been to collect and assemble relevant statements that Ogden has given in interviews and personal communications over the years and give them a logical coherence useful to a reader who desires to understand how his approach to psychoanalysis has evolved over time.

At the end of this volume *Why Read Ogden?*, readers will also find a timeline in which I have ordered Ogden's works according to their date of publication. My intention is that this timeline may be used as a guide for studying and reading Thomas Ogden's body of writing. I believe it is important to read Ogden chronologically because he has produced a very systematic *oeuvre* that gradually builds upon itself through additions: subsequent constructions depend on the sedimentation of ideas previously presented in earlier works.

Life and Work

Thomas Henry Ogden was born on December 4, 1946, on the island of Manhattan, in the state of New York. He was born into a family of Reform Jews, who celebrate Jewish holidays, but do not consider themselves religious. Ogden's father was a life insurance broker who became a producer of Broadway shows. Among his productions, he staged Robert Shaw's *The Man in the Glass Booth* in 1968–1969. Ogden's mother was a social worker who became a psychoanalytically oriented psychotherapist and maintained a

DOI: 10.4324/9781003423188-1

private practice. Ogden has a brother two years younger who is a psychotherapist, with a PhD in clinical psychology (Ogden, 2022, 2023b).

Ogden attributes the development of his interest in psychoanalysis to a few events and experiences. Firstly, when Ogden was around three years old, his mother went into analysis herself. His own hypothesis is that, during this experience, his mother sharpened both her personal sensitivity and her capacity for self-reflection, and the result of this process somehow permeated the way she communicated and interacted with her children, leading her to become a very affectionate and emotionally attuned and attentive mother (Ogden & Di Donna, 2013, p. 625; Gougoulis & Driffield, 2021, pp. 223–224). Secondly, at the age of six, Ogden himself was referred to a child psychoanalyst and underwent therapy for three years, a process that he describes as a fruitful experience:

> It was necessary for me to begin psychoanalytic child therapy when I was six, and this continued for about three years. I have many memories of that therapy, and was keenly aware, even at the time, that it (just talking and playing) had helped me greatly with the difficulties I was having.
>
> (Gougoulis & Driffield, 2021, p. 224)

Finally, in the early 1960s, when Ogden was 16, teachers at his high school produced a list of compulsory summer reading options, from which each student had to choose three books. Ogden chose Brill's translation of Freud's *Introductory Lectures to Psychoanalysis*, which led him to "immediately know" that he wanted to become a psychoanalyst (Gougoulis & Driffield, 2021, p. 224.). About the experience of reading Freud for the first time, he recalls:

> I can remember beginning to read it on a bus in New York City, and how I became so absorbed that I missed my stop, which didn't bother me at all since it meant that I could read undisturbed for as long as I chose. I was far more taken by the voice in the book than I was by the ideas. The book is written as an imaginary lecture to a skeptical audience. The way Freud speaks to the audience about their doubts and fears concerning what he is saying was far more interesting to me then, and now, than the ideas, for instance the unconscious psychology of jokes or even the unconscious psychology of dreams.
>
> (Ogden & Di Donna, 2013, p. 625)

Here we also note the awakening of Ogden's interest in the theme of an author's literary voice and writing style, an appreciation of *how* ideas and feelings are expressed, alongside *what* is expressed (Ogden, 1998). His passion for literature will largely inform his way of reading the psychoanalytic bibliographic repertoire, and literature will also constitute a repository from which he will extract many of his insights into psychic functioning.

But Ogden, with keen personal insight, deepens his understanding of his interest in Freud's "voice" through its intimate internal echoes and resonances:

> In retrospect I think that there were two reasons why the voice in [Freud's *Introductory Lectures*] was what interested me most [...] First, voice is a literary creation, and I loved Freud's writing as writing. I loved all good writing that my 16-year-old mind could be touched by. The other reason I took to the voice in the book so thoroughly and readily was, I suppose, that it felt as if the voice I was hearing in the book was the voice of my mother's analyst, a voice I had been very curious about, and, of course, had never heard directly, but nonetheless was in my bones. So my introduction to psychoanalysis was through object relations – my early relationship with my mother, and through her, my early relationship with her analyst and with psychoanalysis. This early experience with psychoanalysis was of a wordless sort, a sort that had to do with my very being and my mother's very being.
>
> (Ogden & Di Donna, 2013, p. 626)

His interest in psychoanalysis having emerged, the second work he read was Michael Balint's *Primary Love and Psychoanalytic Technique* (1956):

> After I 'discovered' psychoanalysis or it discovered me, I read in a random sort of way books that I happened to come upon. The second psychoanalytic book I read was Balint's *Primary Love and Psychoanalytic Technique*, because it was the only book on psychoanalysis in the local library. I could feel the ways in which the voice and the writing style of this book differed greatly from Freud's. Balint was dealing with early forms of love, while Freud was concerned with early forms of sexuality. Even at my early age, I found love a more human event than the dissection of sexuality in which Freud was engaged.
>
> (Ogden & Di Donna, 2013, p. 626)

Although perhaps not initially drawn to Freud's theory of sexuality – he was still quite young after all – Ogden will later reflect on the psychoanalytic theory of human sexuality in a very artful and succinct way:

> Freud claimed not only that sexual desire is a terribly powerful human motivation, but also that it exists from birth [...] Far more radical a proposal was Freud's notion that all human motivations, all human psychopathology, all human cultural achievements, all human behavior, can be understood in terms of *sexual meanings*. From this perspective, the sexual instinct is not simply a striving, an impulse, a desire, but *the* vehicle by which human beings create meaning. In other words, Freud did not simply propose that the sexual instinct be thought of as generating sexual wishes and impulses.

Of much wider significance is the implication that human beings interpret all perceptions in terms of sexual meanings, thereby *creating* experience. One makes sense of one's internal and external perceptions through the lens of the system of sexual meanings. To use still another metaphor, the sexual instinct is the Rosetta stone that allows the human being to translate raw sensory data into meaning-laden experience.

(Ogden, 1986, pp. 18–19)

André Green (1995) famously bemoaned the waning of sexuality in the theoretical constructs of Anglo-American psychoanalysis – especially within the school of object relations – when contrasted with Francophile traditions, but the above quotation might lead future research to readdress Green's caution within the work of such contemporary writers like Thomas Ogden.

When it came time for higher education, Ogden was admitted to the prestigious Amherst College, located in western Massachusetts. Amherst had established itself as a culturally sophisticated city throughout the 19th century and is the birthplace of poet Emily Dickinson (1830–1886), one of the most important American writers and among Ogden's favorite authors. Robert Frost, another of Ogden's favorite poets, taught at Amherst for a number of years before he died, just before Ogden matriculated. Ogden graduated from Amherst in 1968, earning a *magna cum laude* degree in English Language and Literature and becoming a member of the prestigious Phi Beta Kappa society. At Amherst, Ogden had what he considers to be the "single most important educational experience of my life": a freshman writing course that helped him "learn to hear what good writing sounded like" (Ogden, 2022). And it was also here where he honed and sharpened his skills at close reading, in a style sometimes reminiscent of (although not identical to) the techniques developed by the so-called "New Criticism" school (Ogden, 2023b). Ogden employs this technique routinely, especially when scrutinizing classic works of the psychoanalytic corpus, such as in the pieces collected in *Creative Readings: Essays on Seminal Analytic Works* (2012). He is definably an attentive reader of literary works but, when addressing fiction, one can detect a slight shift in his style of inspection: the New Critic in him gives some way to an approach closer to a reader-response criticism, where his own deeply personal reactions to the text gain center stage. This intriguing tension between two widely different approaches to texts – a "distanced", more "remote" approach versus a "warmer", more "merged" or "involved" approach – will be touched upon in the book *The Analyst's Ear and the Critic's Eye* (2013, co-authored by Benjamin H. Ogden), a volume which should be read side by side with the earlier *Creative Readings* (2012).

During his college years, Ogden began analysis with Selwyn Brody (1912–2004), a pioneer of psychosomatic psychoanalysis in the United States. In many ways, Dr. Brody's life was marked by tragedy. His parents, Chibalaya and Chaim Brody, were brutally murdered by a tenant in 1941, in the quiet community of Glace Bay, Nova Scotia (Canada). The crime inspired the

Canadian film *The Bay Boy* (1984), starring Kiefer Sutherland and Liv Ullman. By one of those unfortunate coincidences in life, Brody himself was violently stabbed in New York in 1972, but survived the attack. Thomas Ogden underwent analysis with him for nine years (Ogden, 2023b).

After graduating from Amherst, Ogden decided to study medicine, already knowing he wanted to become a psychoanalyst. Regarding this professional choice, Ogden comments:

> I decided to go to medical school because, at the time, only medical doctors were admitted to psychoanalytic institutes associated with the American Psychoanalytic Association, which dominated American psychoanalysis. I didn't know there were a very few institutes that admitted candidates who were not physicians. I'm not sure if I would have taken the medical route even if I had been aware that I could become a psychoanalyst without doing so. I think that medical training does have value in the practice of psychoanalysis. For me, what was most important about my medical training was the experience of taking responsibility for the life of the patient in the most literal of ways. It is an enormous responsibility, and one that I think some analysts try to deny in their relationships with their patients. Most of the time, in psychoanalytic practice, patients are fully capable of taking responsibility for their own lives. But that is not always the case. For instance, schizophrenic patients and patients with other types of psychoses, along with depressed and suicidal patients, are often not able to take responsibility for their lives. Many analysts and psychotherapists whom I have treated or have consulted with me are frightened of that type of responsibility and try to avoid it by not taking on psychotic or suicidal patients. Unfortunately for both the patient and the analyst, it is not always possible to predict which patients will become psychotic or suicidal in the course of the therapy or analysis. In fact, I believe that every analytic experience worth its salt involves psychotic and deeply depressive feeling states, and those states are avoided by analysts who are afraid of taking responsibility for the lives of their patients.
>
> (Ogden & Di Donna, 2013, pp. 626–627)

Ogden explains that his views on the role of doctors and medicine in society and before patients is admirably expressed in a set of texts that he now considers valuable for the training of any psychoanalyst. These are the "medical stories" of both Anton Chekhov (Coulehan, 2003) and William Carlos Williams (2018), and the book *A Fortunate Man: The Story of a Country Doctor* (1967/2016) by John Berger and Jean Mohr (Berger & Mohr, 1967; Ogden, 2018).

I believe that Ogden's interest in these texts reveals an "Ogdenian" clinical ethics, which would later permeate his scientific works and the way he thinks about the relationship between psychoanalysis and psychiatry. Donald Meltzer, in the first volume of *The Kleinian Development* (1978), points out what he perceives as a revolutionary attitude in the Freudian psychoanalytic project; namely, little by little, Freud begins to conceive of psychoanalysis as distinct from mere symptomatic therapy: psychoanalysis becomes something that investigates the entirety of a personality and the entirety of a life (Meltzer, 1978, p. 63). In *A Fortunate Man*, one of Ogden's valued books, as mentioned above, art critic John Berger and photographer Jean Mohr follow the daily life of a family doctor in rural England in the 1960s. It is a portrait of a simple, good-natured man, struggling to reconcile the imperfect scientific information available in his time with the singularity of clinical cases that escape common medical sense, with the socioeconomic ills experienced by the historical context in which he lives, and with the vices and virtues and unique personalities of each of his patients. Berger writes:

> [T]he patient should be treated as a total personality [...] illness is frequently a form of expression rather than a surrender to natural hazards [...] [The doctor] sees to it that he stays well-informed. But his satisfaction comes mostly from the cases where he faces forces which no previous explanation will exactly fit, because they depend upon the history of a patient's particular personality. He tries to keep that personality company in its loneliness.
>
> (Berger & Mohr, 1967, p. 64)

To "keep a personality company in its loneliness" is both an ethical and clinical posture that will resonate throughout Ogden's clinical thought.

Ogden received his medical degree from Yale University in 1972, where he also completed his residency in psychiatry. Yale's psychiatry department was dominated mainly by psychoanalysis guided by the School of Ego Psychology, but Ogden was supervised by Roy Schafer from 1972 to 1975, who at the time had been dissociating from this school of thought (Ogden, 2023a). In 1976, Schafer would publish the classic *A New Language for Psychoanalysis* (Schafer 1976), in which he provides an epistemological review of psychoanalytic metapsychology, moving psychoanalysis away from the theoretical model of the natural sciences and bringing it closer to the human sciences and hermeneutics, a project that could be reviewed alongside Ogden's ways of conceiving the nature of psychoanalytic concepts. Are psychoanalytic conceptualizations *descriptive discoveries* about the functioning of the mind or *metaphorical constructions and abstractions*? This is another theme worthy of exploration by future academic studies of Ogden's work.

Since the age of 20, Ogden had been developing an interest in the English school of object relations, which he had come across in his readings and personal research. Upon completing his residency in 1975, and under the impression that psychoanalytic training in the United States would be strongly influenced by Ego Psychology and Margaret Mahler's Development Psychology, Ogden decided to apply to the British Psychoanalytic Society in London, to which he was admitted. He, his wife Sandra (an attorney) and their son Peter, aged one-and-a-half, thus moved to England (Gougoulis & Driffield, 2021, p. 224).

Ogden lived in England from August 1975 to June 1976, where he began his training analysis with Nina Coltart (1927–1997). He also worked as an associate psychiatrist at the Tavistock Clinic. But the young family did not adapt to the new country and chose not to stay. About this period, Ogden muses:

> I chose a training analyst from the Independent group, Nina Coltart. In the course of the initial weeks of analysis, I made a very painful decision. I had been looking forward to analytic training in London and had uprooted my family in moving to London for a richer experience in analytic training than I could find in America. During those weeks of analysis, I battled within myself in a way that I had never before done. In the end, I decided, with my wife, to return to America. We did not know where in America we would live or where we would work. My wife is an attorney who worked at a law firm during the time we were in London. After my nine-year analytic experience in America, I knew that once I began analysis in London it would be extremely difficult emotionally to end it prematurely. I am grateful to Nina Coltart for not interpreting my decision to return to the United States as a resistance to beginning analysis.
>
> (Gougoulis & Driffield, 2021, p. 224)

Ogden returned to the United States, and opted to relocate to San Francisco, California. Although their families were originally from the East Coast, Thomas and Sandra Ogden, who had spent happy summers in San Francisco, were attracted to the city and had contacts in the region (Ogden, 2023a).

In 1979, Ogden began his training at the San Francisco Psychoanalytic Institute, now renamed the San Francisco Center for Psychoanalysis (SFCP). During this period, he underwent training analysis with Norman Reider (1907–1989), a psychoanalyst with a very prolific scientific production, with whom he had "a good experience [of personal analysis]" (Ogden, 2023a). His psychoanalysis with Reider also lasted nine years (Ogden, 2023b).

Around the same time, Ogden was hired by the UCSF Medical Center at Mount Zion, the teaching and research hospital at the University of California, in San Francisco. There he established a passing relationship with Erik Erikson (1902–1994), who led the clinical case discussions (Ogden, 2023b) on the ward where Ogden was working. But the greatest influence for him was his interaction at Mount Zion with Otto Allen Will, Jr. (1910–1993), psychotherapy director at Chestnut Lodge and the Austen Riggs Center, prominent centers for the psychoanalytic treatment of patients hospitalized with significant chronic conditions. Ogden learned much about the psychoanalytic treatment of seriously disturbed patients during this period and mentions Otto Will as an "inspirational" figure (Ogden 2023a). His long-lasting interest in the phenomenon of psychosis flourished in this context, and it was also at this time that he developed a personal friendship with James S. Grotstein

(1925–2015), 20 years older than Ogden, and who greatly influenced his analytical thinking:

> I regularly visited [James Grotstein] for more than 35 years, until his death in 2015, in Los Angeles, where we talked for hours about psychoanalysis as we walked around the park near his home. I always returned from those visits feeling that I had learned a great deal from the conversation. As I look back on it, it was not only that I learned much from our talks together, I felt changed in some way I do not have words for, by the experience of those day-long exchanges.
>
> (Gougoulis & Driffield, 2021, p. 225)

Thomas Ogden's first articles were published between 1974 and 1978 in the *International Journal of Psychoanalytic Psychotherapy*, printed from 1974 to 1985. Although Ogden was only 28–32 years old at the time, these articles are surprisingly mature and polished, exuding self-confidence and with a strong clinical focus. However, Ogden never republished these texts in books, and they are not always easy to find (see timeline for the complete list of Ogden's chronologically arranged publications). Between 1979 and 2000, Ogden co-led, with the psychoanalyst Bryce Boyer, a seminar on both the psycho-analytic treatment of schizophrenic patients and on object relations theory. Boyer, who died in 2000, was a pioneer in psychoanalytic anthropology and in the psychoanalysis of schizophrenic and other seriously disturbed patients. That seminar continues to the present (Ogden, 2001b).

Between 1979 and 1986, Ogden published the first works that would have an impact on the international psychoanalytic landscape. The following ideas date from this period:

- His conception of *projective identification* (Ogden, 1979, 1981, 1982).
- His discussion on the nature of the *schizophrenic conflict* (Ogden, 1980).
- An explanation of his understanding of the *object relations theory* (Ogden, 1983).
- The introduction of the concept of *deep psychological structure* (Ogden, 1984).
- His interpretation of Winnicott's concept of *potential space* (Ogden, 1985).
- The publication of his second book, *The Matrix of the Mind* (Ogden, 1986), which compiles, refines and synthesizes his ideas up to this point.

In many ways, it is a body of work in tune with major psychoanalytic concerns of the period. With the refraction of psychoanalysis into "schools" – "Freudian School", "English School", "School of Ego Psychology" – the 1980s witnessed a series of synthetizing efforts around the various schools, com-parative exercises and attempts to establish dialogues and counterpoints between the different paradigms. For example, the following works date back to the 1980s: Jay Greenberg and Stephen Mitchell's *Object Relations in*

Psychoanalytic Theory (1983), the influential article "One psychoanalysis or many?" (1988) by Robert S. Wallerstein, and Judith M. Hughes's *Reshaping the Psychoanalytic Domain* (1989).

Regarding the proliferation of different matrices of thought in psychoanalysis, Ogden comments:

> It is easy to say that it is the analyst's obligation to become conversant with multiple epistemologies and integrate them. I think that in reality, however, the best that we can hope for is an uneasy coexistence of a multiplicity of epistemologies. Our goal is to attempt to escape the pitfalls of ideology and to learn from our awkward efforts at thinking within the context of different systems of ideas that together, in a poorly integrated way, constitute psychoanalysis [...] The understanding of psychoanalysis that I am describing places the natural science model in the position of being one of many of the epistemologies comprising psychoanalysis. In a natural science model, there is a single unifying method (the scientific method) by which the body of knowledge is expanded. In psychoanalysis we have the much more difficult task of attempting to reconcile the diversity of forms of knowledge that we have at our disposal. We must understand the history of these lines of thought, the methods by which they were developed, and the kinds of experience that have served as organizers of this knowledge. Each epistemology is separate unto itself and at the same time stands in dialectical tension with the others. Each is slowly and sometimes painfully being transformed by the others, and, as a result, one is not dealing with a linearly expanding body of knowledge.
>
> (Ogden, 1991, p. 369)

Ogden's works from 1979 to 1986 were important exercises in contrasting epistemologies. He also describes them as efforts to introduce the ideas of Klein, Winnicott, Fairbairn and Bion into the American psychoanalytic environment (Ogden, 2006). But Ogden is an "anthropophagic" author: he swallows the analytical tradition, metabolizes and transforms it, expelling something innovative and authentically his own – his writings are critical and creative readings of the psychoanalytic legacy, and not mere explanations of the concepts developed by seminal authors (Brinholli & Coelho Junior, 2020, seem to agree).

The introduction of the concept of *deep psychological structure* (Ogden, 1984) marks an important milestone and represents one of the rare moments in which he goes beyond the limits of the field of psychoanalytic knowledge. Ogden is not an author who frequently draws on philosophy or other disciplines within the humanities (although literature and literary criticism are a central paradigm for him). On a few occasions, he draws analogies from evolutionary biology. But the notion of "deep structure" is something he absorbed from Noam Chomsky's *Language and Mind* (1968) and Chomskyan linguistics in general. This is where he finds the key to a solution to an epistemological problem presented by Kleinian metapsychology. It is a variation of the blank slate problem, which takes on different configurations in philosophy, neuroscience and psychology: the question of the existence or non-existence of innate mental contents or proclivities, a "human nature" that is "pre-formatted". In psychoanalysis, the Kleinian school was harshly criticized for appearing to postulate, from birth, the presence of highly developed and complex mental activities, particularly phantasy, which would make it "an untenable theory" (Ogden, 1986, p. 21). Ogden sought to escape this logical pitfall through an analogy with Chomskyan linguistics. This is a major step that deserves to be highlighted, as it constitutes one of the touchstones of Ogden's thought.

In this first phase of scientific activity, we can also observe an interest in the clinical and epistemological problems imposed on psychoanalysis by severely disturbed patients. Commentators of Ogden's work have already astutely pointed out that "the clinical matrix that guides Ogden's thinking is that of psychosis, more specifically schizophrenia" (Brinholli & Coelho Junior, 2020, p. 3). Ogden lists the works of L. Bryce Boyer, James S. Grotstein, Harold F. Searles, Peter Giovacchini, Otto F. Kernberg, David Rosenfeld, Hanna Segal, Francis Tustin and Otto Will (Ogden, 1991, p. 363) as his main influences and references in this area.

With the publication of *The Matrix of the Mind* (1986), the characteristic way in which Ogden chose to convey his ideas was also established. He usually publishes his articles in leading English-language scientific journals in the field of psychoanalysis. When a sufficient volume of published stand alone works is achieved, he brings them together in a book with an introductory chapter in which he tries to detect a common thread through the texts. The book titles tend to be sonorously poetic and the literary epigraphs included in the beginning of his books and articles deserve attention from readers, as they offer clues about the "spiritual tone" of the book. Some of these volumes are tightly knitted together and form a logically coherent unit; in other cases, certain readers might consider the result to resemble a relatively "loose" compilation of the most recent articles by this extremely active psychoanalyst. It is always useful for readers to reflect upon the theme and unity (or lack thereof) in Ogden's books.

Ogden becomes a member of the San Francisco Psychoanalytic Institute in 1986, having published his first two books – *Projective Identification and Psychotherapeutic Technique* (1982) and *The Matrix of the Mind* (1986) – while still a candidate.

This marks the beginning of a period where his works revolve around the autistic-contiguous position (Ogden, 1988; Ogden, 1989a; Ogden, 1989b; cf. also: Ogden, 2008). This period culminates with the publication of his third book, *The Primitive Edge of Experience* (1989b). One can ponder what led Ogden to postulate an autistic-contiguous position? What theoretical pressures does it respond to? Ogden conceives his postulate as a natural development of the investigations initiated by Klein, Winnicott, Fairbairn and Bion (Ogden, 1989a, p. 341; Ogden, 1989b, p.4), added by the conjectures developed in the works of Esther Bick, Donald Meltzer and Francis Tustin (Ogden, 1989b, p. 30). If psychoanalysis managed to broaden and/or rethink the concept of "psychosis" to contemplate both psychopathological phenomena and the psychotic dimensions of neurotic functioning, the autistic-contiguous position resignifies the concept of "autism" to describe a pre-symbolic form dominated by sensory impressions of the organization of experience, more primitive than the paranoid-schizoid position. Ogden believes that Bick's, Meltzer's and Tustin's works revealed limitations of Klein's and Fairbairn's paradigms, demanding a review of the understanding of the paranoid-schizoid position. The autistic-contiguous position would represent the "underbelly" or "primitive edge" of the schizoid personality organization (Ogden, 1989b, p. 5). Following the notion of deep psychological structure, I believe that the postulation of the autistic-contiguous position is the second step in the construction of what I will call an "Ogdenian *metapsychology*".

I identify a new phase of Ogden's scientific production in the years 1989 to 1997. The books *Subjects of Analysis* (1994) and *Reverie and Interpretation* (1997) date from this period. It is a period marked by a strong emphasis on intersubjectivity and countertransference phenomena. The fact that Ogdenian psychology is an intersubjective psychology is the third mark of his system. He tells us that "the idea that it takes at least two people to think" is one that "runs through all of [his] work" (Ogden & Di Donna, 2013, p. 628). In his words:

> My own conception of analytic intersubjectivity places central emphasis on its dialectical nature. This understanding represents an elaboration and extension of Winnicott's notion that "There is no such thing as an infant [apart from the maternal provision]. I believe that in an analytic context, there is no such thing as an analysand apart from the relationship with the analyst, and no such thing as analyst apart from the relationship with the analysand."
>
> (Ogden, 1994, p. 63)

Winnicott's formula, "there is no such thing as an infant", is enriched with Bioninan colors. Ogden writes:

> As Bion puts it [in the *Clinical Seminars*], "the human unit is a couple; it takes two human beings to make one."
>
> (Ogden, 2008b, p. 100)

After all,

> "it requires two minds to think one's most disturbing thoughts."
>
> (Ogden, 2008b, p. 100)

Intersubjectivity is a theme that transcends Ogden's work. Jonathan Dunn, reviewing the psychoanalytic bibliography on the subject, outlines a more "classical" and "positivist" tradition in psychoanalysis that postulates the core of mental life as a closed and discrete system, interpretively capturable by a less implicated analyst, and an "intersubjective turn", which would postulate the opposite: mental life and processes of the soul are inseparable from relational matrices (Dunn, 1995). At times, the debate illustrated a clash between supporters of the *intrapsychic* model (sometimes called "monadic models" or "one person psychologies") and supporters of the *intersubjective* model ("relational models" or "two person psychologies"). Much was written on the subject between 1980 and the 2000s (Ghent, 1989; Aron, 1990). In 2000, André Green joined the debate, seeing the new relational focus as a necessary corrective and the foundation of a new paradigm (Green, 2000). The 2004 *International Journal of Psychoanalysis (IJP)* featured in its "Psychoanalytic Controversies" section a debate between Owen Renik and Elizabeth Spilius on the subject (Renik & Spillius, 2004) and the same IJP also published, in its 2012–2013 educational section, robust new articles on the topic (Schwartz, 2012; Bohleber, 2013). In 2021, the *Journal of the American Psychoanalytic Association (JAPA)* also dedicated a section to the topic of intersubjectivity in psychoanalysis (Civitarese et al., 2021).

All of this suggests that there is a potential to examine Ogden's interest in intersubjective phenomena with an eye on these psychoanalytic debates that spill over the boundaries of his work: intersubjectivity became a hot topic in psychoanalysis. Bruce Reis writes about a "phenomenological turn" by Ogden, perceiving in his formulations strategies analogous to those used by Hegel and Merleau-Ponty to deconstruct Cartesian objectivism (Reis, 1999). In Brazil, Nelson Ernesto Coelho Junior published important articles where he examined the intersubjective model proposed by Ogden (Coelho Junior, 2002, 2010, 2012, 2015). It is also worth pointing out that Craig Morton, in the United States, and Marina Ribeiro, in Brazil, published interesting papers detailing how Ogden's concept of "thirdness" has unfolded throughout his work since the period marked by the focus on projective identification (Morton, 2003; Ribeiro, 2020). On the other hand, it is worth considering if Ogden's approach to "subjectivity" and "intersubjectivity" is truly so epistemologically and philosophically charged. There might be a lighter touch to Ogden's use of these ideas that is closer even to everyday usage than to more controlled and refined theoretical constructions. At times, it seems that Ogden is even calling attention to how "intersubjective" human beings are as a species: he is pointing to very common and humdrum experiences and not necessarily engaged (or not consciously engaged) with current wider debates in the field.

A fundamental aspect of Ogden's model of the mind is his emphasis on its *dialectical nature*, a true leitmotif of his work:

> [The] radical nature of the psychoanalytic project [...] [is] the notion that the experiencing subject is simultaneously constituted and decentered

from itself by means of the negating and preserving *dialectical interplay* of consciousness and unconsciousness.

(Ogden, 1994, p. 15, my emphasis)

A formula that Ogden will frequently use throughout his various works, and in multiple contexts, is the idea that the poles of a dialectically operating constellation (conscious/unconscious; the stratifications of the mind; autistic-contiguous, paranoid-schizoid, depressive positions) are in permanent *"dialectical tension"* (Ogden, 1994, p. 6, my emphasis) so that *"each creates, preserves and negates the other"* (Ogden, 1989b, p. 343, my emphasis). Ogden's readers will come across these expressions and arrangement of words at multiple times throughout his writings and in different contexts. It's a turn of phrase that he seems to be deeply attracted to.

Ogden attributes his understanding of the complex concept of "dialectic" to his reading of the preface to Herbert Marcuse's *Reason and Revolution* (1941), and to his reading of the acclaimed *Introduction to the Reading of Hegel* (1947) by Alexander Kojève. Ogden believes that he encountered these texts sometime in the 1980s (Ogden, 2023b). This is one of the rare occasions on which Ogden draws from the philosophic repertoire. The dialectical nature of psychic dynamism is perhaps the fourth mark of Thomas Ogden's metapsychology. But, again, this conception of "dialectics" might not necessarily be so philosophically charged. At times, it seems that what Ogden is trying to convey through the term "dialectics" is to lay emphasis on the profoundly precarious stability of mental organizations of all sorts and at all levels. His emphasis is on the permanent dynamic tension and slipperiness of the scaffoldings of inner life.

Between 2001 and 2009, Ogden published three books that include the words "dream" or "dreaming" in their titles: *Conversations at the Frontier of Dreaming* (2001a), *This Art of Psychoanalysis: Dreaming Undreamt Dreams and Interrupted Cries* (2005), *Rediscovering Psychoanalysis: Thinking and Dreaming, Learning and Forgetting* (2009). The dream paradigm is central to Ogden's thought and will set the tone for his therapeutic project:

> [P]sychoanalysis most fundamentally is a therapeutic enterprise with the goal of enhancing the patient's capacity to be alive to as much as possible to the full spectrum of human experience. Coming to life emotionally is, to my mind, synonymous with becoming increasingly able to dream one's experience, which is to dream oneself into existence.

(Ogden, 2005, p. 8)

Ogden is, of course, working with an expanded notion of "dream" derived from Bion: "Dreaming occurs both during sleeping and waking life" (Ogden, 2005, p. 100). A dream is a type of thought, a *dream thought*, a continuous activity of the mind:

> Dream thinking is the predominantly unconscious psychological work that we do in the course of dreaming. We dream continually, both while we are awake and while we are asleep [...] Just as the light of the stars in the sky is obscured by the glare of the sun during the day, dreaming continues while we are awake, though it is obscured by the glare of waking life. Dream thinking is our most encompassing, penetrating, and creative form of thinking. We are insatiable in our need to dream our lived experience in an effort to create personal, psychological meanings (which are organized and represented in such forms as visual images, verbal symbols, kinesthetically organized impressions, and so on) [...] In dream thinking, we view our lived experience from a multiplicity of vantage points simultaneously, which allows us to enter into a rich, nonlinear set of unconscious conversations with ourselves about our lived experience.
>
> (Ogden, 2010, p. 328)

If, as we have seen, the presence of two minds is necessary for us to be able to think our most disturbing thoughts (Ogden, 2008b, p. 61), then "it takes (at least) two people to think one's most disturbing emotional experience" (Ogden, 2010, p. 330). Ogden will also *metaphorically* (Ogden, 2010, p. 19, p. 21) invoke two sleep disorders – nightmares and night terrors – as "emblematic of the stuff that the full range of human psychopathology is made on" (Ogden, 2004, p. 859):

> Central to psychoanalysis, as I conceive of it, is the analyst's participation in dreaming the patient's "undreamt" and "interrupted" dreams. Interrupted dreams (metaphorical nightmares) are emotional experiences with which the patient is able to dream (to do genuine un- conscious psychological work) up to a point. However, past a certain point, the patient's dreaming is disrupted—the capacity for dreaming is overwhelmed by the disturbing nature of what is being dreamt. At that point the patient "wakes up", that is, ceases to be able to do unconscious psychological work (e.g., as seen in a child's play disruption). The place at which dreaming ceases is marked by the creation of neurotic and other forms of nonpsychotic symptomatology. By contrast, undreamt dreams are emotional experiences with which the patient is able to do little or no conscious or unconscious psychological work. Undreamable experience is held in split-off states such as pockets of psychosis or in psychosomatic disorders and severe perversions.
>
> (Ogden, 2006, pp. 420–421)

Ogden is a prolific author who writes continuously, but with a close examination of this expanded and metaphorical notion of dreaming, I believe that his proposed picture of inner life is complete. It is a metapsychology supported by five pillars:

1. The notion of *deep psychological structure*.
2. The revision and extension of Kleinian metapsychology to include the *autistic-contiguous position*.

3. The advancement of an *intersubjective model* for both psychoanalysis and human nature in general.
4. The insistence on the *dialectical nature* of intrapsychic dynamics.
5. *Dreaming* as a (metaphorical) paradigm for healthy and creative mental functioning with "nightmares" and "night terrors" as symbolic metaphors for psychopathology and mental breakdown.

Ogden writes (2016, p. 47). that a "small handful of psychoanalytic books and papers" have shaped not simply how he thinks about psychoanalysis, but also what he thinks "about what it is to be alive as a human being". The psychoanalytic works he mentions as seminal to him are Freud's "Mourning and Melancholia" (1917), Fairbairn's "Endopsychic structures considered in terms of object relationships" (1944), Klein's "Notes on some schizoid mechanisms" (1946), Bion's *Learning from experience* (1962), Winnicott's "Fear of breakdown" (1974), Loewald's "The waning of the Oedipus complex" (1979) and Balint's *The Basic Fault* (Ogden, 2023d).

However, he prefers not to be seen as a supporter of any specific school of psychoanalysis:

> For me, the thread running through all of what I have said is that my position in the analytic world has not been that of an advocate of a school of psychoanalysis (or as an adversary of "opposing" schools of psychoanalysis). Neither do I view myself as a "lone voice", because that suggests that I think of myself as a renegade. I would much prefer to describe myself as an independent thinker.
>
> (Ogden, 2006, p. 421)

I would like to add two brief comments on Ogden's style as a *psychoanalytic writer*. In the opening pages of *Reverie and Interpretation* (1997), Ogden writes: "Words and sentences, like people, must be allowed a certain slippage." (p. 3). As we have seen, I am sometimes unsure when to read Ogden's conceptualizations with a more rigid and specific meaning in mind and when he is using terms more loosely and fluidly, closer to the usages of natural language. This is a problem or feature of both philosophical writing and psychoanalytic writing. Some writers prefer to exact enormous semantic control over their vocabulary, while others tend to be more pragmatic or playful or allusive. There are advantages and disadvantages to both approaches, and neither constitutes "the correct perspective". But we should perhaps be mindful of Ogden's caution that "words must be allowed a certain slippage". This could possibly be perceived as his way of characterizing the volatility of the psychoanalytic conceptual toolkit in general, which could well be one of its strongest features rather than a weakness.

We should now turn to another aspect of Ogden's output and intellectual temperament. He has stated that his "principle psychoanalytic teachers" have been Freud, Klein, Fairbairn, Winnicott, Bion, Loewald and Searles; but that he has "learned *as much* about psychoanalysis from poets, novelists, and playwrights." (Ogden, 2016, pp. 3–4, my emphasis). Thomas Ogden is a passionate connoisseur of literature. From childhood, he developed a deep emotional bond with E. B. White's classic tale, *Charlotte's Webb* (1952) and as a teenager, his favorite novel was Herman Melville's *Moby Dick* (1851) (Ogden, 2023b). In an interview with Luca Di Donna, he lists "Kafka, Calvino, Homer, Coetzee, Wordsworth, Melville, Beckett, Frost" amongst his "favorite authors" (Ogden & Di Donna, 2013, p. 631). To this list, we would need to add Jorge Luís Borges, William Trevor, Robert Frost, William Faulkner, Wallace Stevens, Emily Dickinson and William Carlos Williams. He holds William Maxwell's novels *The Folded Leaf* (1945) and *So Long, See You Tomorrow* (1980) in high esteem. He frequently mentions the novel *Disgrace* (1999) by J. M. Coetzee and was quite moved by John Williams's *Stoner* (1965). He has recently been enthralled by the novel *The Solid Mandala* (1965), by Australian author Patrick White (winner of the 1973 Nobel Prize for Literature), a novel that is not often republished in English. Still, it is a novel that he describes as "brilliant" and that he revisits with pleasure (Ogden, 2023c). As we can see, it is a predominantly English-speaking literary culture. I believe that this is largely explained by the attention he devotes to the preciousness and musicality of language – translated literature does not resonate for him as much as literature produced in his mother tongue. His youngest son, Benjamin Ogden, is a literary critic (with a PhD in J. M. Coetzee) and father and son have jointly written a book on psychoanalysis and literature (Ogden & Ogden, 2013). Benjamin Ogden later delved deeper into the topic in a book of his own (Ogden, 2018).

In 2011–2012, already over 60 years old, Ogden ventured into literary writing, and published the novel *The Parts Left Out* in 2014, which was the fourth best-selling novel in Israel in 2017 This novel was followed by two additional fictional experiments: *The Hands of Gravity and Chance* (2016) and *This will do …* (2021). In an interview with Maureen Kurpinsky, he says:

> It feels as if I have been an apprentice to fiction for 40 years in writing analytic papers. While it is rarely put so bluntly, analytic papers are fictions, at least the clinical parts. The clinical examples are inventions — things that an analyst dreams up to try to convey something that feels true to the experience with a patient. Virtually no analyst records sessions — if an analyst did so, it wouldn't be an analytic session — so whether it's an hour, a day, or several years after the session has taken place, the dialogue that we read in an analytic paper is fictional, even though we try to pretend it isn't. So, it's in that sense that I've done a long apprenticeship to writing fiction.
>
> (Ogden & Kurpinsky, 2014, p. 81)

Literature can conceivably be viewed as a laboratory of the imagination, and it does not surprise me at all that Ogden is so deeply drawn to it. In a sense, it centrally characterizes his understanding of psychoanalysis itself. In an interview with Noya Kohavi, he states:

> Psychoanalysis is not a natural science – at best it's a social science and probably closer to a literary experience, *an experience in language*.
> (Ogden & Kohavi, 2017, my emphasis)

His overwhelming passion for writing led him to experiment with various textual registers: the psychoanalytic paper, the essay, literary criticism, poetry and fiction. His novels were the focus of a recent study by Jeffrey Berman (2022). Ogden feels that his identity as a literary writer is taking shape and confesses:

> Depending on the kind of writing I am doing, I think of myself as a psychoanalyst who is also a writer, or as a writer who is also a psychoanalyst.
> (Gougoulis & Driffield, 2021, p. 225)

Ogden insists that he will not stop writing psychoanalytic works given his passion for psychoanalysis (Ogden & Kurpinsky, 2014; Ogden & Kohavi, 2017). He published *Reclaiming Unlived Life* in 2016, and released *Coming to Life in the Consulting Room* in 2021. This is how he summarized his career:

> As I look back on it, it seems that I have become a physician who is viewed as working at the margins of medicine; a psychiatrist who is viewed as working at the edge of psychiatry; and a psychoanalyst who is working at the edge of psychoanalysis.
> (Gougoulis & Driffield, 2021, p. 225)

Note

1 This is a slightly modified version of the original chapter as it appeared in the Brazilian edition of this book.

Bibliography

ARON, L. (1990). One person and two person psychologies and the method of psychoanalysis. *Psychoanalytic Psychology*, 7 (4): 475–485.

BERGER, J. & Mohr, J. (1967). *A Fortunate Man: The Story of a Country Doctor*. Edinburgh and London: Canongate, 2016.

BERMAN, J. (2022). The novels of Thomas Ogden. *Journal of the American Psychoanalytic Association*, 70 (5), 1013–1022.

BOHLEBER, W. (2013). The concept of intersubjectivity in psychoanalysis: Taking critical stock. *International Journal of Psychoanalysis*, 94 (4): 799–823.

BRINHOLLI, F. & COELHO JUNIOR, N. E. (2020). A importância de Thomas Ogden para a psicanálise contemporânea. *Psicologia USP*, 31: 1–9.

CHOMSKY, N. (1968). *Language and Mind*. New York, Orlando, FL and San Diego, CA: Harcourt Brace.

CIVITARESE, G., Orange, D. M. & Kirshner, L. (2021). Psychoanalysis and Intersubjectivity. *Journal of the American Psychoanalytic Association (JAPA)*, 69 (5): 853–935.

COELHO JUNIOR, N. E. (2002). Intersubjetividade: conceito e experiência em psicanálise. *Psicologia Clínica (PUC-RIO)*: 14 (1): 61–74.

COELHO JUNIOR, N. E. (2010). Da Intercorporeidade à co-corporeidade: elementos para uma clínica psicanalítica. *Revista Brasileira de Psicanálise*, 44 (1): 51–60.

COELHO JUNIOR, N. E. (2012). Thomas Ogden e a Alteridade em Psicanálise. *Impulso*, 22 (55): 59–76.

COELHO JUNIOR, N. E. (2015). As origens da noção de terceiridade em Green e Ogden. In: Talya S. Candi (Org.). *Diálogos Psicanalíticos Contemporâneos: O representável e o irrepresentável em André Green e Thomas H. Ogden*. São Paulo: Editora Escuta: 235–270.

COULEHAN, J. (Ed.) (2003). *Chekhov's Doctores: A Collection of Chekhov's Medical Tales*. Kent, OH: The Kent State University Press.

DUNN, J. (1995). Intersubjectivity in psychoanalysis: A critical review. *International Journal of Psychoanalysis*, 76 (4): 723–738.

GHENT, E. (1989). Credo: The dialectics of one-person and two-person psychologies. *Contemporary Psychoanalysis*, 25 (2): 169–211.

GOUGOULIS, N. & DRIFFIELD, K. (2021). Interview with Thomas Ogden. *International Forum of Psychoanalysis*, 30 (4): 223–233.

GREEN, A. (1995). Has sexuality anything to do with psychoanalysis? *The International Journal of Psychoanalysis*, 76: 871–883.

GREEN, A. (2000). The intrapsychic and intersubjective in psychoanalysis. *Psychoanalytic Quarterly*, LXIX: 1–39.

GREENBERG, J. R. & MITCHELL, S. A. (1983). *Object Relations in Psychoanalytic Theory*. Cambridge, MA and London: Harvard University Press.

HUGHES, J. M. (1989). *Reshaping the Psychoanalytic Domain: The Work of Melanie Klein, W. R. D. Fairbairn & D. W. Winnicott*. Berkeley, Los Angeles and London: University of California Press.

KOJÈVE, A. (1947). *Introdução à leitura de Hegel*. São Paulo: Contraponto, 2007.

MARCUSE, H. (1941). Prefácio: uma nota sobre dialética. Em: Herbert Marcuse, *Razão e Revolução*. São Paulo: Editora Paz & Terra, 1984.

MELTZER, D. (1978). *The Kleinian Development [O Desenvolvimento Kleiniano I: Desenvolvimento Clínico de Freud]*. São Paulo: Editora Escuta, 1989.

MORTON, C. (2003). Metaphors are us: Countertransference in the writings of Thomas Ogden. *Psychoanalytic Psychology*, 20 (3): 441–455.

OGDEN, B. H. (2018). *Beyond Psychoanalytic Literary Criticism: Between Literature and Mind*. Routledge.

OGDEN, B. H. & OGDEN, T. H. (2013). *The Analyst's Ear and the Critic's Eye: Rethinking psychoanalysis and literature*. London and New York: Routledge.

OGDEN, T. H. (1979). On projective identification. *International Journal of Psychoanalysis*, 60 (3): 357–373.

OGDEN, T. H. (1980). On the nature of Schizophrenic conflict. *International Journal of Psychoanalysis*, 61 (4): 513–533.

OGDEN, T. H. (1981). Projective identification in psychiatric hospital treatment. *Bulletin of the Menninger Clinic*, 45: 319–333.

OGDEN, T. H. (1982). *Projective Identification and Psychotherapeutic Technique.* Jason Aronson.

OGDEN, T. H. (1983). The concept of internal object relations. *International Journal of Psychoanalysis,* 64 (2): 227–241.

OGDEN, T. H. (1984). Instinct, phantasy, and psychological deep structure. *Contemporary Psychoanalysis,* 20: 500–525.

OGDEN, T. H. (1985). On potential space. *International Journal of Psychoanalysis,* 66 (2): 129–141.

OGDEN, T. H. (1986). *The Matrix of the Mind: Object Relations and the Psychoanalytic Dialogue.* Oxford: Rowman & Littlefield/Jason Aronson.

OGDEN, T. H. (1988). On the dialectical structure of experience. *Contemporary Psychoanalysis,* 24 (1): 27–45.

OGDEN, T. H. (1989a). Sobre o conceito de uma posição autística-contígua. *Revista Brasileira de Psicanálise,* XXX (20): 341–364.

OGDEN, T. H. (1989b). *The Primitive Edge of Experience.* Jason Aronson.

OGDEN, T. H. (1991). An interview with Thomas Ogden. *Psychoanalytic Dialogues,* 1 (3): 361–376.

OGDEN, T. H. (1994). *Subjects of Analaysis.* London: Karnac Books.

OGDEN, T. H. (1995). Analyzing forms of aliveness and deadness of the transference-countertransference", *International Journal of Psychoanalysis,* 76 (4): 695–709.

OGDEN, T. H. (1997). *Reverie and Interpretation: Sensing Something Human.* Northvale, NJ and London: Jason Aronson.

OGDEN, T. H. (1998). Uma questão de voz na poesia e na psicanálise. *Revista Brasileira de Psicanálise,* 32 (3): 585–604.

OGDEN, T. H. (2001a). *Conversations at the Frontier of Dreaming.* Northvale, NJ: Jason Aronson.

OGDEN, T. H. (2001b). In place of a Eulogy for L. Bryce Boyer (1916–2000). *Fort Da,* 7: 70–72.

OGDEN, T. H. (2004). This art of psychoanalysis: Dreaming undreamt dreams and interrupted cries. *The International Journal of Psychoanalysis,* 85: 857–77.

OGDEN, T. H. (2005). *This Art of Psychoanalysis: Dreaming Undreamt Dreams and Interrupted Cries.* London and New York: Routledge.

OGDEN, T. H. (2006). Thomas H. Ogden, MD. In: Arnold M. Cooper (Ed.), *Contemporary Psychoanalysis in America: Leading Analysts Present Their Work.* Washington, DC and London: American Psychiatric Publishing.

OGDEN, T. H. (2008a). Working analytically with autistic-contiguous aspects of experience. In: Kate Barrows (Ed.), *Autism in Childhood and Autistic Features in Adults.* London: Karnac: 223–242.

OGDEN, T. H. (2008b). Bion's four principles of mental functioning. *Fort Da,* 14B: 11–35.

OGDEN, T. H. (2009). *Rediscovering Psychoanalysis: Thinking and Dreaming, Learning and Forgetting.* London and New York: Routledge.

OGDEN, T. H. (2010). On three forms of thinking: Magical thinking, dream thinking, and transformative thinking. *The Psychoanalytic Quarterly,* 79 (2): 317–347.

OGDEN, T. H. (2012). Creative Readings: Essays on Seminal Analytic Works [*Leituras Criativas: Ensaios sobre obras analíticas seminais*]. São Paulo: Editora Escuta, 2014.

OGDEN, T. H. (2014). *Meias verdades.* São Paulo: Editora Blucher, 2017.

OGDEN, T. H. (2016). *Reclaiming Unlived Life: Experiences in Psychoanalysis.* Routledge.

OGDEN, T. H. (2018). Personal communication dated July 7, 2018.

OGDEN, T. H. (2021). *Coming to Life in the Consulting Room: Toward a New Psychoanalytic Sensibility*. Routledge.

OGDEN, T. H. (2022). Personal communication by email dated August 10, 2022.

OGDEN, T. H. (2023a). Personal communication by email dated January 13, 2023.

OGDEN, T. H. (2023b). Personal communication by email dated January 24, 2023.

OGDEN, T. H. (2023c). This information was collected from several private conversations that have taken place over the years.

OGDEN, T. H. (2023d). Personal communication dated December 16, 2023.

OGDEN, T. H. & DI DONNA, L. (2013). Thomas H. Ogden in conversation with Luca Di Donna. *Rivista di Psicoanalisi*, 59 (3): 625–641.

OGDEN, T. H. & KOHAVI, N. (2017). An interview with Thomas Ogden by Noya Kohavi: How psychoanalyst Thomas Ogden found his true self in fiction. Ha'aretz, 29 March.

OGDEN, T. H. & KURPINSKY, M. (2014). Conversations with clinicians: Thomas Ogden in conversation with Maureen Kurpinsky. *Fort/Da*, 20 (2): 81–95.

OGDEN, T. H. & OGDEN, B. J. (2013). *O ouvido do analista e o olhar do crítico: repensando psicanálise e literatura*. São Paulo: Editora Escuta, 2014.

REIS, B. E. (1999). Thomas Ogden's phenomenological turn. *Psychoanalytic Dialogues*, 9 (3): 371–393.

RENIK, O. & SPILLIUS, E. B. (2004). Psychoanalytic controversies: Intersubjectivity in psychoanalysis. *International Journal of Psychoanalysis*, 85: 1053–1064.

RIBEIRO, M. F. (2020). Da identificação projetiva ao conceito de terceiro analítico de Thomas Ogden: um pensamento psicanalítico em busca de um autor. *Ágora* (Rio de Janeiro), XXIII (1) (January/April 2020): 57–65.

SCHAFER, R. (1976). *A New Language for Psychoanalysis*. New Haven, CT and London: Yale University Press.

SCHWARTZ, H. P. (2012). Intersubjectivity and dialecticism. *International Journal of Psychoanalysis*, 93 (2): 401–425.

WALLERSTEIN, R. S. (1988). One psychoanalysis or many? *International Journal of Psychoanalysis*, 69 (1): 5–21.

WILLIAMS, W. C. (2018). *The Doctor Stories*. New York: New Directions.

2 Tradition and Innovation

The Style of Thomas H. Ogden[1]

Nelson Ernesto Coelho Junior

For Octavio Souza

Introduction

Over the past 30 years, the reading of each new text by Thomas H. Ogden has gradually allowed a recognition of the consolidation of a *psychoanalytic style*. To avoid misunderstandings, I would like to make it clear that, in a broad sense, psychoanalytic styles have their origins in Freud and his way of putting into practice a method and technique that anchors the clinical model characteristic of psychoanalysis. Based on the fundamental rules of free association and a likewise free-floating attention, a relatively stable psychoanalytic setting was established and, above all, so was a stereotype of psychoanalytic practice that inundated the imaginations of the 20th and 21st centuries. However, paradoxically, Freud conceived the possibility of making the setting flexible according to the personality of each analyst. The risks of this flexibility, even if considering the requirements of the analyst's neutrality and abstinence, were always of concern to Freud and his most faithful followers. Thus, I think that part of the history of psychoanalysis can be considered based on the impasses between strict faithfulness to the prescribed techniques and a style attributed to Freud (tradition), and the inevitable innovations demanded by both the distinct personalities of each analyst, as by the transformations in the psychopathological conditions of the patients seen over the subsequent generations.

These considerations require an initial differentiation to be made between the notion of style and the notion of psychoanalytic technique. I follow Ogden (2009) in the proposal that "important aspects of my way of practicing psychoanalysis are better described as an analytic style than as an analytic technique" (p. 70). Although he admits that technique and style are practically inseparable, Ogden refers to analytic technique as being a way of practicing psychoanalysis, developed by groups of analysts who have preceded us, while style is created by each analyst. In this manner, for him, an analyst's style cannot be defined as a set of principles that determine a practice, but as "a living process that has its origins in the personality and experience of the analyst" (p. 70).

To better configure the horizon of psychoanalytic practice, of each analyst's daily work, it could be useful to consider two distinct dimensions

DOI: 10.4324/9781003423188-2

in the constitution of what we could call psychoanalytic style. The first is tradition – within this dimension, each analyst is marked by and, to a certain degree, determined by the forces of culture. They are the "prior conditions" that constitute the possibilities of interpreting and acting in the world. Secondly, innovation – a dimension within which each analyst, through their differences, seeks to explore shared inheritance in a personal way.

A good part of the mores, habits and ways of life of analysts are unconscious and have their origins in identifications that allow them to function practically and, more or less, coherently. However, considering the identifications and introjections through which an analyst in training must pass through, it could be worthwhile asking at what point do the innovative creations overflow to break with the introjected tradition? Still, this could be a question bereft of meaning, seeing as every creation is part of a tradition and, in that perspective, does not oppose it. Tradition, in turn, is only revived and transmitted when there exists the possibility of creating a style, which is simultaneously original and the result of the presence of tradition in each new act.

Tradition, in our case, must fundamentally encompass the soil from which psychoanalysis (and each psychoanalyst) receives the bounties that make it what it is. And, it must be so even beyond the rules of foundation and the functioning that psychoanalysis seeks to establish for itself. Based on the lineage of Heidegger (1927) and Gadamer (1960), we can think of the cultural soil, of the soup of Culture that precedes and nourishes us, as an existential pre-structure, like the horizon of each practice, of each theory and of each analyst. We can still always walk toward the horizon and, while it will move with us, it is from this point of view that both psychoanalysis and the tradition into which it is inserted contain their own horizons. As we work, our horizon is constantly being formed, testing our prejudices as they meet the past and demanding comprehension of parts of our tradition, without which we would not exist. On the other hand, an excess of "attachment" (whether conscious or unconscious) to tradition would paralyze an analyst in the thick blanket of familiarity, which is the impregnation of habit, a disease made possible when the horizon is both too close and fixed in time and space.

Meanwhile, innovation aims to reveal itself in each original attempt at expression. However, its base, or "soil" cannot be confused with something such as "the analyst's identity". It is based on a pre-subjective extract (tradition, in the sense presented above) that the analyst's own subjectivity will gradually firm in the effort to construct innovations. In addition to tradition as the pre-subjective field, we can think of a "proper body" (*corps propre*), as suggested by Merleau-Ponty (1945), which is the most originating part of subjectivity, revealing itself as a spatial-temporal support for the self. With this, I understand that subjectivity alone only becomes effective in intersubjectivity, which, in turn, will always be first and foremost an intercorporeality.[2] It is from this inaugural and constitutive level that, in the last instance, involves a mutual intercorporeal constitution, where, to my mind, creative possibility emerges. The creative force that sustains an innovation does not find its original drive in psychological determinism or physical causality. Innovation, in this sense, emerges from singular forms of intercorporeal relationships, which themselves occur in a field steeped in tradition.

There is no doubt that Thomas Ogden is one of the main contemporary psychoanalysts. Fully immersed in a psychoanalytic tradition, but at the same time, the creator of new concepts that expand and bring innovations to that tradition.[3] A creative author who is of fundamental importance in the post-school (or transmatricial)[4] period of the history of psychoanalysis. Based on original readings, especially the works of Freud, Klein, Winnicott and Bion (although he cites the works of Green, Fairbairn, Searles, Loewald and Lacan, among others, with regularity), Ogden demonstrates how to be fertile, without being eclectic, with a way of thinking and working ideas in the field of psychoanalysis beyond the strict boundaries so characteristic of its main schools.

Ogden's psychoanalytic production is, above all, a rigorous and detailed theoretical-clinical reflection on (verbal and non-verbal) forms of communication that constitute psychoanalytic practice. The big differentiator can be found in the evocative and descriptive quality of complex clinical situations that provide a fertile soil for the development of original theoretical developments. In addition, his interest in literature (especially Frost's poetry and Borges' works) and in hermeneutics (Ogden uses an original interpretative approach in his essays dedicated to investigating the style that emerges from the works of renowned psychoanalysts who preceded him) are also noteworthy. His relationship with philosophy is more complex, where his use of dialectics, based on Hegel and the notion of intersubjectivity, originating from the phenomenological tradition begun by Husserl, stands out. In this case, Ogden does not always navigate with the same calm and precision he shows when focused on purely psychoanalytic concepts. However, resorting to philosophy is justified by the need to make psychoanalytic theory face the challenges of its own limits.[5]

As Ogden himself affirms, in his first book, published in 1982, "Psychoanalytic theory suffers from a paucity of concepts and language to describe the interplay between phenomena in an intrapsychic sphere and phenomena in the spheres of external reality and interpersonal relations." (Ogden, 1982, p. 11) The texts that appeared regularly in the 42 years since then present an author with an impressive literary ability to expose the intricate weave that dominates daily psychoanalytic practice, always in a constant search for the most evocative forms of communication, of lending vitality to psychoanalytic concepts and in full ethical recognition of alterity (otherness).

The various papers written by Ogden for the field's most important periodicals and later republished in his books can be divided into six main categories. The first are papers focused on concepts that had already been established in psychoanalytic theory, originally created and developed by other authors, such as projective identification, reverie, potential space, and so on. The second is for papers on original concepts he created, of which examples include the autistic-contiguous position, the analytic third and talking-as-dreaming. Papers about forms of communication and those on forms of reading/writing in psychoanalysis comprise the third and fourth categories. The fifth encompasses papers dedicated to a hermeneutic (close and deconstructive) reading of singular texts by important, established authors, while the sixth is made up of papers that connect clinical experience and case studies with the conceptual dimension he developed.

Next, I will delve into the concepts central to Ogden's theorization, the *contiguous-autistic position* and the *analytic third*, followed by two clinical cases he presented. The aim is to highlight his contribution to contemporary psychoanalytic literature and both cases reveal his ways of thinking, based on a third element, seeking to escape the recurrent dualism that structures the majority of Freudian psychoanalytic theories.[6]

The Autistic-Contiguous Position

In his book *The Primitive Edge of Experience* (1989), Ogden presents, for the first time in greater detail, his notion of the autistic-contiguous position. The idea began taking shape in a previous paper (Ogden, 1988). Close to the Kleinian tradition and authors of the British school of psychoanalysis (post-Kleinian and independents), he sought to give form to a very primitive level of psychic experience that, according to him, could already be found in the work of Esther Brick, Donald Meltzer and Francis Tustin and secondarily, in authors such as Anzieu, Bion, Brazelton, the Gaddinis, Mahler, Milner, Rosenfeld, Searles, Spitz, Stern and Winnicott. Ogden states that "This mode of organizing experience is characterized by specific types of defense and forms of object relatedness, and a quality of anxiety and degree of subjectivity" (1989, p. 48). Although it deals with a position whose primacy came during a period before that of the two organizations described by Klein (paranoid-schizoid and depressive), it dialectically coexists with the two so-called "subsequent" positions. For Ogden, psychopathological conditions emerge from the collapse of the dialectic interplay among these three forms of experience.

The autistic-contiguous position is associated with a specific way of attributing meaning to experience, where sensory data predominates in the formation of pre-symbolic connections among different sensory impressions, generating surfaces with specific borders and delimitations. It is in these surfaces that the experience of the self comes from. Ogden remembers the classic passage by Freud, in which he states the ego (the "I") is first a bodily ego, before insisting on the idea that the ego derives from bodily sensations, those that emanate from the surface of the body.[7]

Ogden believes his notion needs to be differentiated from that of Margareth Mahler, of a normal "autism". In contrast to it – which sees the infant in its first months of life as existing within a monadic, closed system self-sufficient in its mode of hallucinatory wish fulfilment – Ogden does not propose the autistic-contiguous position as a closed system in which the infant is isolated from its world of objects. His concept places object relations in this position as experienced in terms of surfaces, generated through interactions between the infant and its objects and through sensory transformations that occur during these interactions. The object (in the form of sensory impressions) is attributed with meaning and is responded to in an organizing and organized manner, a manner that involves a mutually transformative game between the nascent self and object.

Ogden suggests that in the contiguous-autistic position, it is the sensory experience, of the senses, especially that of the surface of the skin, which is the principal medium for the creation of psychic meaning and the initial rudiments of the experience of a self. The sensory contiguity of the skin's surface, alongside the rhythmical element, are the fundamental bases for the establishment of that we can call infantile object relations. It is through touch, the sensation of the skin, in sensory contiguous relations (the infant's face on the mother's breast), that the organization of a rudimentary sense of "I-ness", can be established, gradually generating the sense of a sensory barrier surface, then allowing the subject to have an experience of oneself – what Winnicott called "a place where one lives". It is the place in which the infant feels, thinks and lives: a place that has form, hardness, coldness, warmth and texture, which are the beginnings of the qualities that lead us to be.

It could be said that the nature of the agony that predominates in the contiguous-autistic position is that of agony from the rupture of the sensation of sensory cohesion, generating an absence of barriers. It is an agony of imprisonment in a closed system of bodily sensations of the annihilation of barriers that generates that sensation of shattering, of disappearance in a space without shapes and boundaries, which impedes the formation of a potential space, as described by Winnicott. It is common in patients who have bodily sensations of shattering, of falling into emptiness with neither shapes nor barriers. At the same time, the defensive modes that predominate in the contiguous-autistic position can be described as defenses that seek to reestablish the continuity of barriers through revisiting the sensations produced on the sensory surface. They are also defenses that seek to revisit the rhythmicity in which lies the inaugural integrity of the self. They can be recognized in patients who, during the session, revisit sensory shapes that reconstitute what he calls a "ground" of sensory safety; the rhythmic curling of hair in every session, the foot that taps out a beat, biting of lips, of the inside of the cheek. These are ways of calming oneself through autistic shapes.

A few years later, going a bit further in the use of this notion, Ogden (1994) seeks to tackle pathological experiences of isolation very early in a human being's life, prior to those described by Winnicott, while at the same time highlighting the need for isolation experiences "as a necessary condition for psychological health" (Ogden, 1994, p. 167). The collapse of subjectivity and intersubjectivity is often anchored, according to Ogden, in "a primitive form of isolation that involves the disconnection of the individual not only from the mother as object, but also from the very fabric of the human interpersonal matrix." (Ogden, 1994, p. 167).

In line with his epistemological concepts about the intersubjective experience (as I will demonstrate below), Ogden (1994) refuses the need to choose when faced with the classical opposition from psychoanalytic studies on the infant's first experiences: is the infant is at one with the mother and so has no conscience of her separate existence or of itself, or is the infant capable, from the beginning of its existence, of recognizing the difference between itself and the other? Ogden states that we should consider the "infantile experience (and human experience in general) as the outcome of a dialectical process involving multiple forms of consciousness (each existing with others)". In this way, "it is no longer necessary to cast our question in terms of mutually exclusive oppositions. The question of whether the infant is at one with the mother or is separate from her becomes a question of the nature of the interplay between simultaneous experiences of at-one-ment and of separateness." (Ogden, 1994, p. 172).

To propose the idea of an isolation even more primitive than the one described by Winnicott, Ogden turns to the idea of an auto-generated sensory matrix that would come to substitute the interpersonal matrix. Based on an investigation of autistic phenomena, he proposed "a vocabulary for thinking about the notion of auto-sensuous isolation." (1994, p. 173). To these ends, he revisits the works of Frances Tustin on autism. The central point is that in very primitive experiences, the infant tends to experience objects as sensations, not as things, so in this sense, "autistic shapes" are "sensory shapes", as proposed by Tustin (1984, p. 280). In the infant's inaugural sensorial experiences, the "contiguity of skin surfaces creates an idiosyncratic shape that is the infant in that moment. In other words, the infant's being is in this way given sensory definition and sense of locale." (Ogden, 1994, p. 174). To further exemplify the origin and functioning of this process of auto-sensuous isolation, the author turns to a classic example, but reinterpreting it:

> [...] the comfort that an infant experiences in thumb sucking is not only derived from the representational value of the thumb as stand-in for the breast; in addition, there is a dimension of thumb sucking that can be understood as involving a relationship to an autistic shape through which a sense of self-as-sensory-surface is generated.
>
> (Ogden, 1994, p. 175)

Ogden considers isolation originating from this type of experience as being the most radical disconnection possible between human beings with whom an infant (or a person of any age) lives:

> The type of isolation I have in mind is not a form of psychological death [...] What I am attempting to describe is a suspension of life in the world of the living and the replacement of that world with an autonomous world of "perfect" sensation "relationships".
>
> (Ogden, 1994, p. 178)

Like Winnicott, Ogden believes this form of isolation to be an essential part of an infant's emotional and relational development, stating that "the well timed, periodic letting go and retrieval of the infant from this form of isolation is an essential part of the early rhythmicity of human development." (Ogden, 1994, p. 178).

Establishing Early Levels of Integration in the Analytic Relationship: The Case of Mr. V

Thomas Ogden insists that, as analysts,

> we attempt to assist the analysand in his efforts at freeing himself from forms of organized experience (his conscious and unconscious "know-ledge" of himself) that entrap him and prevent him from tolerating the experience of not knowing long enough to create understandings in a different way.
>
> (Ogden, 1989, p. 1)

Here, I revisit a clinical case published by Ogden in *This Art of Psychoanalysis* (2005), to indicate the recovery of the uniqueness of the analytic pair, on the primordial relationship ground based on which the constitution of the subjects (analyst and analysand) can take place. The patient's agonies and defenses go back to the autistic-contiguous position, expressing themselves in profound isolation and generalizations that distance them from themselves and from contact with the analyst. Through the analyst's reverie (a concept that refers to the forms of daydreaming during the session, as proposed by Bion), experienced in two key moments during an analysand's first session, we see the emergence of what Ogden denominates the truth of an unconscious emotional experience, which can be used by the analytic pair for psychic transformations; that is, for the constitution of the subject. By discussing the events of this session while making use of the notion of the analytic third, the author illustrates constitutive processes of a fundamentally interactional nature. He also tackles the interactional character of the truth of an unconscious emotional experience, in a way that it is not possible to attribute, to either the analyst or analysand, the truth that is communicated by the analyst's interpretation, a truth that emerges and that is also transformed by the experience of the pair as the session progresses.

The clinical vignette related by Ogden comes from the first session with Mr. V, in which the contents of the analyst's interpretations are largely based on two moments of reverie. In this first encounter, the analyst ponders about an event that took place before the session began. Mr. V hesitated before entering the waiting room to the analyst's office, pacing back and forth in the corridor between the front door and that of the waiting room, a few minutes prior to his first meeting with Ogden. Initially, in the session, Mr. V avoids the topic. Over the course of the meeting, however, he feels more encouraged to talk about what happened, making several comments related to the feelings that are named by the analyst.

Between the analyst's first and second moments of reverie, there is a significant change in the emotional atmosphere of the session. This change takes place after the analyst conveys his first interpretation, formulated shortly after the first reverie. Ogden has a vague recollection from his own childhood of an episode with a friend, in the form of an emotionally intense series of static images, like photographs. He and his friend, both aged eight at the time, are playing on a frozen lake, when his friend falls into the water after stepping on ice that had partially melted. The feelings evoked by the memory of his childhood are fear, guilt and shame, experienced in a way that was not shared between him and his friend. However, a profound sense of loneliness, isolation and sadness also emerged.

Amidst the presence of these evoked emotions, Ogden tells Mr. V that he suspected, from the sound of his footsteps in the corridor before coming in for the session, that Mr. V was experiencing a degree of disturbance as their first encounter approached. Mr. V made contributions to what had happened, followed by the analyst's observations about how lonely he must felt at that moment, before meeting him, as if he were in a kind of "no-man's land", in that corridor, unable both to reach Ogden to get to know him and begin analysis (by crossing the glass door), as well as to be part of life out there, where he imagined people were capable of living.

Mr. V tends to generalize, avoiding talking about his deepest feelings, both relating to the episode in the corridor and to the here-and-now of the session. However, in the final half of the session, Mr. V appeared to take interest in discussing what had happened to him and seemed less hesitant about doing so. A few minutes of silence were felt by Ogden as a long time, but did not appear to be an awkward silence. During these minutes, the analyst returns to the episode from his childhood. This time, however, the experience of the memory was completely different, because of the emergence of an emotional context from the relationship with Mr. V, which was also different. There was a greater sensation of seeing and feeling things from within himself and from his friend, instead of from an external and static point of view, like before. There was, thus, greater proximity to the feelings in question and more vividness in his imagination. It was not a series of poses (photographs), but the unfolding of an experience, forcefully realistic and with a strong emotional impact. Ogden felt he had no choice but to become more grown up than he was at the time, someone he feared he would not be able to become. He felt conscious of not being able to even conceive of that version of himself, more grown up. Ogden, in this reverie, was able to have a more comprehensible and shareable version of the event, feeling less wary of experiencing the feelings at play. The feeling of shame of immaturity was a new version of a feeling evoked in the first reverie, in which intense fear, shame, guilt and loneliness arose.

The analyst, in a tone that also communicates the emotions involved, talks about Mr. V's shame of feeling like a child, in the corridor, when he realizes he forgot the note with the information Ogden had passed to him on the telephone and that, for him, feeling or behaving like a child was something truly shameful. The analyst verbalizing this is followed by a visible relief of tension in Mr. V's body, who then goes on to say, in a tone that appeared, there, for the first time and would only reappear rarely over the first few years of the sessions: "Outside there, I felt so lost..." (2005, p. 73). Ogden emphasizes the tone used by the patient to relay this: there was a softness, yet at the same time, vivacity to the words and the words chosen also communicated something essential. There was an outside that conveyed the feeling that there was also beginning to exist an "inside here" of the analytic space and of the vitalized relationship with the analyst, in which Mr. V already felt less lost.

A universe marked by dimensions of experiences opens up when the analyst speaks about Mr. V's brief hesitance when arriving at the office. He, initially, does not mull over this brief, but significant, episode and tends to avoid it through the more automated contact he initially establishes with the analyst. Profundity and vitality arise, however, when the two speak of this experience of what appears to be Mr. V's sterile contact with the world. The defensive relational manner initially lived by Mr. V goes in the opposite direction to the meaningful relational experience established in the session. In his generalizations, there is fundamentally a distancing – of the experience of the subject himself, and of the experiences of others, which seemed so different to his own.

In this clinical fragment, it is possible to identify the implantation of a fertile experience for both, which corresponds to a level of *early* ego-reality integration. The experience of emotional contact with another, experienced by the analyst in his reverie, allows for identification with the patient's feelings of profound loneliness, fear, shame and isolation. In this moment, early psychic and emotional levels emerge in the relationship and are reminiscent of the tender experience an infant has when the mother, in tune with the infant, can identify its states of being. The immersion into this primordial level of relating, a fundamental level of the human experience, allows for the apprehension of primordial meanings.

Ogden's detailed description and discussion, which include the reasons for why he says what he does to the patient, as well as the changes in the session's emotional atmosphere, relayed both by the analyst's reverie and what he says, are attempts by the author to show how the field is being mutually configured by the analytic pair. There is also a concern to show a dimension of the interpretation that goes beyond its content, encompassing sensorial elements that communicate emotional states, proximity, intimacy and distancing between the analyst and analysand.

Next, I will present the second concept, *the analytic third*, in its direct reference to intersubjectivity present in practice. Finally, there is another clinical vignette to highlight the way in which Ogden works relationships between practice and theory in psychoanalysis.

The Analytic Third[8]

The theme of communication between the analyst and analysand in the analytic setting has already been addressed in different ways over the course of the history of psychoanalysis. Freud (1912), in his classic text on technique, proposed an intersubjective form of communication that has been causing, since its publication, endless controversies and an equally endless number of attempts at clarification. The doctor "must turn his own unconscious like a receptive organ towards the transmitting unconscious of the patient. He must adjust himself to the patient as a telephone receiver is adjusted to the transmitting microphone" (p. 175). For Freud, it is about the analyst's fundamental position of listening supported in the concept of an equally free-floating attention, which, in turn, would be the technical recommendation corresponding to the rule of free association proposed to the analysand.

For many authors after Freud, the receiver/transmitting microphone metaphor needs no recommendation by him to make use of any form of "communication between the unconscious and the unconscious". Laplanche and Pontalis (1985/1998) in their arguments regarding the unfeasibility of such a form of communication, point out that "as Freud points out himself when speaking of free association, the suspension of conscious 'purposive ideas' can only result in their replacement by unconscious ones." (p. 75). That is, how is it possible to maintain the position of an analyst with a free-floating attention, without that attention coming to be directed by their own unconscious motivations? Would unconscious motivations not be affected by the other's unconscious motivations? Should the determinism presupposed in Freud's theories demand that this direction always be from the inside, out? I believe that in this point of argument, it could be useful to go deeper in the investigation of communication forms from the works of Freud and those authors who came after him, seeking to analyze the so-called "infraverbal" forms of communication and the different possibilities of conceiving unconscious perceptions. This could, perhaps, lead to expanding the horizon of the theme of communication in analysis to actually go beyond the generally accepted formulation of ego-to-ego communications and the correlated binomial pre-conscious and conscious perception-representation. A strong psychoanalytic tradition admits there is, for example, the communication of certain feelings that cannot be "contained" by the analysand, that cannot be thought or elaborated, or even "felt". They are feelings that are still "without form" and, as such, cannot be expressed in words. For such expression in words and to make the elaboration of these feelings possible, they first need to be transformed in some way and given a "form". This is only possible through the relationship or in the pre-verbal communication with the analyst that occurs in projective identification.

Clearly, there are many questions that can be raised from this point of view. What means would be used so that communication at the pre-verbal level could take place? What conditions are required for it to occur and for the analyst to be able to realize what his unconscious (or pre-conscious) was able to receive from the analysand? Further, how can the analyst distinguish his own feelings from those that are evoked in him by the analysand?

Ogden tackles these questions from a different angle when he proposes the concept of the *analytic third*:

> The analytic process reflects the interplay of three subjectivities: the subjectivity of the analyst, of the analysand, and of the analytic third. The analytic third is a creation of the analyst and the analysand, and at the same time the analyst and the analysand (qua analyst and analysand) are created by the analytic third. (There is no analyst, no analysand, no analysis in the absence of the third).
>
> (Ogden, 1994, p. 93)

For Ogden, projective identification should be understood as "a dimension of all intersubjectivity, at times the predominant quality of the experience, at other times only a subtle background" (Ogden, 1994, p. 99). Or, further:

> In projective identification, there is a partial collapse of the dialectical movement of individual subjectivity and intersubjectivity and a resultant creation of a subjugating analytic third (within which the individual subjectivities of the participants are to a large degree subsumed). A successful analytic process involves the superseding of the third and the reappropriation of the (transformed) subjectivities by the participants as separate (and yet interdependent) individuals. This is achieved through an act of mutual recognition that is often mediated by the analyst's interpretation of the transference-countertransference and the analysand's use of the analyst's interpretation.
>
> (Ogden, 1994, p. 106)

With this, we can state that the problem which would present to analysts regarding differentiating, in their own emotional reactions, the elements that belonged exclusively to their own subjectivity from those evoked in them by the analysand, now has a solution that is fundamentally different from those that could be identified in other authors:

> In both the relationship of mother and infant and the relationship of analyst and analysand, the task is not to tease apart the elements constituting the relationship in an effort to determine which qualities belong to which individual participating in it; rather, from the point of view of the interdependence of subject and object, the analytic task involves an attempt

to describe as fully as one can the specific nature of the experience of the interplay of individual subjectivity and intersubjectivity.

(Ogden, 1994, p. 64)

It should be noted that, here, we have more than one new response to the same questions, there is a new set of presumptions, based on which new questions arise. This is how Ogden creates an interesting inversion in the problem of analytic communication and relations. Albeit, from a realist and/ or empirical point of view, the analytic situation is never anything other than the situation of two separate and distinct subjects in communication with one another, what Ogden proposes is that we abandon this point of view in our attempt to understand psychoanalytic phenomena. In this manner, that which we used to identify as feelings and thoughts unconsciously *communicated* or *induced* by the analysand in the analyst, Ogden describes as feelings and thoughts that are simply *felt* and *thought* by the third intersubjective subject. Thus, the problem is no longer of the nature and means of unconscious qualified communication; it becomes the problem of the nature of this "intersubjective subject". The relation between analyst and analysand as fully constituted and separate subjects continues to take place on the verbal and conscious levels. However, when considering intersubjectivity as conceived by Ogden, *relation* or *communication* are no longer found to be involved. Intersubjectivity, understood as a "third intersubjective subject" is not a *relation between two subjects*, it is precisely a *new subject*. That which, from a certain point of view, occurred in the relation between the subjects, now occurs as an *experience* of a third subject.

It does seem unjustified to simply say that the problem of communication and of the relation between analyst and analysand has been transferred to a problem of communication and of the relation between analyst and the third subject. It is the situation as a whole that transfigures when one comes to consider the creation of the third: the analyst and analysand no longer exist purely as isolated subjects, with their constitution now being based on the dialectic (or rather *the logic of supplementarity*– as French philosopher Jacques Derrida (1967) suggests – or even *dialectics without synthesis* – as another French philosopher, Merleau-Ponty (1964), proposes) relationship between subjectivity and intersubjectivity. To emphasize, this dialectic relationship is one of *mutual constitution*, where it makes no sense to speak of communication or any other form of relation between two poles that are purely exterior to one another. This is where we clearly find the possibility of a transubjective intersubjectivity[9] in Ogden's work.

Moreover, it is worthwhile remembering that, for Ogden, analytic communication always remains at an ego-to-ego level. Even so, his proposal contains a true novelty that could suggest the defense of the idea of communication between the unconscious of the analyst and analysand: the proposition that all communication always occurs over the background of a series of dialectic relations involving the isolated subjectivities of the analyst, analysand

and third intersubjective subject. These relations primarily take place at an unconscious level, but this is only valid from a descriptive point of view: there is no transmission of repressed representations from one subject to another. "Analysis is not simply a method of uncovering the hidden; it is more importantly a process of creating the analytic subject who had not previously existed." (Ogden, 1994, p. 47).

With Ogden, we can affirm that what is involved in the formation of intersubjectivity (transubjective) is a level of existence and experience that is still pre-representational and even pre-personal (based on which the subject is created), in which one cannot and should not attempt to "determine which qualities belong to which individual participating in it." (Ogden, 1994, p. 64). In the experience of the analytic third, what is at play are:

> … symbolic and protosymbolic (sensation-based) forms given to the unarticulated (and often not yet felt) experience of the analysand as they are taking form in the intersubjectivity of the analytic pair (i.e., in the analytic third).
>
> (Ogden, 1994, p. 82)

"Below" the level in which communication and interaction takes place between analyst and analysand, there is the structuring of an intersubjective field *in which it makes no sense to speak of communication*, not even unconscious communication, or that between the unconscious of the analyst and analysand. The question, here, is that Ogden's intersubjectivity does not refer to the in-between subjectivities, but on what might be called a primordial intersubjectivity – a situation in which the subjectivities constitute themselves mutually, in a manner whereby the individual subjects do not come before the intersubjectivity or vice-versa. This is visible in the fact that the analyst enters into contact with this intersubjective field precisely through "the ways in which he is inextricably given to himself" and through his "very private dimensions" (Reis, 1999, p. 390)

This comprehension of intersubjectivity also involves a corresponding revision of the concept of individual subjectivity:

> The analytic conception of the subject has increasingly become a theory of the interdependence of subjectivity and intersubjectivity. The subject cannot create itself; the development of subjectivity requires experiences of specific forms of intersubjectivity. In the beginning, subjectivity and the individual psyche are not coincident: 'There is no such thing as an infant'. The constitution of the subject in the space between mother and infant is mediated by such psychological-interpersonal events as projective identification, primary maternal preoccupation, the mirroring relationship, relatedness to transitional objects, and the experiences of object usage and truth. The appropriation by the infant of the intersubjective space represents a critical step in the establishment of the individual's capacity to generate and maintain psychological dialectics (e.g., of consciousness and

unconsciousness, of me and not me, of I and me, of I and Thou) through which it is simultaneously constituted and decentered as a subject.

(Ogden, 1994, p. 60)

It is important to emphasize that the affirmation that there is an "appropriation by the infant of the intersubjective space" at a given moment, suggests that the constitution of subjectivity becomes permanent and that the dialectic between subjectivity and intersubjectivity is never interrupted. The same fact is pointed out by Ogden, when dealing with the analytic process:

> The termination of a psychoanalytic experience is not the end of the subject of psychoanalysis. The intersubjectivity of the analytic pair is appropriated by the analysand and is transformed into an internal dialogue (a process of mutual interpretation taking place within the context of a single personality system).
>
> (Ogden, 1994, p. 47)

However, it should also be noted that Ogden is not alone in defending the idea of a pre- and intersubjective level of existence permanently sustaining the existence of the subject as an isolated and defined entity. Bruce E. Reis (1999), for example, has ideas close to the work of Merleau-Ponty,[10] defending that the Hegelian dialectic model, used amply by Ogden, is not capable of accounting for the actual experiences he seeks to describe and comprehend:

> The mirroring metaphor [is] problematic for not taking into account the unique subjectivity of the other [...] Interdependence established through identification with the other is not yet intersubjectivity. For Hegel, subjectivity remains equated with the conscious subject in competition with the other. By contrast, the model I want to introduce here treats intersubjectivity as such an element and primary condition that competition would already represent a differentiation of subject from object.
>
> (Reis, 1999, p. 378)

According to this author, Ogden had overcome both the limits of a model based on a simple mirroring as well as the insufficiency of the Hegelian dialectic relations model:

> The baby is aware of a plurality of subjects in what Ogden termed a 'relationship of relative sameness and therefore of relative difference' before being aware of individual subjects. Intersubjective experience precedes personal experience and is [...] rooted in bodily experiencing.
>
> (Reis, 1999, p. 384)

The presence of Merleau-Ponty's "shadow" in interpretations of Ogden's work, like this one by Reis, inevitably imply that it is necessary to abandon even the actual notion of intersubjectivity, replacing it with intercorporeality, or even co-corporeality, as I have suggested previously (Coelho Junior, 2010).

Furthermore, I point out the proximity of Ogden's concept of the third analytic subject to contributions by Willy and Madeleine Baranger relating to the analytic field. Ogden (2004) accepted the Barangers' ideas as similar to the ones of his investigations only ten years after publishing, for the first time, his article on the analytical third, in a footnote:

> It is beyond the scope of this paper to offer a comprehensive review of the literature concerning an intersubjective view of the analytic process and the nature of the unconscious interplay of transference and counter-transference. See Bion's (1962) and Green's (1975) work concerning the analytic object and [the] Barangers' (1969/1993) notion of the analytic field for conceptions of unconscious analytic intersubjectivity that overlap with what I call the analytic third.
>
> (Ogden, 2004, p. 169)

The preceding ideas close to those of Ogden's, whether Green's, Bion's or the Barangers', in no way diminish the importance of his contribution. However, recognizing these different influences and their roots in the history of psycho-analysis help us to gain a less naïve comprehension of the division between tradition and innovation in the complex constitution of a field of investigation and practice that is psychoanalysis.[11]

Next, I present another of Ogden's clinical cases in which the questions raised so far about the third analytic subject gain new dimensions.

Talking-as-Dreaming: The Case of Mrs. L

This clinical case was published by Ogden in 2007, in the paper "On Talking-as-dreaming", in the *International Journal of Psychoanalysis* and republished in his book, *Rediscovering Psychoanalysis*, in 2009.

Ogden provocatively opens his text with the following:

> I take as fundamental to an understanding of psychoanalysis the idea that the analyst must invent psychoanalysis anew with each patient. This is achieved in no small measure by means of an ongoing experiment, within the terms of the psychoanalytic situation, in which patient and analyst create ways of talking to one another that are unique to each analytic pair at a given moment in the analysis.
>
> (Ogden, 2007, p. 575)

Based on his clinical experience, the author suggest that many patients are incapable of engaging in daydreaming while in the analytic setting, whether in the form of free association, or in any other way. Due to this, Ogden came to recognize ways of working, of talking, that at first glance,

> [...] appears to be 'unanalytic' in that it may seem to consist 'merely' of talking about such topics as books, films, etymology, baseball, the taste of chocolate, the structure of light, and so on. Despite appearances, it has been my experience that such 'unanalytic' talk often allows a patient and analyst who have been unable to dream together to begin to be able to do so. I will refer to talking of this sort as 'talking-as-dreaming.' Like free association (and unlike ordinary conversation), talking-as-dreaming tends to include considerable primary process thinking [...] When an analysis is 'a going concern,' the patient and analyst are able to engage both individually and with one another in a process of dreaming.
>
> (Ogden, 2007, p. 575)

Furthermore, for the author:

> The area of 'overlap' of the patient's dreaming and the analyst's dreaming is the place where analysis occurs (Winnicott, 1971, p. 38). The patient's dreaming, under such circumstances, manifests itself in the form of free associations (or, in child analysis, in the form of playing); the analyst's waking–dreaming often takes the form of reverie experience. When a patient is unable to dream, this difficulty becomes the most pressing aspect of the analysis.
>
> (Ogden, 2007, p. 576)

Ogden understands "dreaming as the most important psychoanalytic function of the mind: where there is unconscious 'dream-work,' there is also unconscious 'understanding-work'" (2007, p. 576).

Ogden suggests that Bion's ideas are the theoretical basis for this work, having determined the radical transformation in psychoanalytic conception about dreaming and the incapacity to dream. Like Winnicott, who modified the focus of psychoanalytic theory and practice from the content of playing (as the symbolic representation of the child's internal world) to the experience of playing, Bion changed the focus from the symbolic content of thoughts to the process of thinking and from the symbolic meaning of dreams to the process of dreaming (Ogden, 2010).

Based on these notions, Ogden gives his own view (definition) of what psychoanalysis is as a therapeutic process:

> I view psychoanalysis as an experience in which patient and analyst engage in an experiment within the analytic frame that is designed to create conditions in which the analysand (with the analyst's participation) may be able to dream formerly undreamable emotional experience (his 'undreamt dreams'). I view talking-as-dreaming as an improvisation in

the form of loosely structured conversation (concerning virtually any subject) in which the analyst participates in the patient's dreaming previously undreamt dreams. In so doing, the analyst facilitates the patient's dreaming himself more fully into existence.

(Ogden, 2007, p. 577)

He insists that this is very different to a situation in which the analyst dreams for the patient (or does the work of dreaming for the patient) regarding what the patient is still not capable of dreaming. Likewise, he insists that for this form of work to actually happen, one must be even more strict (not less) in terms of the analytic setting. The essential difference between the roles of analyst and analysand needs to be maintained as a solid presence throughout the treatment, given that, otherwise, patients would be deprived of the analyst and the analytic relation they need.

In the text, Ogden then presents two clinical fragments; however, we will only focus on the first of these.

They are two vignettes of cases in which the patients were very limited in their ability to dream their emotional experiences, whether through free association or any other form of dreaming. In both cases, the patients were eventually and with the participation of the analyst able to begin to engage with the genuine ability to dream in the form of "talking-as-dreaming".

The first case was that of Mrs. L, an intelligent and successful woman who began analysis due to intense agony that the fear of her seven-year-old son falling and dying caused her. She also suffered greatly from the fear of her own death, which would leave her unable to function. This fear was accompanied by the feeling that her husband, a very selfish man, would be incapable of raising their son if she were gone. During the first year of the sessions, this was all she was able to relate. All the other aspects of her life seemed to have no emotional meaning or importance. For Mrs. L, analysis was not for thinking about her life, it was for the analyst to cure her of her fears. Her dreaming was basically comprised of "dreams" that were not dreams, rather, she did not transform with the repetitive experience of dreams and nightmares in which she was unable to impede one catastrophe after another.

Ogden revealed that his own capacity for reverie in the sessions was limited and useless for the psychological work. A characteristic of Mrs. L, since the beginning of the treatment, was a spasmodic, abrupt way of speaking, expelling words as if she were trying to fit in the maximum number possible in the same breath. The author suggests that it is as if Mrs. L has a fear of running out of breath or of being interrupted by him, affirming that he is unable to stand another minute or word from her (Ogden, 2007, p. 578).

In the second year of analysis, the patient seemed to have lost all hope that it would be of any use. She continued speaking abruptly, not leaving any opportunity, for herself or the analyst, to genuinely think and dream. In this stage of the treatment, Ogden tells the patient that he thinks she feels like someone who is so small, so weak that she lacks the substance to be able to make changes through her thoughts and voice. After this observation, the patient started taking longer pauses than she used to, before continuing to talk. Ogden then comments that she must have found what he just said useless (Ogden, 2007, p.578).

Over the months preceding the session that he then relates, the patient seemed to have a slightly less hurried way of speaking: "Up to that point, it was as if the patient felt that there was not 'time' (i.e. psychological room) for thinking and talking about anything other than her efforts 'to cope', to keep herself from losing her mind" (Ogden, 2007, p. 579). However, the patient's fears of dying or of the death of her son receded to the point that she was able to start reading again, something Mrs. L had not done since the birth of her son. She had given birth to him a few months after having finished her doctorate.

The session Ogden relates took place on a Monday and Mrs. L tells him that, over the weekend, she re-read the novel *Disgrace*, by J. M. Coetzee, published in 1999. Ogden mentions that they had briefly talked about Coetzee's work the year before and that like her, he also admired Coetzee as a writer and that she would have noticed that during that brief conversation they had.

Mrs. L said there was something about the book, which takes place in post-apartheid South Africa, that makes her want to return to him. The narrator is a university professor who is trying to redirect things to a more vitalized life – if he had, in fact been living like that at any time before – through a sexual relationship with one of his students. It seems inevitable that the girl will report him and, when she does, he refuses to defend himself. He even refuses, during his audiences with the dean, to repeat the words (an acceptable lie) that would help him in that situation. Thus, he ends up being dismissed from his position. It is as if he felt his entire life as a series of dishonorable events, with this incident being just the most recent proof of his state, proof that he is unable to refute. (Ogden, 2007, p. 579).

Ogden comments that, although the patient spoke using her usual mannerism, the change that had taken place was very noticeable: Mrs. L was speaking with a genuine vitality in her tone about something that was not directly related to her fears of the death of her son or herself. (Of course, Ogden describes, this change did not take place overnight, only in this moment of the session. It was something that had been happening over the years of analysis, at first with some humor appearing now and then during a session, or through an occasional dream with a degree of vitality, etc.)

He also comments that he did not tell the patient what he went on to think after she spoke, that when she spoke of the novel's narrator, she could have been talking to herself and to him about her own psychic conflict. Ogden did not think it was the case to tell her that an aspect of her (identified with the narrator's refusal to lie) seemed to be in conflict with another of her aspects (the fear of death impeding the possibility of genuine thinking, feeling and speaking). According to him, telling Mrs. L would be the equivalent of waking the patient from what could be one of her first dream experiences in analysis, only to tell her his understanding of the dream. However, Ogden writes that making the interpretation, silently, was fundamental for himself, because, as he shows later, he was engaging with something very similar to Mrs. L's experience at that moment; that is, he was also trying to escape the forms of thinking and feeling (Ogden, 2007, p. 579).

Ogden goes on to tell Mrs. L that Coetzee's voice in *Disgrace* is one of the most destitute of emotions he has read in his life. Coetzee makes it clear in every sentence that he has no wish to even skirt the edges of any human experience at all. An experience is what it is, neither more, nor less. When saying this, Ogden felt as if he were entering a form of thinking and feeling with the patient that was different to all the other exchanges they had so far in the treatment (Ogden, 2007, p. 579).

To his surprise, Mrs. L continues the conversation, saying there was something that took place *between* the characters and *inside* the characters – regardless of how bizarre it may seem – that is strangely correct. Ogden replied with what seemed like a non sequitur: "You can hear in Coetzee's early books a writer who did not yet know who he was as a writer or even as a person. He's awkward, trying this and trying that. I sometimes feel embarrassed with him" (Ogden, 2007, p. 580). (The analyst writes that this was related to what he was feeling in the session, about the awkward movements they were making to start thinking/dreaming/talking in this new form.)

Mrs. L continued with another apparent non sequitur: "Even after the rape of the narrator's daughter and the shooting of the dogs that the daughter loved so much, the narrator found ways to hang on to the fragments of his humanity that remained alive for him" (Ogden, 2007, p. 580). (In this passage, the patient mentions the way in which the narrator from Coetzee's book comes to work with a woman who functioned as veterinarian and sacrificed the animals no one was brave enough to kill, thus avoiding greater suffering.)

At this moment in the session, the author writes that he began to remember that the patient had told him, initially in the treatment and again about three months before this session, about the great losses she had endured in her life: her father lost his first wife and three-year-old daughter to a car accident (the patient loved her father deeply and felt very loved by him). Ogden realized how he needed to forget this account, being unable to think/dream/talk/remember the truth for the emotional experience taking place. In his work with the patient, for a long time he was unable to think/dream/remember and maintain alive within himself the enormous (and unimaginable) pain that the patient's father and the patient herself experienced because of these deaths. Being unable to maintain alive within himself the emotional impact of these irreparable losses left him completely perplexed.

Ogden began to feel capable of dreaming (that is, of doing the conscious and unconscious psychological work) what he now perceived to be the feeling of disgrace and shame lived by the patient who survived in place of the father's first wife and daughter, and in the place of the parts of the father that had died with them.

Next, Mrs. L says:

> In Coetzee's books dying is not the worst thing that can happen to a person. For some reason, I find that idea comforting. I don't know why, but I'm reminded of a line I love from Coetzee's memoir. He says near the end something like: 'All we can do is to persist stupidly, doggedly in our repeated failures.'
>
> (Ogden, 2007, p. 581)

She then laughs loudly in a way the analyst had never heard her do before, after which she becomes more serious and continues:

> There's nothing glamorous about repeated failures while they're happening. I feel like such a failure as a mother. I can't lie to myself and pretend that my obsession with Aaron's dying isn't felt by him and doesn't scare the life out of him. I didn't intend to put it that way—'scare the life out of him'— but that is what I feel I'm doing to him. I'm terrified that I'm killing him with my fear—that I'm scaring the life out of him, and I can't stop doing it. That's my 'disgrace.'
>
> (Ogden, 2007, p. 581)

Mrs. L cried as she said this. In that moment, Ogden writes, it seemed clear that her father's emotional response to his "unthinkable" losses scared the life out of her.

Ogden then said:

> I think that you've felt like a disgrace your whole life. Your father's pain was unbearable not only to him, but to you. You couldn't help your father with his unimaginable pain. His pain was such a complicated thing for you—you're still in the grip of it with him—pain beyond what anyone can take in.
>
> (Ogden, 2007, p. 581)

This was the first moment in the treatment that Ogden was able to talk of the impossibility of the patient helping her father, but also of her inability to dream her experience in response to her father's pain.

The rest of the session showed Mrs. L evolving in her associations, making more directly transferential mentions based on characters from other books by Coetzee that she compares with the relationship she has with Ogden as an analyst. They also talked of Coetzee's choice to live in Adelaide, Australia, their disappointment with his latest books and many other things that Ogden was unsure whether they were said in that same session or the following ones, or even who said what.

Ogden concludes that revisiting how the conversation with the patient about books served as a form of "talking-as-dreaming". It was an experience of dreaming that was not exclusively his or the patient's.

Advancing in these clinical questions, Ogden (2016), based on Winnicott's ideas, focuses on the importance of the unlived dimensions of experiences had by severely traumatized patients. These are patients who have what he calls "unlived lives", with whom it is necessary to cocreate a very specific emotional contact. In a paper from 2017, Ogden indicates that the ability to dream (and eventually dream together – for the analyst and patient to dream the session) as a way of imbuing vitality (injecting some form of vitality into patients with unlived lives): "First there was deadness: the deadness of time, interminable time, time that passed for time, but in fact was time that did not pass, because there was no past, no history, no death. Instead there was a void: the absence in the patient, the absence of the patient. We were able to begin to dream the session [...]" (Ogden, 2017, p. 18). Several contemporary authors, whether or not inspired by Ogden, have been dealing with the theme of death in life, of mortified states and the clinical practice needed to face these states. This research direction, in my view, is one of the most important contributions Ogden has made to contemporary psychoanalysis. By revisiting Ferenczian and Winnicottian tradition and placing them in dialogue with the Kleinian-Bionian tradition, Ogden heads toward innovative thinking and practice that, when faced with the power of disconnection of the forces of Thanatos, recaptures vitalizing capacities, those of connecting (*binding*), of the forces of life.

Clearly, Ogden's ideas are not reduced to what is presented here. There is no doubt his contribution to the contemporary importance of Bion's notion of reverie is massive and has been pointed out by many of the commentators of his work, just as has his rereading of various of Winnicott's insights, which have since seen a resurgence. However, it is his most creative verve, that of proposing new concepts, like those of the autistic-contiguous position and the third analytic subject that might be his greatest strength. That is, it is in these concepts that add value to the tension (or dynamics) between the intrapsychic and intersubjective dimensions, in the dialectics between them as Ogden seems to prefer, that I believe lies his greatest contribution to contemporary psychoanalytic thinking and practice. Far from just someone who continues tradition, a protector of it, but also far from being a creator who produces a sharp break with tradition, Ogden points out a path that is able to simultaneously treasure tradition while risking necessary and vitalizing innovations in a theoretical and clinical field.

Notes

1 This text is a modified and expanded version of the paper "Thomas Ogden e a alteridade em Psicanálise" (Coelho Junior, 2012).
2 Cf. Coelho Junior (2010).

3 Cf. Brinholli & Coelho Junior (2020).
4 Cf. Figueiredo & Coelho Junior (2018).
5 In his latest book, *Coming to Life in the Consulting Room: Toward a new analytic sensibility* (Ogden (2022)), the author points out the transformation of emphasis that has taken place in psychoanalysis, from an epistemological to an ontological investigation and practice, based on the contributions of Bion and Winnicott. Despite the effectiveness of this way of conceiving the history of psychoanalysis, there is no doubt that Ogden seeks, in resorting to philosophical concepts, a way of challenging psychoanalysis regarding its own limits and meanings.
6 Cf. Coelho Junior (2016).
7 Cf. Coelho Junior (2019b), for a discussion on the contemporary theoretical and clinical developments of this notion.
8 These notions were originally published by Coelho Junior (2002) and are presented here with some modifications.
9 Cf. Coelho Junior & Figueiredo (2003).
10 For a dialogue between the ideas of Merleau-Ponty and Ogden, see Coelho Junior (2018).
11 Cf. Coelho Junior (2019a).

References

BARANGER, W. & BARANGER, M. (1969/1993) *Problemas del campo psicoanalítico.* Buenos Aires: Ed. KanEd. Kargieman .

BION, W. R. (1962) *Learning from Experience.* London: Heinemann.

BRINHOLLI, F. & COELHO JUNIOR, N. E. (2020) A importância do pensamento de Thomas Ogden para a psicanálise contemporânea. *PSICOLOGIA USP*, v. 31, pp. 1–9.

COELHO JUNIOR, N. E. (2002) Intersubjetividade: conceito e experiência em psicanálise. *Psicologia Clínica (PUC-RIO)*, v. 14, n. 1, pp. 61–74.

COELHO JUNIOR, N. E. (2010) Da Intercorporeidade à co-corporeidade: elementos para uma clínica psicanalítica. *Revista Brasileira de Psicanálise*, v. 44, n. 1, pp. 51–60.

COELHO JUNIOR, N. E. (2012) Thomas Ogden e a alteridade em Psicanálise. *Revista Impulso*, v. 22, n. 55, pp. 59–76.

COELHO JUNIOR, N. E. (2016) The origins and destinies of the idea of thirdness in contemporary psychoanalysis. *International Journal of Psychoanalysis*, v. 97, pp. 1105–1127.

COELHO JUNIOR, N. E (2018) Lenguajes de la Filosofia, lenguajes del psicoanálisis In: F. MARTIN GÓMEZ & J.M. TAUZIK. *Psicoanálisis latinoamericano Contemporáneo.* Buenos Aires: APA Editorial, 2018, v. 1, pp. 892–910.

COELHO JUNIOR, N. E. (2019a) From Ogden to Ferenczi. The constitution of a contemporary clinical thought. *The American Journal of Psychoanalysis.* v. 79, pp. 468–483.

COELHO JUNIOR, N. E. (2019b) Do Afeto ao Pensamento ou do corpo à simbolização In: T. CANDI & A. ROCHA BARROS. *Diálogos psicanalíticos Bion e Laplanche: do afeto ao pensamento.* São Paulo: Editora Escuta, pp. 363–38.

COELHO JUNIOR, N. E. & FIGUEIREDO, L. C. (2003) Patterns of intersubjectivity in the constitution of subjectivity. Dimensions of otherness. *Culture and Psychology.* London & Thousand Oaks, CA: v. 9, n. 3, pp. 193–208.

DERRIDA, J. (1967) *Grammatology*. Baltimore, MD: Johns Hopkins Paperbacks edition, 1976.

FIGUEIREDO, L. C. & COELHO JUNIOR, N. E. (2018) *Adoecimentos Psíquicos e Estratégias de Cura*. São Paulo: Blucher.

FREUD, S. (1912) *Ratschäge für den Arzt bei der psychoanalytischen Behandlung, Ergänzungsband*. Frankfurt: S. Fischer Verlag, 1970.

GADAMER, H.-G. (1960) *Truth and Method*, 2nd rev. ed., trans. J. Weinsheimer & D. Marshall. New York: Continuum, 2004.

GREEN, A. (1975). The analyst, symbolization and absence in the analytic setting (on changes in analytic practice and analytic experience). *International Journal of Psychoanalysis*, 56, pp. 1–22.

HEIDEGGER, M. (1927) *Being and Time*, trans. John Macquarrie & Edward Robi. Oxford: Blackwell Publishers Ltd, 1962.

LAPLANCHE, J. & PONTALIS, J. B. (1985/1998) *Vocabulário da Psicanálise*, São Paulo: Ed. Martins Fontes – 3ª edição.

MERLEAU-PONTY, M. (1945) *Phénoménologie de la Perception*. Paris: Gallimard.

MERLEAU-PONTY, M. (1964) *Le Visible et L'Invisible*. Paris: Gallimard.

OGDEN, T. H. (1982) *Projective Identification and Psychotherapeutic Technique*. New York: Jason Aronson.

OGDEN, T. H. (1988) On the dialectical structure of experience: Some clinical and theoretical implications. *Contemporary Psychoanalysis*, n. 24, p. 17–45.

OGDEN, T. H. (1989) *The Primitive Edge of Experience*. Northvale, NJ: Jason Aronson.

OGDEN, T. H. (1994) *Subjects of Analysis*. Northvale, NJ: Jason Aronson.

OGDEN, T. (2004) The analytic third: Implications for psychoanalytic theory and technique. *Psychoanalytic Quarterly*, 73, pp. 167–195.

OGDEN, T. H. (2005) *This Art of Psychoanalysis*. London: Routledge.

OGDEN, T. H. (2007) On Talking-as-dreaming. *International Journal of Psychoanalysis*, v. 88, pp. 575–89.

OGDEN, T. H. (2009) *Rediscovering Psychoanalysis*. London: Routledge.

OGDEN, T. H. (2010) On three forms of thinking: Magical thinking, dream thinking and transformative thinking, *The Psychoanalytic Quarterly*, v. LXXIX, n. 2, pp. 317–347.

OGDEN, T. (2016) *Reclaiming Unlived Life*. New York: Routledge.

OGDEN, T. (2017) Dreaming the analytic session. *The Psychoanalytic Quarterly*, v. LXXXVI, n. 1, (pp. 1–20.)

OGDEN, T. (2022) *Coming to Life in the Consulting Room: Toward a New Analytic Sensibility*. New York: Routledge.

REIS, B. (1999) Thomas Ogden's phenomenological turn. *Psychoanalytical Dialogues*, v. 9, n. 3, pp. 371–393.

TUSTIN, F. (1984) *Estados autísticos em crianças*. Rio de Janeiro: Imago.

3 Thomas H. Ogden, Reader of Freud

Érico Bruno Viana Campos

Introduction

The task to outline or minimally characterize the reading of Freud by any author in Psychoanalysis is certainly an impossibility, since it cannot take into account the whole horizon that limits our field. The Freudian legacy is basic and fundamental. Every psychoanalyst faces it in their training and refers to it to follow their own path. However, each person has a particular reading of Freud, which in seminal authors becomes a certain perspective and position that configures the foundations of their originality in psychoanalytic theorization and practice. This is how there is a certain reading of Freud in the configuration of the epistemological matrices of the great psychoanalytic schools in Lacan, Klein, Bion and Winnicott, for example. Each person chooses their objects and preferences within the complex theoretical-conceptual building of the area. However, this reading is only endorsed retroactively, as the unique contributions of these authors gain amplification, support and relevance in the particular analytical community that gives it the due consistency.

These initial considerations are important, as there is a certain academic notion of "reading" or "work" that tends to be, so to speak, *canonical*. In this sense, there are excellent readers of Freud, not only in the dogmatic reconstruction of his concepts, but also in the questioning of his demands. In our colonized Brazil, this deference was often imposed and remains on the question of who and how can anyone really read Freud, as a means for legitimizing a certain inheritance in the game of power. Readings with a more academic bias, whose mark is evident in the university context of the recent history of Brazilian Psychoanalysis, are configured as readings of a close and reproductive nature or "in the order of reasons", mainly in the approach to the Freudian legacy that we find in the so-called "philosophy of psychoanalysis" or in Lacanian groups.

There are few authors who approach Freud more freely, without the hallmark of deference, but mainly from an effectively more *dialogical position*, that is, in a more horizontal debate in which differences are put to work in contradictions of meaning within the scope of theoretical-conceptual discourse, but also in its clinical and literary strata. Thomas Ogden is an author

DOI: 10.4324/9781003423188-3

of this type and does so in a different style. He is effectively an author of contemporary Psychoanalysis, who, therefore, transcends the scholastic matrices of the field and dialogues with diverse traditions in an original perspective. His work is relatively extensive in time and in the weight of contributions, being multifaceted, although defined by some axes of questions and interests. Its greatest merit is precisely that it does not propose itself as dogmatic or systematic and, in this sense, it does not exactly constitute a metapsychological or clinical model in Psychoanalysis. It is closer to an aesthetic and existential aim than to the great conceptual systems and, in this sense, its readings, appropriations and articulations are specific and often implicit. Because of this, the work of answering the question of what could be Ogden 's reading of Freud becomes relatively more complex. Without wanting to be exhaustive, I will simply address what I consider to be two illustrative moments in this author's work in his dialogue with the Freudian legacy.

Discourses on the Subject

Our first moment will aim the beginning of Ogden 's original work, in which his training path as a psychoanalyst and as an internationally renowned author is consolidated, between the years 1980–1990 (please see Chapter 1 and the Appendix on the life path and work by the author, and a chronology, in the present volume). To this end, it is worth considering its insertion and contribution a little.

North American Psychoanalysis is marked by the so-called "Ego Psychology", which is more than a school in the strict sense that was formed between the years 1940–1960 (around Hartmann, Kris and Lowenstein) and is a perspective that sets the tone of this tradition. This tone has two characteristics that I consider most relevant: the first is the attempt to maintain Psychoanalysis in the epistemological reference of medical and psychological knowledge, that is, in a naturalistic and functionalist conception with the intention of making Psychoanalysis a general Psychology. The second is the focus on the drive dimension as the main axis of psychosexual development, valuing the logic of progressions, fixations and regressions of libido, and the dynamics of defense mechanisms in the organization of psychic structures. Hence the "developmental" tendency in this perspective, seeking support for the psychoanalytic theory of personality in descriptive empirical studies on emotional and cognitive conditions in childhood (such as the work of Spitz and Mahler). This alliance ends up valuing the intrinsic dimension of development in a strongly adaptationist strand to the environment and is rooted in a classic clinical matrix, based on neurotic personality organizations and a more pedagogical approach to child psychotherapy. Thus the Freudian legacy in North American Psychoanalysis in the era of schools consists of a particular section with very orthodox characteristics. This means that the Freud with whom Ogden begins his dialogue and has as his training horizon is basically the one who was consolidated in the reference of Otto Fenichel's manuals on psychoanalytic theory and technique.

Ogden makes his initial journey trying to separate himself from this trad-ition, whether through his consistent and systematic work with the clinic of psychoses, or through his study of the English theory of object relations. North American Psychoanalysis has undergone a renewal since the 1970s, with movements that begin to value the historical, relational and intersubjective dimension of subjectivity. The book, *The Matrix of the Mind* (Ogden, 1986/2017), needs to be understood in this context.

In general terms and explicitly, the text intends to present and make a con-tribution to the theories of object relations, especially Klein and Winnicott at that time, to American Psychoanalysis. Noteworthy is the effort to polish the edges of Kleinian conceptions in their insertion in the general plan of the development of cognition and the distinction between subject-object, in order to build a path that can locate the intersubjective experience at the cultural and clinical level. To this end, it proposes a reinterpretation of the Freudian and Kleinian notions of "phylogenetic inheritance of ideas" (which is nothing more than a representative of the innatist and instinctivist weight of the drive paradigm) in the light of Chomsky's deep linguistic structures.

Already at this moment, a stance has emerged that we can recognize as effectively contemporary in the approach to linguistic phenomena and their operations at the level of clinical experience and theorization: a position where the interlocutions that support the different levels of the psychoana-lytic field take place in an interplay of dynamic interpretations, which are alive, fertile and present, looking back on the past in a truly historical per-spective. This is a position that we can recognize as *dialectical*, since it takes the game of contradictions as necessary for the institution and consolida-tion of meanings and actions, going beyond the subject-object and rational-irrational dichotomy. The author's definition is clear and consistent with the general Hegelian notion and the critical theory of society in particular (he refers directly to Marcuse's work below):

Dialectics is a process in which opposing elements create, preserve and deny each other, each in a dynamic and always changing relationship with the other. The dialectical movement tends towards integrations that are never completely realized. Each potential integration creates a new form of opposition, characterized by its distinctive form of dialectical tension. That which is generated dialectically is continually in motion, perpetually in the process of being created and denied, of being decentered from static self-evidence.

(Ogden, 1994/1996, p. 12)

It is in this spirit that he will discriminate between analytical *dialogue* (what takes place between analyst and analysand, in the context of clinical work) and psychoanalytic *discourse* (what takes place between thinkers and authors, in the context of theoretical systems and institutional logics of psychoanalysis) as dimensions of this necessarily relational field. This is the tone of the psychoanalytic debate that the author proposes:

> The isolation of any portion of the analytic dialogue between analyst and analysand, or of the discourse between analytic thinkers, results in individual or cultural alienation. It's not like a part of the past disappears; This cannot happen because the past is immutable. However, we can isolate ourselves from our history. History differs from the past in that the latter is simply a collection of events, while history is a creation that reflects our conscious and unconscious memory of our individual and collective representations, distortions and interpretations about the past. By isolating ourselves from the dialogical history that preceded us and, in a way, created our present, we find it more difficult to know and understand ourselves fully through symbols, meanings, ideas, feelings, art and the work we create.
>
> (Ogden, 1986/2017, p. 13)

I think that this hermeneutic and ethical positioning is fundamental to understanding the way Ogden interprets, including his reading of the Freudian legacy.

Ogden 's initial reading of Freud is shaped by the orthodox tradition of North American Psychoanalysis and the contribution it proposes of object relations focusing on the drive paradigm in the Freudo-Kleinian matrix (Figueiredo & Coelho Junior, 2018). Freud is summoned not in the filigree of his texts or in the permanence of his concepts, but in the contribution to a certain conception of the *subject* in which mental structures can be thought in a new light: "Freud's contribution is not a static text, but rather a set of ideas in constant evolution and transformation in the context of subsequent dialogue" (Ogden, 1986/2017, p. 15). The Freud who appears in this reading appears alongside Klein in a conception of personality that is based on psychological contents, functions and structures that are constituted intrapsychically and that are expressed interpersonally through transference.

In his journey in constructing the proposal for a matrix of the mind, Ogden advances in the characterization of internalized object relations and the positioning of internal objects in relation to the *self*. He is particularly concerned with reshaping Klein's contribution of a paranoid-schizoid position to highlight the idea that in the initial moments of psychic and emotional life, objects are experienced as things in themselves (*self*-objects), not referred to an integrative condition and in an active ego stance, that is, below a *subject position*. Another concern is to integrate the Winnicottian contributions of potential space in the construction of a theory about the mind that can compose a dialectical interplay between intrapsychic and interpersonal contents and spaces.

Ogden thus proposes moving towards an intersubjective theory of the psychoanalytic subject. To this end, it starts from the two most fundamental

Freudian contributions to Psychology, namely, the unconscious condition of the mind and the role of sexuality in motivation. However, in this characterization, it is first necessary to resituate the notion of phylogenetic inherited "knowledge", that is, of specific contents that are transmitted between generations: "Freud's theory of psychological development is built on the concept of the innate expectation of constellations particular meanings (including specific dangers at each stage of development), where expectations do not depend on actual experience" (Ogden, 1986/2017, p. 28).

This is where a more structural view of the deep and original content of the unconscious mind emerges, in which the potential of instinctual assemblages give rise to a plurality of meaning constellations (fantasies) on a universal basis that comes not from the acquired archaic heritage, but from an originary matrix in the sense of generational grammar. This indicates that Ogden updates the Freudian conception of the subject, but bypasses French linguistic and anthropological structuralism. In this way, his notion of otherness comes from an approach to an original intrapsychic coding matrix that is updated and configured in the intersubjective relationship.

The psychoanalytic subject for Ogden is, therefore, not an effect of the Other's discourse. Nor is it a mere psychic apparatus of intrapsychic contents and objects, or even of internalized object relations. It is a fundamentally interpersonal conception of the subject, whose first step in its construction consists of defining its original matrix.

Following his studies on the original dimension of subjectivity, Ogden continues his dialogue with the logic of development, seeking to add tension to the static view of mental structures. Beyond supporting Kleinian metapsychological constructs towards the developmental psychology of psychic functions, he seeks to deepen the originating dimension, proposing in his next book the notion of an *autistic-contiguous position* as a structuring dynamic complementary to the paranoid-schizoid and depressive positions. From this step onwards, the author will seek a new attempt at systematization, advancing in the proposition of an effectively intersubjective matrix of the mind. This is the transition from the matrix of the mind to the subjects of psychoanalysis, where the position of the *analytical third* emerges in all its originality as the author's greatest contribution to the history of Psychoanalysis.

The book, *Subjects of Analysis* (Ogden, 1994/1996), is effectively a masterpiece, for several reasons. First, because it is the work from which Ogden will become known worldwide for his original propositions for Psychoanalysis. There is a coherent and sufficiently systematic approach to development, based on a dialectical approach to the three subjective positions. There is also a theory of technique and a conception of dynamic transfer, which goes beyond the subject-object dichotomy and endorses a relational and positional notion of the analytical field. It is not the scope of this chapter to present this entire journey (for which we rely on the other chapters of the book), but rather to highlight where Freud's reading fits into this proposition.

Ogden draws on the Freudian legacy to construct his proposal, but this time the general position of appreciation of the psychoanalytic conception of the subject is much less orthodox. Let's see:

> For Freud, the subject does not coincide with the conscious, thinking, speaking *self*, nor is it the subject located 'behind the barrier of repression' in the 'unconscious mind'. On the contrary, the Freudian conception of subjectivity is, in my view, fundamentally dialectical in nature and is rooted in the idea that the subject is created, maintained and simultaneously decentered from itself through the dialectical interrelationship between consciousness and the unconscious. The principle of presence-in-absence and absence-in-presence underlies the Freudian conception of this dialectical movement.
>
> (Ogden, 1994/1996, p. 7)

This quote is clear in reiterating the dialectical view of the subject that Ogden proposes, but it raises some questions that should be explored further. It is noted that there is a recognition that subjectivity is organized and configured in the interplay of relationships dependent on intrapsychic instances, that is, it is neither the psychology of the id nor the psychology of the ego. As he insists later: "The subject, for Freud, must be sought in the phenomenology of what is found in the relations *between* consciousness and unconsciousness" (Ogden, 1994/1996, p. 15). But was there actually a metapsychological conception of the Freudian subject or was it just an existential descriptive category or kind of "spirit" of a dialectical philosophical anthropology? What "Phenomenology" is the author referring to?

We know that Freud does not enunciate a conception of the subject in his own epistemological terms (Psychoanalysis follows the scientific worldview and the unconscious is the object of psychoanalytic science, for example). Even in terms of a psychodynamic or structural theory of personality, the issue boils down to recognizing this split in the subject and its dynamics shaped by conflict. In other words, Psychoanalysis speaks of a split and conflicting subjective experience, detached from the ego and repressed contents. There is a constitutive alienation and a tragic dimension as the ethical foundation of the psychoanalytic understanding of subjectivity. But is there, in fact, a Freudian subject?

In a chapter of his book, which seems central to this work, Ogden proposes to explain this implicit theory of the subject in Freud. For him, the Freudian conception of the subject refers not to an epistemological or discursive dimension, but above all to a dimension that we could call existential. This is because it is the feeling of identity, belonging and substantiality of an active *position* on the reference and feeling of oneself that would mark this notion: "When I speak of the subject of psychoanalysis, I refer to the individual in his capacity to generate a sensation of 'selfhood' that experiences [subjectivity], however rudimentary and non-verbally symbolized this sense of selfhood may be" (Ogden, 1994/1996, p. 12).

From this, he resumes a path of criticism of Freudian metapsychological conceptions in their claims of materiality and universality, but above all of causality and progress in development. It retraces the path of humanist and phenomenological-existential philosophical criticism on the Freudian conception of the human being, but based on the tradition of English-speaking authors and in a more strictly dialectical vision. The linearity and diachrony of Freudian schemes (from the unconscious to the conscious, from the primary to the secondary process, from the pleasure principle to the reality principle and from the id to the ego, to stay with the basics) are understood as deviations or concessions to a conception of human nature that would go against the radicality of the psychoanalytic project in denouncing the plurality and processuality of the conception of subjectivity, that operates in the interplay of preservation and denial in a continuous decentering and recentering between consciousness and unconsciousness.

He then rescues Freudian indications about the decentering of human consciousness through the analogy of the three narcissistic wounds, and then moves on to the notion of intrinsic dialectic between conscious and unconscious, each defining, denying and preserving the other and communicating through operations of construction and deconstruction of meaning. For Ogden, this logic that is already established in the topographic model is intensified in the structural model, as the psychic instances of ego, id and superego define each other also in dialectical terms: the self, the internal non-self and the internalized and idealized other. Thus, "the subject of the structural model is situated in the stereoscopic illusion of unity of experience dialectically constituted by the discourse, denier and preserver, of the id, ego and superego" (Ogden, 1994/1996, p. 17).

The dialectical principle operative in Ogden's reading of Freudian subject is clearly Hegelian. The author quotes Hyppolite's famous comment on the *Aufhebung* as the essence of Hegelian dialectics, meaning simultaneously to *deny*, *suppress* and *conserve*, as well as its application to the understanding of the Freudian defense mechanism of *denial* as a form of suppression or lifting the barrier of repression. It is this reading of the fundamental logic on repression dynamics that Ogden will rely on to defend the move beyond a linear understanding of causality between conscious and unconscious in the subject towards a dialectic between presence and absence:

> The idea of a dialectic of affirmed and denied meanings, which is expressed phenomenologically in the form of the simultaneity of conscious and unconscious meanings, is perhaps the most fundamental analytical statement regarding the concept of mind. Presenting one's own being in the form of not being one is what is in fact at issue in this *Aufhebung* of repression, which is not an acceptance of the repressed. When speaking one says: 'This is what I am not' (Hyppolite, 1956, p. 291).
>
> (Ogden, 1994/1996, p. 18)

It is therefore, within the framework of continental European phenomenological-existential criticism (France and Germany) that Ogden seeks elements for his reading of the Freudian subject. This evidently involves the choice of term to speak of this intangible and unsustainable condition of dialectical transit of the experience of "self-ness", which he chooses to call *subject*. It is a term foreign to the tradition of the English language, which tends to work with the binomial ego and *self*. The term *ego* is clearly insufficient to name this transit – since it directly concerns a specific instance of the psychic apparatus – but the idea of *self* as the totality of subjective experience or its activity position is not only a notion in common use in the English language, but also an established use in the tradition of North American Psychoanalysis to provide a counterpoint to the more restrictive idea of ego (from Hartmann to Kohut, passing through humanist criticism). However, Ogden considers that the use of the term in the English-speaking psychoanalytic tradition is also already sufficiently worn out and fixed by static and mainly reifying meanings. With the reservation of stating that no word can account for the multiplicity and ambiguity of meaning necessary for the concept,he relies on the term *subject* to account for the "psychoanalytic conception of the 'I' that experiences [again the emphasis on experience], both in a phenomenological as well as metapsychological" (Ogden, 1994/1996, p. 23). His preference is justified by the etymological ambiguities of the term, which refers to the condition of subjectivity as semantic reflexivity and with the denotation of simultaneity between the positions of subject and object. In view of this, the notion of subject in Psychoanalysis is configured, comprising the plurality and multiplicity of expressions and implications that are inherent to it.

A final consideration is necessary to clarify this conceptual characterization for readers in the contemporary community: how does all this relate to the Lacanian proposal of the subject and, by derivation, with the tone of French Psychoanalysis regarding subjectivity? Our author does not shy away from taking a position on this issue, albeit briefly and clearly.

Ogden recognizes that Lacan's thought is also based on dialectical thinking to understand the analytical process and the constitution of a decentered subject (the topology of the Symbolic, Imaginary and Real registers). However, he understands that, unlike the Freud-Klein-Winnicott trunk, there would be a *deconstructionist tendency* in Lacan. This "deconstruction" – a term that comes strongly from literary criticism (although it is not directly cited, it is Derrida's position) – speaks above all of an appreciation of *difference* over *essence* and *discontinuity* over *continuity* in understanding subjectivity.

This is truly an epistemological discussion, anchored in a theory of language as support for the idea of subject. The whole issue refers to the overcoming of a representational and psychic conception of subjectivity. Freudian metapsychology is strongly based on a representational metapsychology, although pushing its limits (Campos, 2014). Theories of language throughout the twentieth century reposition the understanding of the subject no longer in possession of a reflective representational consciousness, but in the linguistic and cultural condition in which it needs to be inserted to constitute itself. Hence the structuralist theories based on the disjunction between signifier and signified, or the arbitrariness of the linguistic sign, in which meaning is mainly the effect of structure (the Other as a systematic repository of cultural codes) on people's mental and bodily experience. The structuralist solutions diverge from most of the phenomenological and existential solutions to the problem of subjectivity. This is because these philosophies do not completely give up the more personalistic and experiential conception of mental life. It is the intentionality of consciousness that is highlighted in the link between subject and object, overcoming intrapsychic solipsism and denouncing the imaginary illusion of experiences. However, this position does not completely deny the place of mental and individual subjective experiences, on the contrary.

It is at this point that Ogden takes a stand against Lacan, denouncing that the French author's "deconstructionist" stance, supported by the radical split between signifier and signified, characterizes subjectivity as an illusory slippage of meaning prioritizing the negativity of the interval (the "gap" or hiatus) in the establishment of human understanding. Consciousness and the self would be imaginary illusions, which are crossed by an unconscious subject that is the effect of the Other's speech and, in this sense, "acephalous". It is this absolute primacy of the unconscious subject and the disregard of the intrapsychic and mental scene that the author does not recognize as a Freudian position. Therefore, Ogden highlights in his criticism of Lacan the rescue of an epistemological, metapsychological and clinical Freudian position, even if to expand it in another direction:

> The Lacanian project can be equated with an effort to see through the gaps or grooves of a pictorial image behind which there is another picture. In contrast, the Freudian project can be conceived in terms of a hermeneutic circle in which the foreground is contextualized by the background and vice versa; the Freudian text assumes an integrity in which each part is related to, informs and is informed by each of the other parts of the text. There *is* no radical discontinuity between portions of the web of meanings, whether conscious or unconscious, manifest or latent, intentional or unintended [...] The fundamental logic that underlies the discordant elements of the text is the logic of the dialectical interrelationship between presence and absence discussed above.
>
> (Ogden, 1994/1996, p. 26)

The quote clarifies the position that does not give up a psychic dimension for the subject, even if understood in a dialectical key and based on discursive effectiveness (note the emphasis on the Freudian "text"). The Freudian subject is not headless or mindless and is not the effect of the discourse from the Other.

What is not so clear and which I think needs to be highlighted is that the conception that Ogden defends also implies a specific conception of alterity, of an *intersubjective nature* (See Chapter 1 of this book). This is because in the Lacanian subject, alterity is radical, manifesting itself either in the traumatic and nameless enjoyment of the Real or in the paradigmatic effect of the Symbolic structure. The imaginary Other is a pure delegate of the radical otherness of the lack of the Other. Thus the subject is "barred" and marked by lack because the Other is also "hollowed". In the same way, there is no "other of the Other" and therefore the intersubjective dimension does not have a fundamental ontological status for Lacan.

Therefore, it is possible to affirm that in addition to protecting the intrapsychic and mental scene as a stage for subjectivity, Ogden also indicates the interpersonal and intersubjective dimension as part of its constituent field. To do this, it is necessary to follow another path based on what is implicit in the Freudian conception of the subject, which does not go through the Lacanian *subject of the unconscious* but rather follows the English tradition of the school of object relations. It is following this path that Klein and Winnicott will be called upon to compose the intersubjective plot of the subjects of Psychoanalysis in the psychoanalytic field, but this is a matter for the next chapters. For now, it is enough to conclude this topic by stating that Ogden sets the tone for his journey as a great author of Psychoanalysis, expanding and explaining the Freudian conception of the subject beyond a strictly instinctual and developmental view towards an intersubjective conception through the contribution of theories of object relations and a dialectical approach, renewing North American Psychoanalysis and contributing to launching it into the contemporary era. In the schematic terms proposed by Mezan (2014), it can be said that Ogden makes a reading of Freud in which the conception of the subject and, therefore, the metapsychological characterization, goes beyond the *drive* paradigm towards the *objectal* to the detriment of the *subjectal*.

However, more than that, Ogden's path considers the mutually constitutive relationship between theory, clinic and culture, through their condition as fields of linguistic interaction, interpretative and communicative action. The path of the subjects of Psychoanalysis leads to the valorization of the transference-countertransference field in the sense of pre-verbal or paraverbal *events* (Figueiredo, 1994) that result in the consistency of the analytical third:

> [...] the concept of interpretative action is understood as the analyst's use of the activity to communicate specific aspects of his understanding of transference-countertransference that cannot be transmitted to the patient only in the form of a verbally symbolic speech in the moment of analysis in which the interpretation-in-act is made. The understanding of transference-countertransference transmitted by an interpretative act derives from the experience of the analyst and the analysand in the intersubjective analytical third.
>
> (Ogden, 1994/1996, p. 132)

Ogden's work increasingly moves towards a concern at the ethical and aesthetic level of the use of language, in which the artisanal weave of the interpretative actions of dialogue in the psychoanalytic field stands out. It is the effect of shifting the matrix of the mind to the matrix of transference-countertransference, in which the psychoanalytic discourse takes effect within the scope of a theory of technique fully based on the contributions of the school of object relations. In this new context, a question arises: will there still be a place for reading Freud?

Creative Readings

I will now approach a second moment of Ogden's work, where already with significant theoretical contributions to psychoanalytic theory (deep structural mental matrix, autistic-contiguous position and analytical third) and having already matured a style of reading and writing, the author begins to increasingly direct towards psychoanalytic practice through a rescue, resignification and expansion of the theory of dreams (please see Chapter 1 and the Appendix that present the author's life and work in this book). The book, *This Art of Psychoanalysis*, comes from this period of his work; the book's subtitle, "Dreaming undreamed dreams and interrupted screams", indicates the centrality and originality of his approach (Ogden, 2005/2010). In its first chapter, Ogden presents, with a unique style of writing, the general lines of this art of the authentic clinical encounter, which goes back to the origins of Psychoanalysis: "The invention of a new form of human relationship may be Freud's most significant contribution to humanity. Being alive in the context of the analytic relationship is different from being alive in any other form of human relationship" (Ogden, 2005/2010, p. 27).

It is in this tone of remission to the fundamentals that Freud begins to appear at this moment in Ogden's work. This is because it is an unorthodox theory of dreaming that supports this proposed technical approach. At this point, the author is already very far from Freudian metapsychological conceptions. The conceptions of continence and *reverie* become central to thinking about psychic elaboration through symbolization work in which dream thoughts and the alpha function stand out. Not only is the very notion of thought radically transformed in this transition from Freud to Bion, but so is the direction and function of dream work itself. In Freud, the dream work involves encoding latent thoughts into the manifest contents of consciousness and its inverse work of decoding through interpretation. In Bion, the lived experience needs to be metabolized through thought in order to be used and incorporated into unconscious chains. It is in this sense that "learning from experience" (the title of Bion's book) occurs, whose form of metabolization into thought symbols is dreamlike:

> Bion's conception [] of the work of dreaming is the opposite of Freud's 'dream work' [...] The latter refers to the set of mental operations that serve

to disguise unconscious dream thoughts through means such as condensation and displacement. Thus, in a derivative/disguised way, unconscious dream thoughts are made available to consciousness and secondary process thought. In contrast, Bion's dream work is that set of mental operations that allows conscious lived experience to be altered in such a way that it becomes available to the unconscious for psychological elaboration (dreaming). In summary, Freud's dream work allows derivatives of the unconscious to become conscious, whereas Bion's dream work allows conscious lived experience to become unconscious (that is, available to the unconscious for psychological elaboration). of generating dream thoughts and for the dreaming of those thoughts).

(Ogden, 2005/2010, p. 129)

The emphasis is on figurability and meaning that is constituted in the dialectic between presence and absence, in a game that is no longer by means of representation and communication of intrapsychic contents, but of what is presented in an expressive way and is configured intersubjectively. We are definitely far from the metapsychological and technical framework of orthodox Freudian Psychoanalysis. We are no longer in the frame of reference of ego psychology but rather in an innovative theory of object relations and the clinic, where psychoanalytic dialogue takes place in this intersubjective dreamlike movement. The psychoanalytic technique here truly becomes an ethics of human fabrication based on the intersubjective encounter marked by the most radical collaborative creation of meaning, through a dialectical game of incarnated language.

This position is clearly evident in the conditions of analytical work that are presented in the chapter entitled "What I wouldn't give up". The topics largely highlight this living and embodied vision of psychoanalytic dialogue becoming discourse: 1) Human being; 2) Face the music; 3) Be responsible; 4) Dreaming about being; 5) Think out loud; 6) Not knowing (Ogden, 2005/ 2010, pp. 39–47).

Reading these topics is very fruitful and important for establishing a clinical position that is fundamentally ethical and far removed from the technical concerns of Freudian texts. In fact, we are far from being concerned with the setting rules and the positions of neutrality and abstinence typical of classical technique theory. It is within the framework of analysis as a *total situation*, typical of the developments of the object relations school, that Ogden's position can be recognized. The analyst's listening position is effective based on how he/she is existentially situated in the openness to the singularity, generativity and authenticity of the psychoanalytic dialogue.

In this new frame of reference, the very notion of psychoanalytic discourse (that which occurs among psychoanalytic authors, it is worth remembering) gives way to the dialectical game of appropriation, denial and resignification, but now in the production of the theoretical-conceptual truths of the psychoanalytic field. The question then arises about what truth is and the effective origin of an idea. Distancing himself from a positive hermeneutics, which seeks the correspondences and rational chains that make an idea sustained and linked from its own identity, Ogden approaches a hermeneutics in which dialectical negativity imposes itself. It would then be necessary to think in terms of temporal bidirectionality in the influences and derivations in the horizon of meaning that supports the interpretations, that is, the arduous path of contemporary hermeneutics (Campos & Coelho Junior, 2010), to understand this notion of the relativization of truth and its co-creation in the psychoanalytic field.

The greatest wealth of this consists in confirming the author's general proposition that the support for this interplay of truths is presented not by the academic order of reasons and concepts, but by clinical experience. Ogden generally supports his hypotheses and propositions by discussion of detailed clinical excerpts and vignettes, which illustrate quite effectively his point of view on the ground of practicing that special form of human relationship that is Psychoanalysis.

The central point for our discussion is that the notion of truth becomes a consistent fabrication of the psychoanalytic field, which, evidently, is elaborated at different levels of theorization and conceptualization, from dialogue to discourse, so to speak. This, in turn, authorizes a radically creative perspective on subjectivities and their discursive expressions, which now affects psychoanalytic *texts*. This is the path that leads to the proposition of *creative readings*, in which this question of the origin of truth and its intrinsic relationship with its styles of enunciation and production are central:

> Whether or not we believe that anyone has the right to attach their name to an idea or a poem or an essay or a specific form of 'word music' [...] human truths must be repeatedly discovered in new forms; otherwise, these truths become clichés that stem the flow of genuine creativity and thinking. The renewal of thinking and originality of expression are mutually dependent: writing is a unique form of thought; and originality of writing is originality of thought. Content and style do not exist without each other [...] Together, style and content encompass the living, active body of writing that awaits reading.
>
> (Ogden, 2012/2014, p. 28)

It is in this new context that Ogden will progressively undertake creative readings of seminal texts, revisiting and giving new meaning to the weight of the seminal authors of Psychoanalysis in his own path of formation and authorship. Interestingly, it is at this moment that we will once again encounter a direct confrontation with the Freudian legacy.

It is worth noting that the path of creative readings of seminal texts is done in the usual way of Ogden's production: articles that are first published in prominent periodicals (at this stage practically all of the *International Journal of Psychoanalysis*), and are then published in compilation books in revised and expanded form. Sometimes the chapters are re-edited as well. This is the case of what is observed in the transition from the book on the *Art of Psychoanalysis* to that of *Creative Readings*. The order of readings also draws attention: Freud, Bion and Winnicott in a first compilation; then a more chronological compilation with Isaacs, Fairbairn, Loewald and Searles. From this, it can be inferred that it is effectively in the work of reading and rereading that the classic legacy of Psychoanalysis can be given new meaning and kept alive, indicating the specificity of the idea of textual reading as an organizer of Ogden's proposal and attesting to its alignment with the contemporary psychoanalytic tradition. In this sense, Elias da Rocha Barros' preface to *Creative Readings* is quite illustrative and pertinent:

> Thus, when examining a text by Susan Isaacs or Bion or even Winnicott or Loewald [Freud does not appear in the highlights, which may indicate that it is sufficiently established as an organizing reference for the problematization and not its point of incidence], I believe that I can define our objective being to place my interlocutor *'there'* where the very analytical problematic that mobilizes this particular author was generated and, then, to bring him to *'today'* and with him reflect on the degree to which the objectives were achieved and what new problems this problem generated. It is this stance that makes this work by Thomas Ogden so valuable.
>
> (Ogden, 2012/2014, p. 14)

Ogden himself, in his introductory text, tries to clarify that his texts are rather an attempt to *grasp the experience of reading*, that is, the intersubjective textual experience in which something new is necessarily produced, rather than *writing about an author's reading*, that is, the characterization of the apprehension of discursive and conceptual categories that exist by themselves, independent of the reading experience or their contextual horizon in the psychoanalytic field. In this reading process, the focus is not on what the text says, in terms of content and semantic categories, but rather on the *way of saying it*, in terms of "how" it is said, that is, the *style* of its pragmatics. In short, reading is a process that takes effect in the interpretative action of reading the seminal text and of which the authorial offspring is a testimony. Although he does not make the usual deferences to an explicit hermeneutic theory – since his objective is precisely to highlight the authentic dimension of experience from its field of tacit references – it is certainly in the field of the *function author* of Foucault, the Laplanchian methodology of problematization, as well as in the deconstructive strategies of literature that his reading is supported by, as Barros (2014) warns us in his preface.

I'm characterizing all of this first so we don't take Ogden's texts naively. For this author fits well all those warnings with which one usually introduces the reading of Winnicott's texts (Ogden's apparent simplicity in the use of common sense, the lack of systematic presentation of ideas and indication of the path of theoretical-conceptual references, the recognition and support of ambivalence and paradox, the style of writing that shades the dimensions of experience in strange ways, etc.). I even believe that in this sense Ogden is one of the authors who most converges with the Winnicottian style of writing and reading.

Secondly, because this puts us in a different relationship with Ogden's authorship, in which the conceptual summary by the "order of reasons" ends up becoming very poor in relation to the reading experience that is reported, whose effectiveness only happens when we allow ourselves to be in the place of the author's poetics and to be summoned and seduced by it. In short, only by opening the mind to contain the flow of thoughts that arise through what is written can the reader grasp the process of creative reading that the author proposes. In this sense, rereading and rewriting are the very means through which the process of transmitting the psychoanalytic experience can take place. This certainly places serious limits on the explicit task we have in this chapter, which would be to present the content and tenor of Ogden's reading of Freud. Furthermore, it calls into question the very limits that psychoanalytic communication texts find in the current scientific-academic environment, in which matters of authorship, originality and referencing are questioned and becoming a point of pressure.

Well, with that said, let's get back to Freud. Ogden publishes in three versions what he considers a seminal reading of the Freudian text. The original version that appeared in the *IJP* (Ogden, 2002) and its version latter in the book on the art of psychoanalysis (Ogden, 2005/2010), both focusing in their title on a *new reading on the origins of object relations theory*. The third is in the book on creative readings and its title already focuses more explicitly on the reference object of reading, the text *Mourning and Melancholia* (Ogden, 2012/2014). Despite the varied contexts of insertion, these are texts that do not present significant differences in content or style in their writing. I chose to quote the last version, which is supposedly the best finished to date and which is more committed in its title and context to the interpretation of the legacy of seminal Freudian texts.

Right from the start, we find the basic positions that I have been pointing out as the axis of Ogden's work in his reading of the Freudian legacy: not only a set of ideas and models, but also a new way of conceiving human experience that gave rise to a new form of subjectivity. Furthermore, the recognition that the study of thought is above all a study of writing, in which the content is not separated from the form and the reading experience itself. In addition to the initial contextualization and definition of the reading exercise that he will present to us, the author also indicates his motivation in rescuing this particular text to indicate it as one of the most seminal contributions to Freud's work. The first reason is perhaps the most objective or theoretical, arguing that the article "develops, for the first time, in a systematic way, the line of thought that would later be called 'object relations theory'" (Ogden, 2012/2014, p. 34). The second reason is the reading process itself, an invitation to the extraordinary opportunity "not only to listen to him think, but also, through writing, to enter this process of thinking with him" (Ogden, 2012/2014, p. 34). The second method is what allows us to understand more closely the new way of conceiving subjectivity that begins at this moment in Freud's work.

For everything we have discussed so far, my comments will not explain the richness of Ogden's reading, but I think they are relevant for a retrospective look at the trajectory of motivations for this chapter.

The first point is the reduction in the weight of Kleinian theory in establishing the field of object relations theories, or, as we have already mentioned, the object paradigm in Psychoanalysis (Mezan, 2014). From a rhetorical point of view, it is also an emblematic inversion of the consolidation of the contemporary psychoanalytic field. If in the beginning the concern was to bring the Kleinian contribution to the orthodox developmental drive-libidinal model of North American Psychoanalysis, now it is a question of making one of the precursors of Freudian revisionism the embryo of a conception of subjectivity that is truly based on relationships of internalized objects.

In this movement, the focus is on Fairbairn and not Klein. Despite the historical and terminological landmark of the Scottish psychoanalyst's work, it is curious to see that the effective origin of a theory of object relations is referred to in the 1950s, without considering the intense discussion that took place between the wars, involving not only Klein, but also Abraham and Ferenczi, on the matter of the weight and the way in which objects affect the structuring of the ego and its derivatives. Ogden makes a single more explicit mention in his text about the resonances of the Freudian text in Klein's work. It is in a footnote, but it recognizes that the entire clinical definition of manic defenses (control, contempt and triumph) is already in germ in the Freudian characterization, which is a strong indication of the consonance of Klein's work with the Freudian legacy of object relations. Furthermore, none of Ogden's initial concerns appear at this point and the displacement of the authorship reference is yet another indication that that initial reading of the psychoanalytic legacy has been transformed.

There is tension here about who actually started the movement of object relations. I have already tried to demonstrate and discuss in other works that Freudian theory effectively breaks down and finds a turning point based on the questions that appear around the theory of narcissism and its clinical expressions, which focus on the metapsychology of the constitution of personality structures through identification processes (Campos, 2014, 2020). In this sense, there is a theory of object relations that already operates in the last moment of Freud's work and whose legacy will, through the era of debates, converge strongly towards the Kleinian and intermediate groups in the United Kingdom. Ogden's reading certainly corroborates this point of view, but his contribution to the topic comes from another place, where the question of the origins of the theory arises in a very different way, as he is not at all concerned with the rights of birth.

It is at this point that the second motivation and path of Ogden's text proves to be truly original in approach. In an artisanal weave, the author arrives at some important categories from a close reading of the Freudian text, which he indicates as *principles* for a revised model of the psychic apparatus, in which the conception of an object becomes a model. The quote is long, but it summarizes the analysis undertaken in the reading:

> 1) the idea that the unconscious is organized mainly in stable internal object relations between excised pairs of parts of the ego; 2) the idea that it is possible to defend oneself from psychic pain by replacing an external object relationship with a fantasized unconscious internal object relationship; 3) the idea that pathological bonds of love mixed with hate are among the strongest bonds that bind internal objects to each other in a situation of mutual imprisonment; 4) the idea that object relations psychopathology often involves the use of omnipotent thought in order to prevent dialogue between the unconscious internal object world and the world of real experience with real external objects; and 5) the idea that ambivalence in relations between unconscious internal objects involves not only conflicts between feelings of love and hate, but also conflicts between desires to remain alive in object relations and desires to be in tune with their dead objects.
>
> (Ogden, 2012/2014, pp. 59–60)

How can we briefly understand these principles? I suggest the interpretation that Ogden is trying to bring the understanding of the intrapsychic psychic scene to a new basis, demonstrating, in general, how this psychic apparatus is no longer a set of representational systems under the metaphor of optical devices (telescope, microscope, projector, etc.), but a space of objects internalized and animated into characters, under the metaphor of a stage structure. Mainly, that they are not just objects, but objects in relationship and a relationship that informs and shapes objects. It is these internalized relationships that configure the web of dynamic structures that we will recognize in the structural model of personality. Stable object relations are precisely this dynamic balance, whose general logic of organization is through the split and interplay between introjection and projection. The general logic of organizing subjectivity is then one of structures that oppose each other vertically (side-by-side) and not horizontally (top-bottom), but these structures are actually internalized bonds (object relations). This is what we read in principle 1 and it is fundamental, as it removes Freud from the paradigm of neurotic organization of mental structures through the operation of repression and the model of thinking about locations: they are not individualized representations, but internalized links that are in contact with externalized links. The following principles deepen this vision of the intertwining between internalized and externalized relationships, leading to the recognition that this bond is necessarily ambivalent and multifaceted. The ways of dealing with conflicts in this intertwining indicate solutions that are of the order of refuge in internalized fantasy (2), of fixation in mutual imprisonment (3), in the omnipotent denial of the shared bond with reality (4). Principle 5 has less immediate understanding. I understand that the expansion of the notion of ambivalence beyond fantasies of love and hate to objects that are not identified with the ego is at stake, that is, at the level of object relations themselves and symbolization processes at the level of word representations. The desire is not to have, or not to have, the object, but to be, or be with, the objects with which it is identified in multiple bonds. Therefore, it is at the level of narcissistic relationships and an anguish that is not of the order of castration, but of what we currently call loss of the object or separation. In fact, they are important indications for what will come next in psychoanalytic thought, which is not ours to develop here.

From a reading of a Freudian point of view, we can, by contrast, consider whether there is a transition from a position on the dialectic between the psychic instances of the Freudian subject to the dialogue between internal and external that is necessarily based on object links. This makes effective the transition from a notion of intrapsychic personality to a more contemporary conception of subjectivity in which the classical dichotomies between unconscious and conscious, external and internal, innate and acquired are not only relativized, but effectively dissolved.

Ogden's reinterpretation of the narcissistic identification problem is therefore fundamental in this sense, but there is still one last dimension to consider: the Oedipus Complex. In the light of a new theory of object relations, wouldn't it be appropriate to consider the path of subject constitution and then reintroduce the problem of object relations and identifications in subjectivity? Yes, because today we understand that this resolution is expanded and constitutive in the structural conformation of the subject, but the orthodox Freudian text is not flexible enough to accept our contemporary vision.

It is in the reading of Loewald's work that this issue appears, as this author was important in the context of North American Psychoanalysis for the revisionism of the most orthodox conceptions of ego psychology. His work focused on some themes that converge to a broader discussion of the conception of reality, with important contributions to the contemporary understanding of the constitution of the subject (Sigler & Coelho Junior, 2009). Ogden seeks to defend Loewald's reading of the decline of the Oedipus complex as a watershed in the development of psychoanalytic thought. Evidently, the division is with the "canonical" Freudian view, which justifies us ending our chapter with this last reading.

The core of Loewald's proposition is to resituate the issue of Oedipus in a larger psychosocial framework of understanding the constitution of personality, in which the core lies in the idea that "the task of the new generation is to use, destroy and reinvent the creations of the previous generation

" (Ogden, 2012/2014, p. 195). To do so, it would be necessary to re-examine the premises of the conception of Freudian theory. To know:

All human psychology and psychopathologies, as well as all human cultural acquisitions, can be understood in terms of impulses and meanings that have their roots in sexual and aggressive drives; 2) The sexual drive is experienced as the driving force that begins at birth and develops sequentially into its oral, anal and phallic components over the course of the first five years of life; 3) Of the multiplicity of myths and stories that human beings have created, the myth of Oedipus, for psychoanalysis, is the most important singular narrative in the organization of human psychological development; and 4) The triangular set of conflicting homicidal and incestuous fantasies that constitute the Oedipus complex 'is determined and established by heredity' [...] .

(Ogden, 2012/2014, pp. 196–197)

In fact, it is the orthodox Freudian conception that appears here: its centrality as a conflicting structure of personality in a frame of reference of the psychosexual development of libido in chronological phases in which determination is intrinsically instinctual and hereditary. Loewald's article rescues Freudian theorization to work on the tension between influence and originality, focusing mainly on the premise of genetic origin. To this end, he criticizes the idea of dissolution as merely the repression of parricidal and incestuous intrapsychic fantasies. The core is to reinterpret the conflict in broader terms of a struggle for emancipation, autonomy and responsibility. Once again, Ogden takes a careful approach to close reading, considering the ambiguities of the text and context, the multiple levels of theorization about Oedipus. From a stylistic point of view, the commentator captures a certain irony in the text, Loewald's subservience and timidity in being able to assume the originality of his use of Freud's ideas, but which denotes the weight of orthodoxy in the American establishment at the dawn of a contemporary era of the psychoanalytic movement.

We are interested in highlighting what Ogden considers the difference between Freud and Loewald, in which we can interpret the referendum itself as a break with the Freudian legacy. The point is the displacement of primary sexual and aggressive tendencies towards a tendency towards emancipation and autonomy, through an innovative vision of the internalization and dissolution of Oedipal fantasies, in which a sense of reparation and responsibility stands out:

The incestuous component of the Oedipus complex contributes to the maturation of the *self* to serve as a form of ambiguous, transitional object relationship, which maintains the differentiated and undifferentiated dimensions of mature object ties in tension with each other. The Oedipus complex is not brought to an end by the fear-incited response to the threat of castration, but by the child's need to atone for the parricide and to restore to the parents their (now transformed) authority as parents.

(Ogden, 2012/2014, p. 218)

The author ends with the statement that he does not consider Loewald's proposition to be just an "update" of the Freudian version. Rather, he considers that they are different interpretations of the same phenomenon and equally indispensable for a contemporary psychoanalytic understanding. This means that Ogden does not fall into the traps of expanding psychoanalytic theory to the psychosocial dimension, implicitly criticizing the North American tradition itself, which often softened these and other proposals (such as Erickson's) to compose with a more "updated" vision of human development. The same movement can be noticed in the dialogue with the psychoanalytic tradition of object relations. It manages to indicate the fundamental moral components of the transgenerational limit of culture without falling into a vision that demands systematizations and theoretical-conceptual locations, that is, one that is inserted as a proposition in psychoanalytic discourses.

I understand that this project of Ogden's seminal readings precisely repositions the question of the legacy and transmission of psychoanalytic discourses and their connection with clinical dialogue. Furthermore, they tell us something retrospectively about this author's career.

Considering the historical and institutional circumstances that have shaped the North American psychoanalytic movement since the mid-1980s, we can recognize the implementation of a proposal to resituate the Freudian-Kleinian legacy in the light of contemporary Psychoanalysis. Ogden detaches himself from the explicit bases of Freudian thought to rescue its implicit or tacit spirit. Its initial dialectical reference increasingly becomes a hermeneutics, in which dialogue imposes itself as a matrix of subjectivation.

Final Considerations

This chapter aimed to characterize and discuss the Freudian legacy that appears and persists as a reference in the work of Thomas Ogden. To this end, I proposed a focus on two moments in the author's work, addressing two of his first and two of his last writings, through the notions of dialogue, discourse and creative reading. I started from the idea that the author initially positions himself in the task of reintroducing the theory of object relations in the context of North American Psychoanalysis, in dialogue with Developmental Psychology and Neurosciences, in addition to heavily referring to the Freudian reading of Ego Psychology.

During this period, the search for organizing structures of subjectivity stands out, in which the dialogue with psychoanalytic theories allows us to propose a matrix of the mind as a deep linguistic generational structure, based on Chomsky, and a more primitive autistic-contiguous subjective position than the paranoid-schizoid one, based on Klein. The dialogue with

Freud in this first moment is more indirect, where he appears either in the place of a general psychoanalytic frame of reference, or in the place of representative of a strongly drive-based psychodynamic conception, based on the conflict between impulses and defense mechanisms. However, it is noted that this path results in the explanation of an innovative characterization of the Freudian subject, pointing to the dialectical relationship between intrapsychic, interpsychic and analytical third.

In the second moment of his work, Ogden effectively finds himself in the position of a world exponent, fully integrated and protagonist of a contemporary transmatricial Psychoanalysis, working in a broader dialogue with the different psychoanalytic traditions in which the tension between the object model and the drive model meets overcome and given new meaning. The metapsychological debate at the level of theoretical discourses gives way to the outcomes of clinical dialogue and the creative reading of seminal texts. In this new frame of reference, Freud is revisited as an exponent of the artisanal, singular and human dimension of the psychoanalytic craft, as well as a pioneer of a theory of object relations within classical Psychoanalysis. The central reference is the precursor texts from the turn of the 1920s, in the articulation between Narcissism and the Oedipus Complex.

A more heterodox Freud emerges from these last readings, demonstrating not only his original fertility, but also his constant reference as a horizon in Ogden's production as a great author of Psychoanalysis.

References

BARROS, E. M. R. (2014). Prefácio. In: T. H. Ogden, *Leituras criativas: ensaios sobre obras analíticas seminais*. Trad. Tania Mara Zalcberg. São Paulo, SP: Escuta.

CAMPOS, E. B. V. (2014). *Limites da representação na metapsicologia freudiana*. São Paulo, SP: Edusp.

CAMPOS, E. B. V. (2020). Constituição do eu e identificação narcísica: o debate de Freud, Ferenczi e Abraham acerca da melancolia. *Sofia*, 9(2): 12–42.

CAMPOS, E. B. V., & Coelho Junior, N. E. (2010) Incidências da hermenêutica para a metodologia da pesquisa teórica em psicanálise. *Estudos de Psicologia* (Campinas), 27(2): 247–257. https://doi.org/10.1590/S0103-166X2010000200012

FIGUEIREDO, L. C. M. (1994). *Escutar, recordar, dizer: encontros heideggerianos com a clínica psicanalítica*. São Paulo, SP: Escuta/EDUC.

FIGUEIREDO, L. C., & Coelho Junior, N. E. (2018). *Adoecimentos psíquicos e estratégias de cura: matrizes do sofrimento psíquico*. São Paulo, SP: Blucher.

MEZAN, R. (2014). *O tronco e os ramos: estudos de história da psicanálise*. São Paulo, SP: Companhia das Letras.

OGDEN, T. H. (1986/2017). *The Matrix of the Mind* [*A matriz da mente: relações objetais e diálogo psicanalítico*]. Trad. Giovanna Del Grande da Silva. São Paulo, SP: Blucher (Originalmente publicado em 1986).

OGDEN, T. H. (1994/1996). *The Subjects of Analysis* [*Os sujeitos da psicanálise*]. Trad. Claudia Berliner. São Paulo, SP: Casa do Psicólogo (Originalmente publicado em 1994).

OGDEN, T. H. (2002). A new reading of the origins of object-relations theory. The International Journal of Psychoanalysis, 83(4), 767–782. https://doi.org/10.1516/LX9C-R1P9-F1BV-2L96

OGDEN, T. H. (2005/2010). *This Art of Psychoanalysis* [*Esta arte da psicanálise: sonhando sonhos não sonhados e gritos interrompidos*]. Trad. Daniel Bueno. Porto Alegre, RS: Artmed (Originalmente publicado em 2005).

OGDEN, T. H. (2012/2014). *Creative Readings* [*Leituras criativas: ensaios sobre obras analíticas seminais*]. Trad. Tania Mara Zalcberg. São Paulo, SP: Escuta. (Originalmente publicada em 2012).

SIGLER, R., & COELHO JUNIOR, N. (2009). Hans W. Loewald: a importância da realidade na constituição do sujeito e na clínica psicanalítica. *Ágora: Estudos em Teoria Psicanalítica*, 12(2): 229–243. https://doi.org/10.1590/S1516-1498200900 0200005

4 Thomas H. Ogden, Reader of Klein

Understanding Klein to Move Beyond Her

*Janderson Farias Silvestre Ramos
and Elisa Maria de Ulhôa Cintra*

Thomas Ogden (1986/1990) states that Klein's ideas and the reactions thereto form a large part of the dialogue "underlying the development of object relations theory" (p. 10). So much so that, for Ogden, the work of such authors as Winnicott, Balint, Guntrip and Fairbairn can be considered reactions and responses to Klein's thought. With this affirmation, Ogden seems to be saying something similar to Elizabeth Lima and Elias Mallet Rocha Barros (2018) when, speaking about the benefits of Melanie Klein as an author, they say, "What defines a creative author is the introduction of a new problematic which can no longer be ignored, and so never ceases to generate impacts that form fresh seeds for the advancement of thought" (p. 14).[1] Klein's writings introduced problematics which other theorists studying object relations could not ignore, and these proved so pivotal that the originality of the resulting work came to rest, to a large degree, upon Klein's provocations. Much of Ogden's own contribution can be read from this perspective.

As an avid reader of Winnicott (Kupermann & Neves, 2023),[2] Ogden knows one can only be original vis-à-vis a base of tradition (Winnicott, 1971/2017). Any builder will tell you that no matter how unusual a house or building may be, even the most inventive architectural design can only withstand gravity if raised on solid foundations. Ogden's originality is built upon many cornerstones, one of which is, without doubt, Klein's *oeuvre*. As Ogden himself says (1986/1990): "One must understand Kleinian theory in order to move beyond it" (p. 10). Ogden makes Winnicottian use of Kleinian theory: he keeps dismantling and reassembling it until he finally transcends it.

In this chapter, we will look at how Ogden avails himself of Klein's concepts of unconscious phantasy, projective identification, and the paranoid-schizoid and depressive positions, and shows how they form important bedrock on which the Californian analyst was able to raise conceptions of his own.

Unconscious Phantasy

In her introduction to the work of Melanie Klein, Hanna Segal (1964/1975) says that the elucidation of the concept of unconscious phantasy is essential

DOI: 10.4324/9781003423188-4

to any understanding of Klein's theories. Ogden (1986/1990) says something similar when he states that "In discussing Klein, one must begin with the concept of phantasy, for this is the hub of the mind-body system she envisions" (p. 10). In fact, while Klein never wrote a book or paper specifically devoted to the theme of phantasy, the notion permeates her entire work. Hardly surprisingly, Susan Isaacs' paper about the nature and function of phantasy served as a bastion of defense for Kleinian thought during the controversial discussions at the British Psychoanalytical Society between 1941 and 1945 (King & Steiner, 1991/1998). Isaacs' rigorously grounded defense of the idea that phantasy exists in the mind since the very beginning of the child's life was extremely important in validating the pertinence of child analysis through the technique of play.

Ogden (1986/1990) presents an understanding of the concept of unconscious phantasy that reveals how the notion reverberates productively in his thought. He eschews the facile, seductive approach taken by other theorists, who simply discard the Kleinian notion as irrelevant based on a superficial understanding that it hinges upon a defense of the existence of thoughts inherited by the infant, and/or of an infant that thinks from the very outset.

Ogden's chapter (1986/1990), titled "Instinct, Phantasy and Psychological Deep Structure in the Work of Melanie Klein", is similar to Isaacs' paper (1952/1978) in some respects. Just like the English Kleinian, Ogden draws from other fields of knowledge in supporting the pertinence of the concept of unconscious phantasy. One such field is linguistics. Noam Chomsky's linguistic deep structure serves as a model for a proposed *psychological deep structure*. Ogden (1986/1990) explains that the American linguist's concept refers to a pre-existent system out of which we select, organize and interpret the multiplicity of sounds to which we are exposed. It's an innate code that enables each and every human being to learn at least one of the world's languages. This conception indicates that human beings do not organize experiences randomly, that is, unfiltered by preconceptions. On the contrary, we have innate, pre-existing schemas that orient the way we organize incoming stimuli.

Ogden goes on to present a series of examples from linguistics and other fields. For instance, he shows that the way we catalogue sounds into phonemes does not occur passively, that is, the distinction between certain phonemes such as "ba" or "pa" is not based solely on the intrinsic quality of the stimuli themselves. We have a system for processing stimuli that enables us to arrange them in this particular way: "The human being is incapable of perceiving any sound as existing between these two phonemes" (Ogden, 1986/1990, p .14).

Ogden (1986/1990) offers an interesting example from the field of ethology: even without possessing any prior experience of predation, chicks instinctively recognize predators from their wing-shape, and this enables them to flee to safety. This indicates that the animal has some innate coding that enables it to organize stimuli independently of any real prior experience.

These ideas ground, if not explicitly support, the pertinence of Kleinian logic as elucidated by Isaacs (1952/1978), according to which the phantasy relative to a given instinct is conducive to the very nature of that instinct and does not depend on there having been any experience in reality. As such, the phantasy of suckling does not, in a sense, require the experience of suckling. Another example would be that a baby does not need to have seen someone cut to pieces or drowned to be able to phantasize, when enraged, that it is orally dilacerating the mother or drowning her in its urine. Likewise, the phantasy of offering feces or urine as gifts does not, according to Isaacs (1978/1952), derive from the act itself (which may be reinforced by the loving mother), but from the child's *desire* to offer these substances as things that are good to give.

From Ogden's perspective (1986/1990), we can assume that, while the baby is not born with the phantasy or knowledge of tearing the breast, it is *predisposed* to organize experience along certain predetermined lines. Whether the lines in question are those proposed by Klein is an open question, says Ogden. However, the notion of a psychological deep structure confers robust plausibility upon the idea of unconscious phantasy operating from the very onset of life, even if it does not provide proof of the existence of any specific determined contents of phantasy.

Using the notion of psychological deep structure, Ogden (1986/1990) reformulates certain Kleinian ideas. If unconscious phantasy is the interpretation the baby makes of reality, the relative constitution of the life and death instincts is the core determinant of which code will be used to interpret experiences. In other words, whether the experience is interpreted aggressively (through the lens of the death instinct) or lovingly (through that of the life instinct) depends on which code is applied to the experience. What's more, while the meaning is influenced by real experiences, it is not created by experiences alone, as these merely strengthen or attenuate the expectations.

Ogden (1986/1990) argues that Kleinian thought was not such a drastic change in relation to the Freudian concept of "'inheritance' of knowledge" (p. 21), as Freud's most fundamental contribution to the theory of sexuality, as Ogden sees it, is not about postulating sexuality as a powerful human driver, or its presence from birth, but rests upon the understanding that "the sexual instinct is not simply a striving, an impulse, a desire, but *the* vehicle by which human beings create meaning" (p. 19). As such, "the Oedipus complex as a whole is understood by Freud as a universal mode of organizing and responding to experience, and not simply as a feature of the family environment to which the child responds" (p. 20). For Ogden, Klein "merely" extended the idea of "inherent readiness" (p. 21) to pre-Oedipal inheritance, characterizing the forms of *preconception characterizing oral, anal and early phallic levels* of development.

A discussion about unconscious phantasy in the earliest phases of development should, inevitably, entail reflection on the level of symbolization possible in a baby. Ogden does not shirk this task, and, in tackling the subject, evokes Isaacs, who argues that the mind/body division does not exist in the infant mind, but comes later:

> It is easier for adults to observe the actual suckling than to remember or understand what the experience of the suckling is to the infant, for whom there is no dichotomy of body and mind, but a single, undifferentiated experience of suckling and phantasying.
>
> (Isaacs, 1978/1952, p. 85)

Ogden (1986/1990) also highlights the fact that Klein's descriptions of unconscious phantasies are necessarily rendered in verbal terms. She is, after all, an adult using adult language to describe the experience of a baby. The infant, however, does not think verbally. On this, Isaacs stresses that the earliest phantasies are wholly distinct from words, which "are a means of referring to experience, actual or phantasied, but are not identical with it, not a substitute for it" (Isaacs, 1978/1952, pp. 83–84).

For Ogden (1986/1990), to begin to understand the activity of infantile phantasy we must "attempt the impossible" (p.25), that is, step outside the system of verbal symbols in which, as adults, we find ourselves trapped, and imagine ourselves "in a system of nonverbal sensory experience (including kinesthetic and visceral experience). This act of imagination involves, in part, an attempt to think without words" (p. 25). Further on, in discussing a clinical case handled by Ogden himself, we will see how, through the analytic third, we can at least partially accomplish this impossible feat. We will perhaps never fully know the content of infantile phantasies, but, as the analytic third is gradually formed through the entwinement of the unconscious phantasies of the analyst and analysand, we will find ourselves approximating in some measure to non-verbal experience much as it might occur in the infant. By this means we can catch a glimpse of the "child in the adult" (Minerbo, 2009/ 2019, p. 40).[3]

It seems to us that the way Ogden (1986/1990) understands the relationship between the degree of subjectivity and the mode of symbolization in the primitive activity of phantasy speaks to certain aspects of his elucidation of the concept of the analytic third. The author points out that Klein never clarifies how she sees the baby's experience in its relationships with partial objects. However, the manner in which Klein expresses herself in her descriptions of primitive phantasies (mostly using the passive voice[4]) is certainly an indication, as Ogden sees it, that "Klein conceives of early infantile experience as nonsubjective" (Ogden, 1986/1990, p. 27). He also argues that later works by Kleinian authors such as Bion, Meltzer, Segal, Tustin and Bick move towards an understanding of early infantile experience as being "devoid of subjectivity" (p. 27). That is, the baby's feelings, perceptions and thoughts are lived as "things in themselves, events that simply occur. The infant does not experience himself as having a point of view or perspective. There is no infant as thinker or interpreter of his experience" (p. 27). This could be considered something of an initial stage in the analyst and analysand's experience of/in the analytic third, as we hope will be clear from the clinical case discussed below.

Unconscious Phantasy and the Analytic Third

Commenting on the Kleinian conception, so well described in Isaacs' article, that unconscious phantasy is originally bodily, Ogden says:

> The newborn infant's world at the outset is a bodily world, and phantasy represents the infant's attempt to transform somatic events into a mental form. Even into adulthood, phantasy never loses its connection with the body. Phantasy content is always ultimately traceable to thoughts and feelings about the workings and contents of one's own body in relation to the workings and contents of the body of the other.
>
> (1986/1990, p. 11)

This affirmation reminds us of the appeal issued by Cintra and Ribeiro (2018), for whom the analyst working with the concept of unconscious phantasy in clinical practice "should tap into her oldest bodily memories so as to tune into and synch with the patient's pre-verbal communications" (p. 65).[5] The authors stress that having the concept of unconscious phantasy at her disposal enables the analyst to simultaneously listen for representations whilst remaining open to "the *unrepresentable* and to *unconscious bodily memories*" (p. 68, original emphasis).

In other words, the concept of unconscious phantasy as it appears in Kleinian practice, and in the theorization presented by Isaacs, figures as an important tool which the analyst can use to listen out for meaning that lies beyond what has been represented and symbolized, that is, the most primitive phantasies, rooted in bodily experience. This idea is present at various moments in Ogden's own practice, and his clinical notes recurrently mention bodily sensations evoked by intersubjective interaction with the patient. For example, a clinical vignette which the author titled "The woman who could be given no consideration" begins with a detailed description of the bodily sensations the analyst felt in the build-up to and first moments of a session with a patient:

> My stomach muscles tensed and I experienced a faint sense of nausea as I heard the rapid footfalls of Mrs. B. racing up the stairs leading to my office. It seemed to me that she was desperate not to miss a second of her session. I had felt for some time that the quantity of minutes she spent with me had to substitute for all the ways in which she felt unable to be present

while with me. Seconds later, I imagined the patient waiting in a state of chafing urgency to get to me. As she led the way from the waiting room into the consulting room, I could feel in my body the patient's drinking in of every detail of the hallway. I noticed several small flecks of paper from my writing pad on the carpet. I *knew* that the patient was taking them in and hoarding them "inside" of her to silently dissect mentally during and after the session. I felt in a very concrete way that those bits of paper were parts of me that were being taken hostage. (The "fantasies" that I am describing were at this point almost entirely physical sensations as opposed to verbal narratives.)

(Ogden, 1997/ 2013, pp. 182–183)

The word *knew*, which Ogden himself highlights, brings to mind the following statement by poet Manoel de Barros: "Our knowledge wasn't the kind that came from books. It derived from touch and the other senses. Was it, perhaps, some primordial knowledge?" (Barros, 2010, p. 450).[6] The poet's question underscores his intuition that primordial knowledge is bodily knowledge. In other words, it is apprehended viscerally. Isaacs (1952/1978) muses that while unconscious phantasy can perform defensive functions, that is not its primordial function. Phantasy is not originally an escape from reality (though it can be in certain contexts). It is the lens through which the child interprets reality. It is a form of primordial thought,[7] a visceral sort of knowledge. Ogden's description of the physical sensations experienced shortly before and during his session with the patient reveals his openness to listen out for what lies beyond the representable; listen, that is, with the "whole body" (Cintra, 2017, p. 24), just as a mother open to her baby's unconscious fantasies might feel them echo in her own corporality (and through her own fantasies).

In another clinical account, in the chapter of *Subjects of Analysis* devoted to his seminal concept of the analytic third, "The Psyche-Soma and the Analytic Third", Ogden (1994) focuses exclusively on bodily experience. In this section, he offers an account of

an analytical interaction in which a somatic delusion experienced by the analyst, and a related group of bodily sensations and body-related fantasies experienced by the analysand, constituted a principal medium through which the analytic third was experienced, understood, and interpreted.

(Ogden, 1994, pp. 83–84)

In the second year of analysis, Ogden's sessions with this patient, referred to as Mrs. B., began to stall, often descending into 15–20-minute silences. The analyst's interpretations of the transference-countertransference failed to alter the situation, which saw the patient constantly apologize for "not having more to say" (p. 85) and express concern that she was disappointing the analyst. Ogden says that, as time went by, the apologies grew less verbal and were conveyed more by

> her facial expression, gait, tone of voice, and so on. Also, at this juncture in the analysis, Mrs. B. began to wring her hands throughout the analytic hours, but more vigorously during the silences. She pulled strenuously on the fingers of her hands and deeply kneaded her knuckles and fingers to the point that her hands became reddened in the course of the hour.
>
> ((Ogden, 1994, pp. 85–86)

During this period, Ogden began to develop a mild case of the flu, but nothing that kept him from seeing patients. In the weeks that followed, though the flu had passed, he continued to feel unwell, specifically during his sessions with Mrs. B. In addition to a certain nausea and dizziness, he also found himself feeling like an old man, a sensation that was at once comforting and a source of resentment. Ogden began to experience a pervading anxiety during his sessions with the patient, a state which he says was indissociable from these physical sensations. The analyst realized that he was now putting off Mrs. B.'s sessions, often finding something to do shortly before their hour so he would arrive late. He also noticed that he had great difficulty remembering the woman's first name. At this same time, it struck Ogden that the patient would stare fixedly at him at the beginning and end of each session, and it became clear that her associations tended to orbit around possible emotional problems her children were having. On that score, the analyst floated the interpretation that Mrs. B. was perhaps experiencing self-doubt about her value as a mother and as a patient.

At one particular session, Ogden leaned over the arm of his chair to take a drink of water, something he often did during his sessions with Mrs. B. and others. However, before he could reach the glass, Mrs. B. turned suddenly on the divan, looked at Ogden with a panicked expression, and said: "I'm sorry, I didn't know what was happening to you" (Ogden, 1994, p. 84). The author says:

> It was only in the intensity of this moment in which there was a feeling of terror that something catastrophic was happening to me that I became able to name for myself the terror that I had been carrying for some time. I became aware that the anxiety that I had been feeling and the (predominantly unconscious and primitively symbolized) dread of the meetings with Mrs. B. (that was reflected in my procrastinating behavior) had been directly connected with an unconscious *sensation/fantasy* that my somatic symptoms of malaise, nausea, and vertigo were caused by Mrs. B. and that she was killing me. I now understood that I had for several weeks been emotionally consumed by the unconscious conviction (a "fantasy in the body") [Gaddini, 1982, p. 143] that I had a serious illness, perhaps a brain tumor, and during that period had been frightened that I was dying.

I felt an immense sense of relief at this point in the meeting as I came to understand these thoughts, feelings, and sensations as reflections of transference-countertransference events occurring in the analysis.

(Ogden, 1994, p. 88, our italics)

We have highlighted the words "sensation/fantasy" in the above passage so as to emphasize the relationship between this manner of understanding the clinical experience with the way unconscious phantasy expresses itself in early infancy, as described in Isaacs' article (1952/1978). In its more primitive dimension, unconscious phantasy pertains to a blurred borderland between representation and sensation. It is through openness to this primitive mode of grasping experience, in the intersection between fantasy and sensation, that the analyst can access something unrepresentable in the patient that is expressed, nonetheless, in nonverbal gesture:

My own and the patient's capacity to think as separate individuals had been co-opted by the intensity of the shared unconscious fantasy/somatic delusion in which we were both enmeshed. The unconscious fantasy reflected an important, highly conflicted set of Mrs. B.'s unconscious internal object relationships that were being created anew in the analysis in the form of my somatic delusion in conjunction with the patient's delusional fears (about my body) and her own sensory experiences (e.g., her handwringing).

(Ogden, 1994, p. 89)

In response to Mrs. B.'s stunned comment, Ogden says that he thought she had been afraid that something really horrible was happening to him, and that he may even be dying. The patient confesses that, crazy though it might seem, when she heard him shifting in his chair, she got the distinct impression he might be having a heart attack. She also remarked that she had, for some time, thought him somewhat pale. This made Ogden realize that it was not her eldest son who Mrs. B. wanted to take to see a doctor, but the analyst himself. Her fear was that "something catastrophic" (p. 89) was happening between them (she and the analyst). Ogden then tells Mrs. B. that he suspected she was not only afraid that he was going to die, but that she was actually the cause of his ill-health. He said he thought she feared having a damaging effect on him in the same way she believed herself to have on her son, to the point that she thought she might actually be the death of him. At this point, "Mrs. B.'s handwringing and finger-tugging subsided" (p. 90). The patient then admitted to Ogden that all of that rang true to her, but that she was afraid she would forget everything that had happened during that session:

Mrs. B.'s last comment reminded me of my own inability to remember her first name and my fantasy of being a mother unwilling to fully acknowledge the birth of her baby (by not giving it a name). I now felt that the ambivalence represented by my own act of forgetting and the associated fantasy (as well as Mrs. B.'s ambivalence represented in her anxiety that she would obliterate all memory of this meeting) reflected a fear jointly held by Mrs. B and myself that allowing her "to be born" (i.e., to become genuinely alive and present) in the analysis would pose a serious danger to both of us. I felt that we had created an unconscious fantasy (largely generated in the form of bodily experience) that her coming to life (her birth) in the analysis would make me ill and could possibly kill me. For both our sakes, it was important that we make every effort to prevent that birth (and death) from occurring.

(Ogden, 1994, p. 90)

This understanding derived from an interpretation (which Ogden attributes to Mrs. B.) that her long silences during analysis represented an attempt on her part to make herself invisible, annul herself as a source of tension for the analyst, and so prevent him from falling ill. The patient admitted that she was aware that she apologized to him way too often, and that it actually bugged her to such an extent that she regretted ever starting analysis in the first place, and suspected the analyst felt the same about taking her on. She added that the sensation was similar to a feeling she had carried with her since childhood. Despite her mother's assurances that she had been a very welcome and wanted child, she herself had never felt that her parents' home was a place for children. Her toys, for example, were always stowed away in her bedroom so as not to bother her father. Based on this, Ogden began to understand Mrs. B.'s silences as a way she had found not to strew her "toys" (thoughts, behaviors, feelings) around the analyst's "home" (the analysis itself). This led Ogden to understand that his fantasy that he had developed a brain tumor (and the sensory experiences that accompanied it) was a reflection of the unconscious fantasy that Mrs. B.'s very existence was a sort of "growth that greedily, selfishly, and destructively took up space that it had no business occupying" (p. 92).

The patient reiterated her concern (expressed at the start of the analysis) that she was not presenting a fair and accurate picture of her parents, especially her mother, though she added that "this felt more reflexive than real this time" (p. 92).

Ogden mentions feeling that these exchanges with Mrs. B. were "the first time in the analysis that there were two people in the room talking to one another" (p. 92). It seemed to him now that not only was Mrs. B. able to talk and think "more fully as a living human being" (p. 92), but that he too was "feeling, thinking and experiencing sensations in a way that had a quality of realness and spontaneity of which [he] had not previously been capable in this analysis (p.92):

In retrospect, my analytical work with Mrs. B. to this point had sometimes felt to me to involve an excessively dutiful identification with my own analyst (the "old man"). I had not only used phrases that he had regularly used, but also at times with the intonation I associated with him. It was only after the shift in the analysis just described that I fully recognized this. My experience in the phase of analytic work being discussed had "compelled me" to experience the unconscious fantasy that the full realization of myself as an analyst could occur only at the cost of the death of another part of myself (the death of an internal object analyst/father). The feelings of comfort, resentment, and anxiety associated with my fantasy of being an old man reflected both the safety that I felt in being like (with) my analyst/ father and the wish to be free of him (in fantasy, to kill him). The latter wish carried with it the fear that I would die in the process. The experience with Mrs. B., including the act of putting my thoughts, feelings, and sensations into words, constituted a particular form of separation and of mourning of which I had not been capable to that point.

(Ogden, 1994, pp. 92–93)

This clinical account indicates how the analyst can, through fantasy grounded in corporality, plumb the very depths of understanding while proceeding beyond representation. Openness to unconscious phantasy enabled the analyst to listen empathically to "crazier" aspects of the patient (an adjective she herself used with reference to the fantasy that the analyst was having a heart-attack). Through the concept of the analytic third, as demonstrated through this particular case, Ogden shows that there is a road-less-traveled, off the grid of superficiality and standard interactions, which leads into deeper layers (formed by primitive unconscious phantasies) of the intersubjective experience shared with the patient.

Projective Identification as Freedom from Imprisonment within Phantasy

For Ogden (1986/1990), underlying Klein's vision of unconscious phantasy is the understanding that the baby is, initially, a prisoner of its own state of mind. The baby sees in the world only confirmations of its expectations based on its own preconceptions, that is, on innate codes derived from the life and death instincts (psychological deep structure). The infant is therefore incapable of learning from experiences, as they can only be interpreted in accordance with these innate codes. Seen in these terms, we are presented with a rather bleak outlook regarding the psychic possibilities open to infants and subjects in general.

An extremely important question arises out of this context, one which Ogden formulates as follows: how can the baby break out of the imprisonment of its own phantasies and learn from its experiences? One of Klein's replies, seconded by later Kleinians, is that positive experiences with the primary object can attenuate the infant's belief in its "badness" and that of things in general (though the opposite holds just as true):

Through being loved and through the enjoyment and comfort he has in relation to people his confidence in his own as well as in other people's goodness becomes strengthened, his hope that his 'good' objects and his own ego can be saved and preserved increases, at the same time as his ambivalence and acute fears of internal destruction diminish. Unpleasant experiences and the lack of enjoyable ones, in the young child, especially lack of happy and close contact with loved people, increase ambivalence, diminish trust and hope and confirm anxieties about inner annihilation and external persecution.

(Klein, 1940, p. 128)

Ogden (1986/1990) considers this explanation unsatisfactory, because if the prevalent code acting upon a baby's experience is based on the death instinct, we might wonder why the baby would ever accept a good experience as being truly good, as opposed to a manipulation or deception.

Another Kleinian attempt to explain this lies in the innateness of the life and death instincts. If the constitutional endowment of the life instinct predominates over that of the death instinct, the projection of the derivatives of that instinct would foster the creation of good objects that serve, in turn, as a defense against the bad. For Ogden, this line of explanation is no less unsatisfactory, because

[it] does not explain the capacity of the infant to alter his relationship to bad objects other than by relying on idealized good objects to protect him against the danger. By analogy, the adult paranoid patient does not emerge from paranoia by developing a mental police force to protect him against danger.

(Ogden 1986/1990, p. 33)

Ogden (1986/1990) sees in Klein's concept of projective identification a far more convincing clarification of how the baby can break through this imprisonment in fantasy and start to learn from experience. The author notes that while Klein stresses the intrapsychic aspect in her discussions of the concept, that is, she emphasizes projective identification as a shield against the anxiety deriving from the death instinct, the examples she gives and the language she uses offer up a glimpse of an interpersonal conception. For example, she says things like "expelling dangerous substances (excrements) out of the self and *into the mother*" (Klein, 1946/1997a, p. 8, our emphasis), rather than "onto the mother", and "The projection of good feelings and good parts of the self *into the mother* is essential for the infant's ability to develop good-object relations and to integrate his ego" (p. 9, our emphasis).

For Ogden (1986/1990), if the mother allows herself to be used as the screen for the baby's projections, something new is created, something that is more than just mother and baby, but is a mother-infant entity in itself. This enables the baby to process its experience in a way that would be impossible to do on its own. In this sense, Ogden thinks that the idea of metabolization is insufficient to explain the dynamic involved in projective identification, which is more than just the mother giving back digested mental content to the baby in a more assimilable form, but involves the baby also acquiring the capacity to live experiences differently. In other words, it's not only the projected content that is transformed, but also the way in which the baby sees itself and the world. In fact, there is a change in expectations, the emergence of a possibility of relating to the world in a way that transcends the innate codes deriving from the life or death instincts, because "the mother-infant of successful projective identification is an entity greater than either individual alone and is capable of generating a quality of being that neither individual alone could have generated" (Ogden, 1986/1990, p. 36). This understanding of projective identification clearly constitutes one of the understructures of the concept of the analytic third, something Ogden explicitly states when he refers to the analytic third as "the subject of projective identification" (p. 101). So, the concept of the analytic third can be understood, at least in part, as fruit of the intersubjective reading Ogden makes of projective identification. As he sees it, projective identification is more than just a turbo-charged form of projection or identification, or even a blend of both, because these concepts refer to intrapsychic aspects of experience. In Ogden's conception, projective identification can only be comprehended "in terms of a mutually creating, negating, and preserving dialectic of subjects" (p. 101).

For Ogden (1994), a successful analytic process involves the re-appropriation of the individual subjectivities of the analyst and analysand, "which have been transformed through their experience of (in) the newly created analytic third (the subject of projective identification)" (p. 101). As such, the projective identification involves a central paradox: "the individuals involved in this form of relatedness unconsciously subjugate themselves to a mutually generated intersubjective third (the subject of projective identification) for the purpose of freeing themselves from the limits of who they had been to that point" (p. 101).

If in the text from 1986 Ogden posits projective identification as a way in which the infant (projector) can break the bars of phantasy, roughly ten years later (1994), while presenting the concept of the analytic third, he goes further still, arguing that it is not just the projector (infant or patient) who experiences psychological growth through projective identification-mediated interaction. Here, Ogden affirms that no intersubjective relationship is ever unilateral. In other words, the recipient of the projective identification (analyst or mother) is always also a projector. The recipient implied in the experience of projective identification is negating its individuality. However, this negation is not a purely passive event, as the recipient is not only contained or limited. On the contrary, the negation occurs, in part, "with the purpose of disrupting the closures underlying the coherence/stagnation of the self" (Ogden 1994, p. 102). In short, the path toward liberation from the fantasies spun from the codes deriving from the life and death instincts is available to both the projector and recipient in a projective identification relationship.

In projective identification, the recipient is offered the possibility of generating a new form of experience grounded in otherness to himself, and so create "conditions for the alteration of who he had been to that point" (p. 102). The recipient does not merely identify with the projector (the individual projecting onto/into him), but actually becomes, himself, something else (neither projector nor recipient). Ogden sees the projector and recipient in a projective identification as allies in the aim of using the tools of their individual subjectivities and of intersubjectivity itself "to escape the solipsism of their own separate psychological existences" (p. 105). In other words, to escape from the unconscious phantasies in which they are imprisoned.

In an earlier text, Ogden (1979) says that the first stage (or first aspect of the same psychological unit) of a projective identification takes the form of the unconscious phantasy of projecting oneself into another. The second phase, which Ogden calls the "induction phase", consists of the projector applying pressure upon the recipient through interpersonal interaction in a bid to make the other think, feel and behave in accordance with the projector's fantasy. Lastly, in the third and final phase, once the recipient has processed the projected feelings, these are re-internalized by the projector. In this sense, Ogden recognizes projective identification as, at once, a form of communication, a kind of defense, a primitive mode of object relation, and a pathway toward psychological change.

Considering the first and second phases, Ogden (1979) warns that, while the fantasy is operationalized and concretized by means of the pressure which the projector exerts upon the recipient, what occurs is not a transfer of content from one to the other. In the analytic context, for example, the patient can bring the analyst to feel something close to what he or she feels, but will never transplant that feeling into the analyst, because the analyst/recipient is a human being in his own right, with his own past and set of psychological conflicts, fears and difficulties. So, even if the feelings a recipient experiences in projective identification are elicited by the projector's pressure, they are the products of an entirely different personality system, with its own strengths and weaknesses. This is precisely what makes it possible for the projected feelings in the recipient to be metabolized in a way the projector himself could never do. For example, the recipient might try to master the feeling through sublimation and understanding. These are different methods of projective identification (the defense employed by the projector), because they are not attempts to negate, be rid of, or forget feelings and ideas. On the contrary, they are attempts to contain or experience those contents.

Ogden (1979) says that if the recipient succeeds in dealing with the feelings projected into him in a way that differs from the projector's own processing of them, a whole new set of feelings arises out of that. This new feeling set may be accompanied by the sensation that the projected content can be experienced without harming the self or any valued internal or external objects. This new experience might even involve the sensation that those formerly projected feelings can now actually be appreciated.

Managing the Technique of Projective Identification

Ogden (1982/1991) notes that while the concept of projective identification was originally formulated by Klein, the Kleinian technique is not the only source of input on how to manage this phenomenon in a clinical setting. Analysts from a number of theoretical schools have developed techniques for working with projective identification, even if they don't always call it that. In a brief description of how other groups handle this clinical phenomenon, Ogden (1982/1991) mentions the modern psychoanalytical group, most specifically Nelson et al. (1968, apud Ogden (1982/1991) and Spotnitz (1976, apud Ogden (1982/1991); the middle group; and even some classical analysts who may not have directly approached the full repertoire the concept of projective identification involves, but nonetheless make important contributions to the understanding of interpersonal phenomena. For example, the author mentions the ideas of Anna Freud, Warren Brodey, Weiss and Sampson, among others. For the purposes of this chapter, we will focus on how Ogden himself understands the clinical management of projective identification, and his own way of using the Kleinian concept.

The psychoanalytical technique Ogden proposes (1982/1991) for projective identification endeavors to open the patient up to a slightly altered version of what was already his, but which could not, in that former form, be used for the purpose of psychological integration and growth. Ogden says that this goal can be achieved through verbal interpretation at certain junctures in the therapeutic process, but that other modes of therapeutic intervention can be employed at less favorable times, particularly with more disturbed patients.

Ogden (1982/1991) makes an important observation about interpretations: working with patients whose transference is connected with the whole object, verbal interpretation functions as a necessary modification of the patient's projected aspect; however, when dealing with patients whose transference is related to the partial object, verbal interpretations, even when correct, can ring strange, with little real relevance to the patient. In this case, the patient finds himself before the following dilemma: he can introject the interpretation in an undigested way, which will create the sensation of having been forced to take it in, and of having relinquished his own individual existence in the process, or he can reject the interpretation, which invites the risk of his feeling alone and disconnected from the analyst. In these situations, the analyst is faced with a patient who is so isolated and defensive that the analyst himself may experience corresponding feelings of isolation, futility and frustration.

For Ogden (1982/1991), an important indication that the analyst is involved in a projective identification dynamic is the development of a shared, unquestionable and inflexible vision of himself in relation to the patient. This is an element that can be clearly seen in the case of Mrs. B., in terms of the phantasies which Ogden harbors about being ill and his attempts to delay their sessions. Another indication is how hard the analyst finds it to comfortably observe the transference as it unfolds. On the contrary, he is disturbed and confused by it. We can see this in the clinical vignette about Mrs. B., as in various other clinical accounts which Ogden gives.

Ogden (1982/1991) believes that once the interaction has begun to take shape as a projective identification, the analyst would be wise not to intervene until he has been able to sift through the feelings evoked. If the analyst can contain those feelings within the analytic situation, the associative connections will emerge with sufficient clarity to be recognized and thought out.

In another clinical vignette, Ogden (1994) shows that the understanding of a projective identification as underlying the analytic interaction sometimes arises in a way that is barely verbally symbolized at all, which places the analyst before the pressing need to contain what is going on. During a preliminary telephone call, a patient who Ogden refers to as Mr. P. had told the analyst about an affair he was having with his best friend's wife, and when he arrived for their first session, he did so carrying a wad of papers which he said were love poems he had written about her, and which he felt would help the analyst understand the feelings he was having towards this woman. In the few seconds in which this initial interaction occurs, the analyst is flooded with sensations and thoughts: the distinct feeling that it would be cruel not to accept the offer of the poems; the impression that there was "something slightly effeminate about the patient's appearance and manner of speech" (p. 125), and the sense that the patient was inviting the analyst to engage in a "type of sadomasochistic homossexual scene" (p. 125). Based on these rapid ideational-emotional responses, Ogden tells the patient it would take some time to understand what had just transpired between them, and that it would be best for him to hold onto the poems for the time being.

After declining to take the poems at that initial session, Ogden was able to formulate a series of considerations that he could then gradually share with the patient in the form of verbal interpretations:

> I feel that these thoughts and feelings would not have been discernible to me had I reflexively acceded to the patient's offer of the poems in an "empathic" effort to accept his expression of his need to be understood. Not accepting the poems allowed a psychological space to be created in which the poems could be created (and eventually understood) as an "analytic object".
>
> (Ogden, 1994, p. 127)

Not immediately accepting the patient's poems enabled Ogden (1994) to open a space in which he could mull over what had gone on between them without any masochistic submission on his part to the evacuation—out of the patient and into himself—of the man's "destructive out of control passion" (p. 128). At the same time, it also allowed him to avoid sadistically defending himself by forcing an interpretation upon the patient. In this brief exchange, we can see an essential aspect of the therapeutic engagement: *processing* the projective identification rather than *acting* on the engendered feelings (Ogden, 1982/1991). The latter would have been a failure of containment, with the analyst potentially forcing back into the patient the aspects of the "I" which he or she was trying to project into him. In this case, the analyst could use interpretations like "you are trying to make me feel your pain (or experience your insanity) for you." For Ogden (1982/1991), while this is a genuine aspect of every projective identification, if that facet of the situation alone is broached by the analyst, the patient will feel punished for doing something destructive or selfish.

In another clinical vignette, we see an intervention that falls midway toward the ideal Ogden (1982/1991) proposes for managing projective identification. The patient's mother had suffered from chronic depression and committed suicide when she—Mrs. N.— was only ten years old. Mrs. N.'s relationship with the analyst was constantly overshadowed by the threat of suicide. In the eleventh month of treatment, soon after the analyst's return from vacation (the first he had taken since their sessions began), the patient attempted suicide by ingesting a large amount of antidepressants. Immediately after taking these pills, she rang the analyst, who arranged for emergency treatment and she was saved. For months afterwards, the analyst was terrified every time the phone rang that it would bring news of the patient's death. It got to the point that he began to wish Mrs. N. would just go ahead and get it over with, so as to end the suffering.

During a certain session, the analyst told the patient that the constant threat of suicide was making it impossible for him to think clearly and work properly with her. Ogden (1982/1991), whom the analyst seems to have approached for supervision, says that this intervention was a partially successful containment of the projective identification. The analyst was being forced to experience the unsustainable responsibility which Mrs. N. had had to bear as a child when told that she was to blame for the death of her depressed mother. For Ogden (1982/1991), the analyst's intervention shone a light on the fact that an identical burden was being foisted onto him, but that he, unlike the patient, had an emotional repertoire and arsenal of responses that were much broader than those available to a ten-year-old girl.

However, Ogden (1982/1991) warns that the intervention risked forcing back into the patient that aspect which she was trying to convey to the analyst through projective identification. He emphasizes that it was important for the analyst to recognize the patient's attempt to communicate something important rather than simply address her controlling, hostile and escapist designs, which are almost always present in a projective identification. In this sense, Ogden (1982/1991) suggests that the analyst might have completed his intervention by saying something like: "I think you'd like me to know what it was like to feel fully responsible for your mother and yet totally unable to help her" (p. 60). In fact, as the analysis progressed, with the analyst working with the supervisor's comments in mind, some clearly discernible changes came about, such as the account Mrs. N. gave of a dream (something she rarely ever did), her realization that there were similarities in the ways she treated her daughter and she herself had been treated by her mother, and a reduction in the frequency of suicide threats.

Ogden (1982/1991) discusses other aspects of the clinical management of projective identification, such as the fact that deeply regressed patients tend to experience very primitive projective identifications based on sensorial precursors of unconscious phantasies that have not yet attained visual and verbal symbolization, saying that it is the task of analysis to help the patient re-elaborate the phantasy in such a way as heightens the clarity and definition of what is being unconsciously ejected by the patient and evoked in the analyst. In this undertaking, the analyst should avail of other means of presenting his impressions to the patient, such as rhythm and tone of voice, facial expressions, way of looking at the patient, etc. We shall stop here, however, as a thorough presentation of Ogden's understanding and use of the concept of projective identification[8] lies beyond the scope of this chapter.

At certain times, Ogden expresses his interest in tapping deeper layers of the intersubjective experience lived with the patient. We frequently find the author nurturing this idea during an encounter with a patient and then discarding it in virtue of its superficial character. We often come across comments on some thought which occurred to him as an explanation for something experienced during a session: "this idea seemed rote and wholly inadequate to the disturbing nature of the claustrophobia and other poorly defined feelings that I was experiencing" (Ogden, 2013, p. 171), or "this formulation made intellectual sense, but felt clichéd and emotionally lacking" (Ogden, 1997, p. 68). At other moments we find him bemoaning the superficiality of an interpretation: "I silently agreed with her that my comment sounded canned" (Ogden, 2018, p. 409).

Something different to this was presented in the case of Mrs. B. (Ogden, 1994). The analysis was steeped in the patient's and the analyst's fantasies, but these only became significant after Mrs. B.'s anxious intervention (expressing her fear that Ogden was on the verge of a heart attack). From that point on, the analyst was able to understand that both he and she were caught up in transference-countertransference events. The patient had never really felt wanted as a child, and had always lived in fear of disturbing her father whenever she played or expressed herself. This unconscious situation had transferred to the analytic context, generating a whole field of shared unconscious phantasies shot through with fears of death, particularly that the patient's recuperation of her vitality would come at the cost of the analyst's life. It was only when these fantasies were finally verbalized that Ogden felt there were actually two people in the room, talking to one another, and that the patient was now finally capable of speaking and thinking in a more fully human way.

When the subject cannot think the disturbing emotional experience out for himself, he requires the help of another to *dream the dreams undreamt and interrupted cries* (Ogden, 2004/2010). In the analytic situation, it's the analyst who can, through reverie, gather up the patient's bodily sensations, emotionscapes, words and silences so that both of their unconscious phantasies can reveal themselves in a meaningful way, and be named by the analyst and recognized by the patient. It is important to live through the perplexity of not understanding what is going on, for as long as that takes, in order to attain the insight and internal understanding which will elucidate the phantasies in which the analyst and analysand find themselves imprisoned. The juncture at which a multitude of earlier impressions finally come together to generate new meaning is something of a eureka moment. This new-minted meaning suddenly blends a manifold of earlier impressions and enigmas that had presented themselves as a blur of indefinite expectations and fears. When insight strikes, something comes unstuck and starts to flow. There is a surge of liquid emotion, an undoing of knots, and with this comes a great sense of relief and liberation. Being able to access the logic of what one has been feeling and thinking through reverie is sometimes experienced as an awakening, a veritable birth that opens onto the possibility of entering into free association so one can finally recount one's own life in a way that makes sense.

This ability to narrate one's life is achieved through the capacity to confer intelligibility upon emotional life, and this is secured by elaborating upon the depressive position. In our view, Ogden here appropriates Melanie Klein's positions in an original and creative way.

A Dialectical Understanding of the Paranoid-Schizoid and Depressive Positions

The human need to know the truth of our psychic life is one way of referring to Melanie Klein's enlightenment aspiration; it reflects the desire to shed the light of reason on the darkest aspects of our psychic life and is a genuine thirst to know the unconscious truth about ourselves and others. This enlightenment trait can be found in her work right from the beginning, from her very first case, when she expressed her desire to see her patient accept the father's participation as something indispensable to the origin of babies (Klein, 1921/1975). Klein always believed that it was essential to draw upon empathy to get as close as possible to human suffering in order to see the construction mechanisms behind the unconscious phantasies that form the bedrock of our beliefs, preconceptions and moral judgments. It is fundamental that we know this network of unconscious emotions and ideas so we can deconstruct them and lay bare the construction mechanisms that engender our violence in the psychic and social spheres. We shall see in what manner these aspirations pervade Klein's theory of positions, and the creative way Ogden appropriates them in his book *Subjects of Analysis* (Ogden, 1994).

First, we will briefly outline Klein's theory of positions. In her earliest sessions with children, Klein found her attention drawn to the archaic anxieties that accompany polymorphic infantile sexuality, tinged with violence and sadism, which is driven by the oral desire to seize and consume the world and its objects, and the sadistic-anal libido, which demands control and triumph over objects, or, in more radical form, harbors the desire to destroy and be rid of them as if they were fecal matter. During the phase of sadistic-oral and sadistic-anal dynamisms, there is a predominant desire to exact revenge for the passional fury of the infant's first forms of love. It's a sort of Talion (*lex talionis*), which demands that this early primitive form of love blow back upon the individual. In this "position"—paranoid-schizoid—there is a radical oscillation between passivity and activity, a feeling of impotence and fantasies of omnipotence, and the things of the world become either ideally good or terribly bad, that is, the psyche defends itself from the intensity of instinct by splitting, idealization and projective identification.

In parallel with this all-or-nothing dynamic, we start to see the first fears of losing the good object, which, on the imaginary plane, is at risk of being destroyed by the instinctual power and urgency of the forms of loving (oral and anal) described above. If the child finds itself alone and unsupported, in need of something that it cannot obtain by itself, and there is no one around who can come to its aid at that moment, the mother's absence will transform into a sense of abandonment. The infant's anxiety in relation to the loss of the mother finds itself confirmed, and this creates an atmosphere of sadness and terrible imaginary suspicions, such as that the child itself was somehow responsible for the mother's abandoning it, and is being punished for that now.

Talion exposes the child to its own instinctual violence. What predominates at this point is the fear of loss, or depressive anxiety, which is a mixture of pining, sorrow, pain, shame, rage and a feeling that one has been harmed and aggrieved. This is the hardest part, because it combines guilt, a lack of self-worth and the feeling of impotence for not being able to prevent the good object's disappearance: this is the archaic anxiety of the depressive position. This imaginary dynamic is inescapable, but it must be worked through and processed through mourning.

Each position is a (re)discovery of the vulnerable side of the human condition: dependence on others, feeling ignorant and impotent with regard to what is happening to oneself and to the world, not knowing how to break the impasse or deal with waiting, frustration, failings and traumas that come from the environment. The best way to understand the "depressive" component of this position is the need to move from the pleasure principle to the reality principle and to transform illusions of omnipotence. Klein believed that the paranoid-schizoid position was a more primitive mode of functioning than the depressive position, but as the latter is always temporary, the former will always return to dominance, even after the successful processing of a depressive position. We can understand this oscillation between positions by imagining a background/foreground system: when the depressive position comes to the fore, the paranoid-schizoid dynamism remains in the background, ready to retake the foreground at any moment, shunting the depressive position back into the blur. This description of one position lingering on the horizon while the other hogs the limelight paints a picture very different to the notion of these positions as "chronological stages".

On the other hand, the stages of libido development in Freud follow a linear chronology, in which one stage gives way to another. While the positions are there from the very beginning of life, they continue being the basic forms of organization behind our emotional life throughout: "Positions neither follow nor precede one another; rather, each coexists with the others in a dialectical relationship". (Ogden, 1988, p. 34).

In addition to these two positions, Ogden introduces the idea of a third pole of human experience, namely the autistic-contiguous position. The autistic-contiguous position is a more primitive psychological organization than the other two and stems from an "elaboration and extension" of the work of Esther Bick (1968, 1986), Meltzer (1975) and Tustin (1972, 1980, 1984, 1990).[9]

> Rhythmicity and experiences of sensorial contiguity (especially at the skin surface) contribute to an elemental sense of continuity of being over time. Such experiences are generated within the invisible matrix of the environmental mother.
>
> (Ogden, 1994, p. 36)

The forms of experience associated with each of these positions need to be understood as poles "of the dialectical process in which each creates, negates and preserves the other" (Ogden, 1994, p. 34). What does that mean? It means that each of the positions *creates* the conditions under which the other position can emerge. And yet, when the depressive position prevails over the paranoid-schizoid, for example, that predominance in a sense *negates* the earlier dynamism, at the same time as it *preserves* it. In order to install itself, all negation must preserve to some degree what it negates:

> Associated with each of the positions is a particular quality of anxiety, forms of defense and object relatedness, a type of symbolization, and a quality of subjectivity. Together these qualities of experience constitute a state of being that characterizes each of the positions.
>
> (Ogden, 1994, p. 35)

The main idea is that Ogden thinks of the paranoid-schizoid and depressive positions as *different forms of attributing meaning to emotional experience*. Klein says that the positions are *two different ways of functioning*. So, to say, as Ogden does, that they are two *forms of conferring meaning upon existence*—one paranoid-schizoid, the other depressive—is something else entirely. It's a case of knowing Klein in order to transcend her: more than modes of psychic functioning, we're now thinking in terms of *different forms of attributing meaning to emotional experience*.

The blossoming of a line of thought lies precisely in these little shifts in meaning. Ogden makes just such a shift when he claims, more explicitly than Klein ever did, that the two forms never exist separately, but in dialectic relation. He imports the Hegelian notion of dialectic into Melanie Klein's intuition. This is a strategy he employs to force the original intuition to go that much further and work in a new way. In his book, he goes so far as to say that each of these ways of lending meaning to existence *demands* the other form as background.

They switch back and forth in the same way that, for Freud, the conscious mind only makes sense in relation to an unconscious mind; they do not exist outside of that tension. The Kleinian subject—he says—"exists not in any given position or hierarchical layering of positions, but in the dialectical tension created *between* positions" (Ogden, 1994, p. 34, our emphasis). From this, we can infer that the subject's place in psychoanalysis is an *empty space*; in fact, it's not a detectable *space* at all, but is best defined by saying that the psychic subject is a *relation* between two spaces, between two ways of giving experience its meaning! In this sense, each position would have to be considered a theoretical fiction that helps us approach psychic functioning and its meaning-bestowing strategies.

And Ogden also explains that the paranoid-schizoid position produces a state of being that he suggests is *a-historical*, devoid of the experience of a subject capable of mediating between the sensation of I-ness and lived sensorial experience: "This paranoid-schizoid mode *contributes to the sense of immediacy and intensity of experience*" (Ogden, 1994, p. 35, our italics).

On the other hand, the depressive position creates a self-narrating subject capable of interpreting the lived, and of mediating between itself and lived sensorial experience; this subject is equipped for historical time, with notions of past and future. Odgen will go on to say that it is the elaboration of the depressive position that enables us to narrate our own lives and slip into the flow of historical time—which allows the subject to enter most fully into his own existence.

A person who cannot narrate himself to himself, and who finds himself at the center of a movement of "letting others speak for him" is someone who, in a sense, "does not exist". This is a tragic and radical observation to make. We might think of those patients who find themselves numbed and in need of revitalization and awakening. They need to break out of a state in which they are inhabited by voices and eyes that are not theirs, by ghosts that prevent them from having a mind of their own. They have not yet fully stepped into historical time, and can only repeat what they have heard said about themselves and the world. Ongoing and systematic analytic work to engender and transform depressive positions is what is required for these subjects to enter historical time. They need to become narrators of themselves, an "I" that gathers up a past, present and future, and wriggles free of the shackles of fantasies of self. Many such patients find themselves trapped inside a fixed idea about themselves, in a thought prison that restricts them to a locked cell of frozen images and representations.

These ideas make us think of a Brazilian patient of Bion's who, at a certain point in the analysis, during a trip to London, began to shout with glee: "I'm being born, Dr. Bion, I'm being born." I think this little analytic anecdote reveals the importance of narrating oneself to oneself, which we consider one of the main achievements of the depressive position and which can actually feel like a birth, a stepping into time, a becoming real.

In addition to entering historical time, the depressive position allows us to recognize others as total, independent subjects with an inner life like our own, thus giving rise to our capacity to feel care and guilt, and to seek non-magical reparations for damage we have done in imagination and reality, while boosting our threshold for pain and frustration; in short, it generates a quality of life possessed of a wealth of symbolic meanings. In fact, following on from Klein's intuition, and considering this constant flitting between these two positions, Ogden sees the subject as emerging out of successive processes of splitting and integration, a subject forged in the chop-and-change of positions, caught between these two ways of conferring meaning upon lived experience. This subject is built because it temporalizes; its process of constitution makes it an errant subject, always passing through, a being that is in constant becoming, between ceasing-to-be and coming-into-being in a new way, that is, forever differentiating itself from itself by incorporating new emotional experiences as these arise.

The writer Noemi Jaffe (2017) gave her book a very suggestive title, one that captures this idea of entering historical time and existing in a perpetual process of mourning the past. The title *Não está mais aqui quem falou* translates roughly as "the person who said that is no longer here". In other words, the simple capacity to narrate one's life highlights the transitory nature of each subjective manifestation. The change demanded by the passage of time keeps the subject churning through new *formulations of her subjectivity*, each unlike the one *that had been up to now*, before the narration. The new subject that emerges out of the story told is the result of many invisible processes of separation and reunion, splitting and integration.

There is no denying that this reading of Klein is a creative way of using her discovery. Ogden promotes a de-crystallization of the idea of the psychic subject when he says that the depressive position, with its historicity and capacity to create symbols, should not be thought of as "the" place of the subject in Kleinian theory, just as the unconscious should not be considered "the" place of the Freudian subject. In fact, in Freud as in Klein, the psychoanalytical subject is always a nomad, perpetually in transit between the conscious and unconscious minds, the paranoid-schizoid and depressive poles, in the *space and tension created by the "dialectical interplay of the different dimensions of experience"* (Ogden, 1994, p. 48, our italics).

Ogden stresses the simultaneous presence of these positions, each functioning as a backdrop to the other. However, the diachronic axis, that is, the sequence of past, present and future, is also held in a dialectical tension with the synchronicity of the positions: "a psychological theory becomes untenable if it does not incorporate a recognition of the directionality of time and of life". (Ogden, 1994, p. 36). A fully processed depressive position enables the development of the capacity to feel guilt, make reparations, mourn, feel empathy and gratitude, and to care for other subjects.

Concluding Remarks: Splitting and Integration of the Subject

Klein believed that living through the depressive position was the most important aspect of infantile development, and that it unfolded, with great intensity, over the course of the first five years of life. It's a way of conferring meaning upon emotional experiences that needs to be revisited constantly throughout life, albeit worked through in a more nuclear approach through the analytic process. But what does living through the depressive position entail? We might say that, in broad strokes, it is about what Freud (1920/1996) called the greatest cultural achievement of humankind. Observing his grandson's game of *fort/da*, Freud witnessed the playful way the boy attenuated his mother's *disappearance* into her *absence*, a concept that carries within it the evocation of a *future presence*, thus making the lack more tolerable through primary symbolization (of play), which, in turn, paves the way for words and inserts the subject into the flow of historical time. It's a process that is, at the same time, extremely good and deeply unpleasant.

So, in order for the depressive position to arise, there has to be a solid introjection of the good object. Introjecting the good object means making a stable record of experiences of pleasure and safety, which come to constitute a relatively stable internal reserve. This reserve functions as an assurance that there will be future pleasures, thereby increasing the subject's capacity to tolerate privation and frustration:

> In this sense, the *good object* is more than just the record of the experience of satisfaction introjected and converted into a source of well-being and safety; it is the name of what derives from the introjection of the experience of an encounter between the child's need [and desire] and what the environment can actually provide. This internal good object will become the source of the instincts of life and love.
>
> (Cintra & Figueiredo, 2004, p. 84)

However, alongside the good objects, there are also bad objects, or internal persecutors:

> But it is because the baby projects its own aggression onto these objects that it feels them to be 'bad' and not only in that they frustrate its desires: the child conceives of them as actually dangerous—persecutors who it fears will devour it, scoop out the inside of its body, cut it to pieces, poison it—in short, compassing its destruction by all the means which sadism can devise. These imagos, which are a phantastically distorted picture of the

real objects upon which they are based, are installed by it not only in the outside world, but by the process of incorporation.

(Klein, 1935, p. 145)

While the good and bad objects exist on the plane of phantasy, the *effect* of the splitting is very real and helps organize the complexity of emotional experiences. Ogden (1994) claimed that Melanie Klein made a huge contribution to psychoanalysis, stressing the importance of this dialectic between moments of splitting (paranoid-schizoid position) and of an (always relative) integration of the subject (depressive position).

Here, the mechanism of projective identification features in a fundamental manner, seeing as it is the means by which the subject simultaneously distances herself from, and binds herself to, that part of herself that is deemed (for now) intolerable. Through projective identification, the subject "steps outside herself" towards the other, hopefully with the support needed to forge ahead with her process of integration (for example, from an analyst who is sensitive to the intersubjective phenomena in play).

On this latter topic, Freud had already effected a decentering of the subject between conscious and unconscious, or between the Id, Ego and Superego. On this, "the systems [Id, Ego and Superego] are pictured as relatively autonomous persons-within-the-person (the superego, for instance, is said to behave in a sadistic way toward the ego)" (Laplanche & Pontalis, 1967, p. 452, apud Ogden, 1994, p. 40).

Melanie Klein broadened this decentering of the subject through the idea that there are internal object relations:

For Klein, the psyche (after an initial hypothetical moment of unity) enters into an ongoing process of splitting of the ego and a corresponding division of the (internal) object. The ego and object are split into components that hold meaning for (are "cathected" by) one another. For example, the hating and hated component of the object is the facet of the (internal) object that (for defensive purposes) holds meaning for and is recognized by the hating and hated component of the ego. In this way, the individual can safely hate the bad object without fear of destroying the object that is loved and beloved.

(Ogden, 1994, pp. 39–40)

Ogden sees that beyond this saga of internal objects loving and hating, the Kleinian subject is formed through these two tendencies—splitting and unification—such that the tendency to split corresponds to the paranoid-schizoid position and a predominance of the death instinct, while the tendency toward unification corresponds to the depressive position and a greater involvement of the life instinct. In this play of deintegration/integration out of which the psychic subject emerges, the movements of splitting and unification occur in the inner world, yet under the influence of what transpires in the world of intersubjective relationships.

The propensity towards splitting and deintegration conjures fantasies that the subject is exploding, as if the world of internal objects were about to be blasted and scattered throughout infinite space, or, on the other hand, fantasies of the subject's implosion, which evoke the sensation of crumbling to nothing and disappearing into an internal vacuum.

Ogden stresses that:

It is important that one not pathologize the negating, desintegrative, decentering pressures associated with the paranoid-schizoid component of the Ps—D dialectic. The intrapsychic pressure for desintegration represents an essential negation of the integrative qualities of the depressive pole of the dialectic. In the absence of the desintegrative pressure of the paranoid-schizoid pole of the dialectic generating experience, the integration associated with the depressive position would reach closure, stagnation, and "arrogance" (Bion, 1967).

(Ogden, 1994, p. 41)

So we can see how this alternance between splitting and deintegration is very important in terms of generating new psychological possibilities and psychic change. Beyond 'integration', the subject also needs to constantly 'break apart' the previously attained arrangements, so that it can put itself back together again.

Ogden also gives us the idea that this game of "integrating" and "deintegrating" our internal world occurs in dreams, through the processes of displacement and condensing. During sleep, dreams sift back through the daytime debris in order to cobble together a conversation we have with ourselves, but, more importantly, the dream is also "an experience of desintegrating one's experience and re-presenting it to oneself in a new form and in a new context (the context of the dream space)" (Ogden, 1994, p. 42).

In order to feel safe throughout this perpetual play of piecing together and pulling apart, it is essential that the subject be able to trust the cohesion of his internal world, something that one achieves through firm introjection of the good object.

In short, through Ogden, we can appreciate Klein's clinical and theoretical intuitions through a "playfully" and creatively lucid gaze. As we alluded in the subtitle to this chapter: to better understand Klein, we have to assemble and dismantle her over and over.

Notes

1 Authors' translation.
2 Chapter 6 of this book: "Ogden, Reader of Winnicott".
3 Authors' translation.
4 There are recurrent examples of this in Klein, for example:

"the breast, inasmuch as it is gratifying, *is loved and felt to be 'good'*; in so far as it is a source of frustration, *it is hated and felt to be 'bad'.*" (Klein, 1952/1997b, p. 62, our italics). Note the expressions "*is loved and felt to be 'good'*" [Klein, 1952/1997b, p. 62]), "*is hated and felt to be 'bad'*" [Klein, 1952/1997b, p. 62]), rather than active assertions such as "the baby loves the breast as good (or hates it as bad)."

Note here the use of *arise*: "In early infancy anxieties characteristic of psychosis *arise* which drive the ego to develop specific defense-mechanisms" [Klein, 1946/1997a, p. 1, our italics], rather than "the early infant experiences anxieties characteristic of psychosis".

5 Authors' translation.
6 Authors' translation.
7 We refer the reader to Chapter 5 of this book, "Ogden: Reader of Bion", in which the authors reflect on the article "Reading Susan Isaacs: Toward a Radically Revised Theory of Thinking" (Ogden, 2012/2014)
8 We refer the reader to Chapter 7 of this book: "From Projective Identification to the Concept of Analytic Third by Thomas Ogden: A Psychoanalytic Thought in Search of an Author".
9 A longer description of this position can be read in Chapter 2, "Tradition and Innovation: The Style of Thomas Ogden", in this volume.

Bibliography

BARROS, M. (2010). *Poesia completa*. São Paulo: Leya.
BARROS, E. L. R. & BARROS, E. M. R. (2018). Prólogo. Melanie Klein ontem, hoje e amanhã. In E. M. U. Cintra, & M. F. R. Ribeiro. *Por que Klein?* São Paulo: Zagodoni.
BICK, E. (1968). The Experience of the Skin in Early Object Relations. *International Journal of Psycho-Analysis*, 49, pp. 484–486.
BICK, E. (1986). Further Considerations on the Function of the Skin in Early Object Relations. *British Journal of Psychotherapy*, 2, pp. 292–299.
CINTRA, E. M. U. (2017). Empatia, identificação projetiva e *rêverie*: escutando o inaudível na clínica do trauma. In E. M. U. Cintra, G. Tamburrino & M. F. R. Ribeiro (Orgs.). *Para além da contratransferência: o analista implicado* (pp. 17–28). São Paulo: Zagodoni.
CINTRA, E. M. U. & FIGUEIREDO, L. C. (2004). *Melanie Klein: E*stilo e pensamento. São Paulo: Escuta.
CINTRA, E. M. U. & RIBEIRO, M. F. R. (2018). *Por que Klein?* São Paulo: Zagodoni.
FREUD, S. (1920/1996). Além do princípio do prazer. In Freud, S. Além do princípio do prazer, psicologia de grupo e outros trabalhos. (J. Salomão, trans.). Rio de Janeiro: Imago.
ISAACS, S. (1952/1978). The Nature and Function of Phantasy. In *International Journal of Psycho-Analysis*, 29, pp. 73–97.
JAFFE, N. (2017). Não está mais aqui quem falou [The person who said that is no longer here]. São Paulo: Companhia das Letras.
KING, P. & STEINER, R. (1998). *As controvérsias Freud-Klein 1941–45*. (N. J. P. Franch, trans.). Rio de Janeiro: Imago.
KLEIN, M. (1935). A Contribution to the Psychogenesis of Manic-Depressive States. In *International Journal of Psycho-Analysis*, 16, pp. 145–174.
KLEIN, M. (1940). Mourning and its Relation to Manic-Depressive States. In *International Journal of Psycho-Analysis*, 21, pp. 125–153.

KLEIN, M. (1921/1975). The Development of a Child. In *Love, Guilt and Reparation: and Other Works, 1921–1945*. New York: The Free Press.

KLEIN, M. (1946/1997a). Notes on Some Schizoid Mechanisms. In *Envy and Gratitude and Other Works, 1946–63*. New York: Vintage.

KLEIN, M. (1952/1997b). On Observing the Behaviour of Young Infants. In *Envy and Gratitude and Other Works, 1946–63*. New York: Vintage.

KUPERMANN, D. & NEVES, P. (2023). Ogden leitor de Winnicott. In M. F. R. Ribeiro (Org.). *Por que Ogden?* São Paulo: Zagodoni.

LAPLANCHE, J & PONTALIS, J. B. (1967/1973). The Language of Psychoanalysis. (D. Nicholson-Smith, trans). New York: Norton.

MELTZER, D. (1975). Adhesive Identification. *Contemporary Psychoanalysis*, 11(3), pp. 280–310.

MINERBO, M. (2009/2019). *Neurose e não neurose*. São Paulo: Blucher.

NELSON, M. C., NELSON, B., SHERMAN, M., and STREAN, H. (1968). Roles and Paradigms in Psychotherapy. New York: Grune and Stratton.

OGDEN, T. H. (1979). On Projective Identification. *International Journal of Psycho-Analysis*, 60, pp. 357–373.

OGDEN, T. H. (1982/1991). *Projective Identification and Psychotherapeutic Technique*. London: Jason Aronson. (Originally published in 1982).

OGDEN, T. H. (1986/1990). *The Matrix of the Mind: Object Relations and the Psychoanalytic Dialogue*. Lanham, MD: Rowman & Littlefield.

OGDEN, T. H. (1988). On the Dialectical Structure of Experience: Some Clinical and Theoretical Implications. *Contemporary Psychoanalysis*, 24, pp.17–45.

OGDEN, T. H. (1994). *Subjects of Analysis*. Lanham, MD: Rowman & Littlefield.

OGDEN, T. H. (2004/2010). This Art of Psychoanalysis: Dreaming Undreamt Dreams and Interrupted Cries. *International Journal of Psychoanalysis* 85, 857–877.

OGDEN, T. H. (1997/2013). *Reverie and Interpretation: Sensing Something Human*. Lanham, MD: Rowman & Littlefield.

OGDEN, T. H. (2012/2014). *Creative Readings: Essays on Seminal Analytic Works* [*Leituras criativas: ensaios sobre obras analíticas seminais*]. (T.M. Zalcberg, trad.). São Paulo: Escuta.

OGDEN, T. H. (2018). How I Talk With my Patients. *The Psychoanalytic Quarterly*, 87:3, 399–413.

SEGAL, H. (1964/1988). *Introduction to the Work of Melanie Klein*. New York: Routledge.

SPOTNITZ, H. (1969). Modern Psychoanalysis of the Schizophrenic Patients. New York: Grune and Stratton.

TUSTIN, F. (1972). *Autism and Childhood Psychosis*. London: Hogarth.

TUSTIN, F. (1980). Autistic Objects. *International Review of Psycho-Analysis*, 7, pp. 27–40.

TUSTIN, F. (1984). Autistic Shapes. *International Review of Psycho-Analysis*, 7, pp. 279–290.

TUSTIN, F. (1990). *The Protective Shell in Children and Adults*. London: Karnac.

WINNICOTT, D. W. (1971/2017). *Playing and Reality*. London: Tavistock Publications. (Originally published in 1971).

5 Thomas H. Ogden, Reader of Bion

From the Theory of Thinking to Intuitive Thinking

Marina F. R. Ribeiro and
Davi Berciano Flores

Bion is considered a difficult and enigmatic author. Presenting Ogden's declared readings of some of Bion's texts is a considerable challenge. Deducing, from Ogden's work, what, even if not formally stated, leads us to think of Bion, may indeed be a truly intuitive exercise. Ogden (2012) identifies himself as "Bionian", but, while being faithful to the author's ideas, he does not aim to express "what he really meant": "I am far more interested in what these authors knew, but did not know they knew—in how these texts are rich in ways their authors did not consciously intend or understand." (Ogden, 2012, p. 24).

From a predominantly theoretical perspective, in revisiting Ogden's vast work, we are aware that labeling him as "Bionian" would mean to reduce him, much as we would if we attributed the same title to Bion himself. Revisiting the authors read and thought of by Ogden, Bion undoubtedly holds a place in the author's thoughtful mind. However, Ogden visited Bion at different points in his journey (and explored different points in Bion's work), delved into the works of authors read by Bion (among them Freud, Klein, and their contemporaries), dissected the works of Bion's contemporaries (such as Susan Isaacs, Hanna Segal, and Fairbairn), and, in addition, he also engaged with commentators, so to speak more specifically, post-Bionians. Throughout his work, he orchestrated a dialogue among them in his predominantly clinically oriented mind, so it would be rather risky to determine where Bion stands in Ogden's work. It might be most accurate to say that, from our theoretical and clinical perspective, there is a field that refers us to Bion in Ogden's work, some points more clearly, others perhaps not so much:

> A philosopher is concerned with understanding and misunderstanding, but he cannot do what a psychoanalyst can do: that is, watch and listen to a person while he is understanding and while he is misunderstanding. This is one reason why I am not greatly interested in psychoanalytic theories. If one gets trained one can go and look them up in a book, but the practice of analysis is the only place where it is possible to read people, not books.

DOI: 10.4324/9781003423188-5

It is, therefore, a pity to spend time which could be spent in reading a person, in reading a book instead.

(Bion, 1973/2014, p. 63)

Taking into consideration Bion's provocation above, we consider that reading a text by Ogden implies, at the same time, reading the theory and reading the person—"at the same time", indeed, being one of the hallmarks of both authors. What we mean is that, beyond the numerous theoretical perspectives presented in his texts, Ogden has found a writing style that presents theory as a living expression of his clinical practice. A style that per- haps also derives from the extended provocations made by Bion throughout his work, asserting numerous times that psychoanalytic writing naturally diverges from the emotional experience of the analytic session, thus striving to find a language that could, if successful, bring the reader closer to the psy- choanalytic experience. Ogden attributes movement to the "black markings on the page:

I attempt not *to write about* my experience of reading their works, but *to write my experience* of reading them: to write what I have let these papers and books do to me, what I have done with these papers and books, and how I have rewritten them and made them my own books and papers.

(Ogden, 2012, p. 9)

Hence, we deduce, within the ideas to be presented by us, traces of Bion within Ogden in us, understanding them as a transformation of Bion's work. And we emphasize that we would not be able to precisely delineate where the author's reasoning ends and his begins, as we run the risk of including our own ideas when we present the ideas of both. "Ideas do not come labeled with the name of their owner" (Ogden, 2012, p. 26)—a statement that reflects his inspiring freedom of thought and his way of creative reading, also being an idea drawn from Bion's texts (1977/2014). This entails a complex and chal- lenging intertextuality, a common practice in both authors' writings.

Having elucidated the complexity of the field of reflection that we are ven- turing into, we emphasize that the intention is to engage in a dialogue with some understandings and expansions that we consider original in Ogden's reading of Bion's texts, rather than presenting Bion's theory from Ogden's perspective.[1] Furthermore, our goal is not to present Ogden's texts,[2] but to highlight creative aspects of his reading and foster a dialogue between the authors. We are inspired by and faithful to Ogden's proposal: a creative and authorial reading of the texts.

From the theory of thinking to intuitive thinking

We shall start with Ogden's text, which we consider a thorough overview of Bion's work, specifically his theory of thinking: "Bion's four principles of mental functioning" (Ogden, 2008/2009).[3] This text was originally published in 2008, a date that we believe is relevant to highlight, as we observed the expansions that occurred in Ogden's reading of Bion's thought, eventually proposing a cross-fertilization of ideas between some texts.

From the very title of the text we are struck by Ogden's ability to present Bion's work succinctly, making a creative pun with Freud's 1911 text, entitled "Formulations on the two principles of mental functioning", a text that is a fundamental reference for Bion's thinking.

Ogden (2008/2009) introduces at the beginning of the text four principles in the Bionian theory of thinking, which are unpacked throughout his explanation and revisited at the end, showcasing a sophisticated aesthetic presentation, a successful effort to articulate the essential points of the theory of thinking into four principles:

(1) Thinking is driven by the human need to know the truth—the reality of who one is and what is occurring in one's life;
(2) It requires two minds to think a person's most disturbing thoughts;
(3) The capacity for thinking is developed in order to come to terms with thoughts derived from one's disturbing emotional experience, and
(4) There is an inherent psychoanalytic function of the personality, and dreaming is the principal process through which that function is performed.
(Ogden, 2008/2009, pp. 94–95)

Considering the first principle, we need, above all, a definition of Truth, that is common to Ogden and Bion, although with limitations in its explanation. It is a laborious definition right from the beginning of this chapter, so we rely on the reader's patience and intuition to grasp the notion of Truth throughout the subsequent concepts on the following pages.

Ogden (2012) points out that Bion uses different terms to capture something in this sense: "'the thing in itself', 'the Truth', 'Reality' and 'the experience'", among others (p. 119). It is, in fact, a search for words capable of naming something that is, at the same time, inapprehensible and ephemeral. It belongs, therefore, to "the realm of the ultimately unknowable, but 'beable' – that is, existent" (Sandler, 2005, p. 834). In the words of Ogden (2003):

> It seems that paradoxically what is true is timeless, placeless and larger than any individual, and yet alive only for an instant and unique to the set of circumstances constituting that moment of lived experienced by one person. In other words, in an analysis, what is universally true is also exquisitely personal and unique to each patient and to each analyst.
> (Ogden, 2003, p. 599)

Considering the first principle, the human need to know the truth, Bion posits that it involves dreaming the lived emotional experience, that is, the dream is the unconscious thought, a way of thinking what has been lived. In a later text,

"Bion's notes on memory and desire" (Ogden, 2015), the author elucidates that Freud and Bion place reality at the core of the theory of thinking, with reality understood as the truth of lived emotional experience. Ogden renames Freud's reality principle as the truth-seeking principle, and the pleasure principle as the truth-fearing or truth-avoiding principle. In other words, the mind is fed, integrated, and expanded by contact with the truth, which, in turn, is also avoided, in a constitutive and continuous paradoxical movement within the psychic realm.

Continuing the exposition on the human need to know the truth of experience, Ogden (2009) revisits Bion's early texts on groups, linking them to the theory of thinking. He introduces as intriguing idea to the reader through a quote from the writer Borges,[4] who stated that throughout his life he rewrote his first book of poetry in different ways. In the same way, Bion would also be rewriting in various ways his first book, *Experiences in Groups* (Bion, 1961/2014). Based on Ogden's consideration, we can reflect that within an author's body of work, there is an invariance,[5] that is, an element that persists amidst numerous transformations.

The idea here is not to reduce an author's work to a single point, but to acknowledge a paradoxical field in which a work is comprised of various forms (styles, concepts, contradictions, revisions, evolutions) and, at the same time, to intuit an essence, an origin, a stable element amid transformations: "My intention is to begin to explore the paradox that human emotional truths are both universal and exquisitely idiosyncratic to each individual, and are both timeless and highly specific to a given moment of life" (Ogden, 2003, p. 593).

According to Ogden (2009), Bion designates as a work group one that is capable of thinking, while the basic assumptions group is one that is not capable of thinking. Bion posits that analyst and analysand form a group of two, and furthermore, the mind itself is a group composed of different parts of the personality. Once again, there is a realm where there is an invariance alongside multiple transformations. Ogden does not explicitly reference this, but Bion's autobiographical books written at the end of his life, *A Memoir of the Future* (1975/2014, 1977b/2014, 1979/2014), recount this internal group, depicting the different characters inhabiting the mental space.

The work group and basic assumptions group[6] are facets of a single experience, where the former involves thinking, and the latter involves predominance of psychotic patterns, leading to the heightened intensity of projective identifications. Basic assumptions are ways of experiencing reality crossed by different fears characterized by psychotic patterns (Ogden, 2008/2009). Ogden then notes that when basic assumptions prevail, magical thinking manifests, and when the work group predominates, genuine thinking presents itself (a concept introduced by Ogden, 2008/2009).

Returning to the text "Bion's four principles of mental functioning", Ogden describes three ideas related to the first principle of mental functioning in Bion: thinking is driven by the human need to know truth. The first idea is that avoidance of thinking and contact with emotional truth are inseparable from thinking, they are facets of the same experience. The second idea is that genuine thinking requires a tolerance for not knowing.[7] The third idea is the Bionian concept of binocular vision, that is, thinking requires an ability to apprehend reality from different vertices or points of view at the same time. "Reality viewed from a single vantage point represents a failure to think" (Ogden, 2008/2009, p. 100):

> In summary, we require what Bion refers to as 'binocular vision' (1962, p. 86)—perception from multiple vantage points simultaneously— to articulate what we mean by the truth in psychoanalytic terms. What is true is a discovery as opposed to a creation, and yet, in making that discovery, we alter what we find and, in that sense, create something new.
>
> (Ogden, 2003, p. 597)

The capacity to apprehend reality from multiple vertices is fundamental to Bion's understanding of sanity and insanity. Sanity involves this multiplicity of vertices, whereas insanity is characterized by attachment to a single point of view. Ogden understands Bion's concepts in a dialectical way, always co-created, interconnected and influencing one another: conscious/unconscious; psychotic part of the personality/non-psychotic part of the personality; basic assumptions group/work group; paranoid-schizoid position[8]/depressive position, and so on.

The second principle of mental functioning, according to Ogden, is the necessity of two minds for thinking thoughts. In other words, Bion conceives thinking as an intersubjective experience that originates in projective identification:[9]

> Bion elaborated the idea that thoughts may destroy the capacity for thinking in his essays that are collected in *Second Thoughts* (1967b/2014), most notably in "Attacks on linking" (1959a) and "A theory of thinking" (1962b). There, Bion introduced the idea that in the beginning (of life and of analysis) it takes two people to think.
>
> (Ogden, 2004b/2005, p. 102)[10]

Roughly speaking, Ogden refers in the quote above to some important developments in Bion's work, in which it is recognizable that the functions of linking, connecting, or binding mental elements are obstructed or corrupted in predominantly psychotic states of mind. These linking functions are fundamental to the capacity for constructing verbal thought, as seen in thought association, communication, contact between minds or, if we extrapolate to a broader definition, in mental processes that enable symbolization. When the attacks on linking are effective, the intolerable content that undergoes the attacks is expelled from mental functioning, finding in projective identification an effective defensive and communicative solution to allocate what was internally intolerable[11]—and precisely because it is intolerable, it causes a rupture in the continuity of thinking processes. Another depositary for this content becomes crucial for reconstructing processes of linking, attachment and, therefore, of symbolization. In this way, Bion attributes recognition, in his theory, to the intersubjective processes of recognizing and elaborating these links attacked by the psychotic part of the personality.

The third principle refers to the anteriority of thoughts to thinking. Thinking imposes itself under the pressure of thoughts, an inversion of the usual logic in which thoughts are considered products of thinking. Ogden resumes Bion's text (1962/2014), reporting that the baby has a preconception of the breast and that in the encounter with the real breast there is a different experience from the preconceived breast, demanding tolerance of frustration in the experience of non-breast which, in turn, becomes a thought imposing the capacity to think, a thinking apparatus. The mother plays an important role in the tolerance of frustration by her capacity for reverie,[12] for dreaming (unconscious thinking) the baby's anxieties.

At this point, we have already encountered a field of fundamentals that can intuitively create points of articulation in the reader's mind. We offer an attempt to articulate them: nourishing oneself with truth, as a present and paradoxical element resulting from emotional experience requires the capacity to tolerate thoughts that can be quite disruptive. To tolerate them, it is necessary to have two minds, so that intolerable elements find a container in which they can lodge, and thus, an intersubjective configuration arises to provide the capacity to think them (alongside the mind of the mother or of the analyst). Both mother/analyst and baby/analysand find themselves in emotional experiences that demand, from both, the exercise of thinking to tolerate frustration in its multiple manifestations.

If frustration cannot be tolerated, even with the mother's containing presence, the tension is evacuated through excessive projective identifications, thus hindering the expansion of the thinking apparatus. The uniqueness of Ogden's reading of Bion's text is evident in some subtleties of his understanding:

> [...] But we must not lose sight of the fact that beta- elements constitute our sole psychological connection with reality. Beta- elements might be thought of as "those unthoughtlike thoughts that are the souls of thought" (Poe, 1848, p. 80). Bion hypothesizes that "alpha-function" (1962/2014, p. 6) (an as-yet-unknown, and probably unknowable, set of mental operations) serves to transform beta-elements into alpha-elements that can be linked to form dream-thoughts. Dream-thoughts are the symbolic representation of the disturbing experience that was originally registered primarily in sensory terms (i.e. as beta-elements).
>
> (Ogden, 2008/2009, p. 104)

New concepts emerge here: beta-element, alpha-element, and alpha-function. The idea of function has already been introduced in the first pages of our text, so it might be more apprehensible now. We talk about "binding function", "linking function" and the mother's function in dreaming her baby's frustrations so that they become less indigestible. The notion of function, in the Bionian scope, is another inheritance of a mathematical concept, the ability to link, to create an image of an element from one group in another group. The alpha-function, in this case, is the attribute to transform beta-elements into alpha-elements.

Beta-element is a concept of Bion's often recurred to by Ogden and consists of raw, non-mentalized sensory impressions associated to emotional experiences. The beta-elements "are unlinkable with one another"[13] and, consequently, "cannot be linked in the process of dreaming, thinking or storage as memory" (Ogden, 2004a/2005, p. 17–18). Beta-elements constitute "the sole connection between the mind and one's lived emotional experience in the world of external reality" (Ogden, 2004a/2005, p. 116).

The understanding of the beta-elements as our connection to reality and as thoughts that do not appear as thoughts, but are the soul of thinking, represents Ogden's creative reading of Bion's text. Not resembling thoughts or reaching the level of dreamlike elements, means that the beta-elements remain at such a level of undifferentiation, blurring the distinction between the sleeping state and waking life. These solely sensory experiences obscure the ability to differentiate perception from hallucination, external reality from internal reality (Ogden, 2010, p. 859). Manifestations corresponding to the predominance of beta-elements involve non-dreamt dreams, aspects that escape the capacity for psychic elaboration. Ogden, in his theoretical great versatility, finds correspondences (associations, links) between the predominance of beta-elements and psychic manifestations, such as night terrors, associating them with other theoretical scopes:

> Among the disorders characterized by such foreclosure are the psychosomatic disorders and severe perversions (de M'Uzan, 1984); autistic encapsulation in bodily sensation (Tustin, 1981); "dis-affected" states (McDougall, 1984) in which patients are unable to "read" their emotions and bodily sensations; and the schizophrenic state of "nonexperience" (Ogden, 1982) where the chronic schizophrenic patient attacks his own capacity for attributing meaning to experience thus rendering emotional experiences interchangeable with one another.
>
> (Ogden, 2004a/2005, p. 20)

Once the successful capacity to think these unthought thoughts is achieved, the alpha-function comes into play, exercised by both a containing mind (such as that of the mother and the analyst), and the internal mental capacity itself, to transform beta-elements into alpha-elements. For Ogden, " [...] alpha-elements are elements of experience that can be linked together in the conscious and unconscious process of thinking and dreaming (both while awake and asleep) (2004a/2005, pp. 18–19).

Along with the theory of thinking, which is born in Bion's thought and illuminates Ogden's original thinking, we also find the idea of "container-contained", which precisely considers the vibrant dynamics of transit and transformation of these elements in mental functioning, being a character-istic of a thinking connected to emotional experience and the conception of truth: "In Bion's hands, the central concern of psychoanalysis is the dynamic interaction between, on the one hand, thoughts and feelings derived from lived emotional experience (the contained) and, on the other, the capacity for dreaming and thinking those thoughts (the container)" (Ogden, 2004a/2005, p. 119).

Bionian theory, as well as Ogden's work, which serves as a container for the elements presented by Bion, shifts its focus to how thoughts are constructed, theories about bonds, the dynamics between mental objects and elements, and the uses of thinking. The very idea of function indicates an observation to the movements of thinking and the transformations the elements undergo. It is not a matter of discussing the elements themselves, but rather the relationship that exists between them. Likewise, it is not a matter of discerning in whose mind a thought resides, but how thoughts are being thought within an inter-subjective condition. Bion points out repeatedly in his work that an emphasis on anatomical structures and concretized images leads to misunderstandings, missing the dynamic dimension of mental functioning:[14] "The idea of the container–contained addresses not what we think, but the way we think, i.e. how we process lived experience and what occurs psychically when we are unable to do psychological work with that experience" (Ogden, 2004a/2005, p. 114).

Take, for example, the vivid and condensed conversation between Ogden, Bion, and the English poet John Keats, interconnected in Ogden's mind:

> The growth of the contained is reflected in the expansion of the range and depth of thoughts and feelings that one is able to derive from one's emo-tional experience. This growth involves an increase in the "penetrability" (Bion, 1962/2014, p. 93) of one's thoughts, i.e. a tolerance "for being in uncertainties, mysteries, doubts, without any irritable reaching after fact and reason" (Keats, 1817, quoted by Bion, 1970, p. 125). In other words, the contained grows as it becomes better able to encompass the full com-plexity of the emotional situation from which it derives.
>
> (Ogden, 2004a/2005, p. 132)

The alpha-function and container-contained theories are understood by Ogden as an extension of the third principle of mental functioning: thinking evolves to enable the handling of thoughts. Containing is a process:

> [...] it is the unconscious psychological work of dreaming, operating in concert with preconscious dream-like thinking (reverie) and conscious secondary process thinking. The term contained (p. 90) refers to thoughts

and feelings that are in the process of being derived from one's lived emotional experience.

(Ogden, 2008/2009, p. 104)

Considering the third principle of mental functioning, the psychoanalyst in the session is attentive to which disturbing thought the patient entails the analyst to think, remembering that contact with emotional truth is the nourishment of the mind, something that integrates and expands the mind, but it is also what the mind avoids: principle of truth-seeking and principle of truth-fearing. Ogden, drawing from this interpretation of Bion's texts, concludes that "[...] the aim of psychoanalysis is to help the patient develop his own capacity for thinking and feeling his experience" (Ogden, 2008/2009, p. 105).

Taking into account the complex and dynamic nature of emotional experiences, and considering we have already seen some concepts that illuminate this apprehension, such as Bion's theory of thinking (alpha-function and container-contained), we can understand that, in analysis, we always seek for creating conditions so that the analysand, in the words of Ogden (2010), can dream "undreamt dreams and interrupted cries". We can consider this idea as a continuous mental expansion, in which analyst and analysand are always in search of undreamt dreams, unthought thoughts, fostering a constant expansion of the capacity for the unconscious work of dreaming (container) and for encountering thoughts and feelings arising from emotional experiences (contained) (Ogden, 2004b/2005, p. 133). In the author's words:

> The analytic situation, though in many ways unstructured, also has a quality of directionality that is derived from the fact that psychoanalysis most fundamentally is a therapeutic enterprise with the goal of enhancing the patient's capacity to be alive to as much as possible of the full spectrum of human experience. Coming to life emotionally is, to my mind, synonymous with becoming increasingly able to dream one's experience, which is to dream oneself into existence.
>
> (Ogden, 2004a/2005, p. 22)

The fourth principle of mental functioning is that "[...] there is an inherent psychoanalytic function of the personality, and dreaming is the principal process through which that function is performed" (Ogden, 2008/2009, p. 76). Ogden emphasizes in this fourth principle what appears in Bion's text subtly, providing a broader scope to an intriguing concept of Bion: the psychoanalytic function of personality, which consists in the human capacity to dream (representation, symbolization) lived experiences or, in other words, to transform raw experience (beta-elements) into alpha-elements, both composing dream-thinking. Ogden, in an earlier article titled "On holding and containing, being and dreaming" (2004b/2005), referenced in the preceding pages, points out that dreaming is the quintessential manifestation of psychoanalysis, understanding that Bion believes humans are equipped with the potential to produce conscious and unconscious psychic work and, through this, generate psychic growth (p. 128).

> [...] for Bion, the unconscious is the seat of the psychoanalytic function of the personality, and, consequently, in order to do psychoanalytic work, one must make the conscious unconscious – that is, make conscious lived experience available to the unconscious work of dreaming. The work of dreaming, for Bion, is the psychological work by means of which we create personal, symbolic meaning thereby becoming ourselves.
>
> (Ogden, 2008/2009, p. 106)

Ogden concludes the text of "Bion's four principles of mental functioning" (Ogden, 2008/2009) by resuming the initial description of the four principles, providing the reader with a sense that the beginning and end of the text are connected and form a circularity that offers the reader an expressive diameter of Ogden's reading experience of Bion's theory of thinking.

In our understanding, there are developments of the 2009 text in the 2010 article, "On three forms of thinking: Magical thinking, dream thinking, and transformative thinking" (Ogden, 2010); and in the 2011 text, "Reading Susan Isaacs: Toward a radically revised theory of thinking" (Ogden 2011/2012). We will now discuss these unfoldings, recognizing that they do not imply a chronological sequence in the writing of these three texts on the theory of thinking, but rather conceptual connection and extensions.

In the 2009 article, the notions of genuine thinking and magical thinking emerge, which, according to our interpretation, unfold into three forms of thinking in the 2010 text: magical thinking, dream thinking, and transformative thinking, the last two being a detailed exploration of what Ogden names genuine thinking in the 2010 text:

> I conceive of the three forms of thinking that I will be discussing [...] as coexisting, mutually creating, preserving, and negating aspects of every experience of thinking. None of these forms of thinking is ever encountered in pure form. Neither is there a linear relationship among these forms of thinking, such as a "progression" from magical thinking to dream thinking. Rather, I see these forms of thinking as standing in dialectical tension with one another [...] .
>
> Moreover, none of these forms of thinking is a single, unitary way of thinking; rather, each "form of thinking" represents a rather wide spectrum of ways of thinking. The particular variation of the form of thinking that an individual may employ is always in flux and depends upon his level of psychological maturity, the intrapsychic and interpersonal emotional context of the moment, cultural factors, and so forth.
>
> (Ogden, 2010, p. 318)

We consider that Ogden understands the concepts through dialectical tensions, embedded in a complex and spectral field,[15] taking into account a plethora of interacting phenomena, as also seen in Bion's work. This includes notions of psychotic/non-psychotic parts of the personality, the theory of positions, the theory of links (K, L, H), and the theory of transformations, among others. The concepts, in a broad way, both in Ogden's work and in the preceding Bionian spectral model, do not serve as limitations to the previously presented models. Instead, they compose the author's work and the capacity for clinical observation.

Magical thinking is an omnipotent thinking, an avoidance of contact with truth, an escape from both external and internal reality. Taken to the extreme, we have delusional and hallucinatory thoughts that create their own reality, making it impossible to learn from experience, since one loses contact with emotional truth and blurs the distinction between being awake and being asleep; a differentiation constantly produced in the mind by the ability to dream one's own experience.[16] In magical thinking, we enter the realm of psychotic functioning; the frustrating external reality is replaced by an invented reality.

Dreaming is a continuous activity of the mind, according to Bion, and constitutes "our most encompassing, penetrating, and creative form of thinking" (Ogden, 2010, p. 328). Ogden resumes in this text an analogy, originally from Bion, to the understanding of this diuturnal oneiric activity of the mind: stars in the sky are obscured by sunlight, the light of waking life, but they persist. Reverie is a way for the analyst to capture waking dream thinking in the session.

Transformative thinking is a form of dream thinking that can bring about intense changes in the way patient and analyst think. What Ogden termed as genuine thinking in the 2009 text, unfolds into both dream thinking and transformative thinking in this text (Ogden, 2010).

To illustrate transformative thinking, Ogden creatively analyzes a biblical passage, treating it as a literary text, a story that has spanned centuries: faced with an adulterous woman about to be stoned, Jesus says, "He that is without sin among you, let him first cast a stone at her." This vertex of understanding of Jesus' speech creates "a radically different way of ordering experience—that had been unimaginable up to that point" (Ogden, 2010, p. 334). As a result, transformative thinking favors what Bion termed a catastrophic change.[17] Taking Ogden's words back, "Transformative thinking—thinking that radically alters the terms by which one orders one's experience—lies toward one end of a spectrum of degrees of change-generating thinking (dream thinking)" (Ogden, 2010, p. 336). It is worth remembering here that Ogden uses the term "spectrum of degrees of change-generating thinking", meaning that along with the dialectical tension and the field of complexity previously presented, both comprising Bion's concepts, we can also think of the psychic elements within a spectrum.

Returning to "Bion's four principles of mental functioning", Ogden (2008/ 2009) makes another interesting observation: basic assumptions justify Bion's term "protomental", as found in the book *Experiences in Groups* (Bion, 1961/

2014), where it refers to a form of thought in which there is no differentiation yet between physical and mental activities. We thus consider a further opening to another text by Ogden originally published in 2011, "Reading Susan Isaacs: Toward a radically revised theory of thinking" (2011/2012), in which the author raises the conjecture that Isaacs' seminal article on unconscious fantasy precedes aspects of Bion's theory of thinking.

In the text *Reading Susan Isaacs*, Ogden (2011/2012) postulates two eras of psychoanalysis: the Freud-Klein era and the Winnicott-Bion era, with Isaacs' text on unconscious fantasy serving as a transitional piece between the two eras, providing an interesting and original understanding:

> [...] Bion does not use the term phantasy to refer to the shared unconscious beliefs of a group and instead invents his own more expressive term, basic assumption. The "basic assumptions" are the fearful orientations to reality that shape group experience so profoundly that it is inadequate to think of them as mere ideas. They are so basic as to warrant the term proto-mental – thinking "in which physical and mental activity is undifferentiated" (Bion, 1959, p. 154).
>
> (Ogden, 2008/2009, p. 96)

The concept of unconscious fantasy in Melanie Klein's texts and in Susan Isaacs' reference article is understood to have a hybrid character, in the sense that it involves psychic representations of bodily sensations:

> [...] fantasizing is the process that creates meaning, it is the way of being of the unconscious psychic life and transforms somatic elements into psychic contents. It is about representing the drives that are close to intensities and forces, making them enter the field of meaning. The unconscious fantasy is a concept of hybrid character, between body and psychism, inside and outside, sensation and word.
>
> (Cintra & Ribeiro, 2018, p. 66)

In the quotation above, it is possible to preview what Ogden (2011/2012) "read" in Isaacs' text that was there as potentiality, a memory of the future: Klein's concept of unconscious fantasy precedes Bion's concept of alpha-function. In other words, the alpha-function is a transformative function that turns raw experience (sensations) into psychic elements, an unconscious thought, much like unconscious fantasies transform somatic elements (sensations) into psychic elements. Ogden (2011/2012) writes that phantasying is the unconscious thinking:

> It seems to me that this aspect of Isaacs' conception of the role of phantasy – that of transforming sensory/bodily experience into elements of "mental life" – anticipates Bion's (1962b) concept of alpha function. Alpha function is an as yet unknown set of mental operations (a form of thinking)

that transforms raw sense impressions into elements of experience (alpha-elements) that can be linked in the process of dreaming, which, for Bion (1962), is synonymous with unconscious thinking.

[...]

While Isaacs does not name that transformative function, her concept of phantasy activity is, I believe, akin to Bion's alpha function, i.e. phantasying is a mental function (a form of thinking) that transforms sense impressions associated with instinct into a mental form that can be linked to create personal, psychological meaning.

(Ogden, 2012, p. 56)

Unconscious fantasy is related to Melanie Klein's epistemophilic drive, which is the impulse to know, represent, and symbolize the world. It aligns with the first principle of mental functioning from Bion (Ogden, 2008/2009): the human need to know[18] the truth of who we are and what happens in our lives.

Bearing in mind this first principle of mental functioning, we resume that the mind is fed by the truth at the same time that the truth is avoided by the mind, that is, it is necessary to tolerate not knowing in order to become the truth.[19] Thus, we delve into Ogden's surprising reading of another Bion's text: "Intuiting the truth of what's happening on Bion's 'Notes on memory and desire'" (Ogden, 2015).

Intuitive thinking: Intuiting psychic reality

The presence of an opening sentence that captures the reader in an overwhelming way is an invariant in Ogden's texts. The same occurs at the beginning of a session or a first interview, a moment that condenses the subsequent unfoldings. The reason for choosing the second epigraph of this chapter is precisely justified by these aspects, demonstrating that just as we see value in the emergence of an idea, we must also attribute value to the different uses given to it.

In the second paragraph, Ogden introduces his conjecture to the reader: Bion's paper "Notes on memory and desire" (1967a/2014) is about intuitive thinking, that is, Ogden posits, based on his reading of Bion, that there exists a form of thinking he considers intuitive, and this will be the idea developed throughout the paper.

Ogden recounts in this text how the numerous readings of Bion's article over the years have not generated understanding in him, but rather transformations. An apparently simple sentence, however, contains a complex theory that we shall try to briefly elucidate.

To achieve this, we shall approach the text "Ontological psychoanalysis or 'What do you want to be when you grow up?" (Ogden, 2019). Epistemological psychoanalysis relates to knowledge and understanding, with Freud and Klein as the primary authors. Ontological psychoanalysis has Bion and Winnicott as references concerning being and becoming. Right at the beginning of the text, Ogden highlights that, while for Winnicott psychoanalysis shifts from being centered on the symbolic sense of play to the experience of playing, in Bion, the experience of dreaming, considered in all its forms, overlaps with the symbolic sense of dreams.[20]

Ogden emphasizes that the text describes what has happened in his own thinking: "from a focus on unconscious internal object relationships to a focus on the struggle in which each of us is engaged to more fully come into being as a person whose experience feels real and alive to himself or herself" (Ogden, 2019, p. 663). His warning about the necessity of mutual enrichment between the analyst and the analysand is crucial, stating that pure forms of either do not truly exist within the analysis room.

Epistemological and ontological psychoanalysis are oscillating vertices of experience—following the spectral logic by not being mutually exclusive but rather supplementary. Thus, at each moment of the session, we observe the clinical phenomenon in order to identify which vertex predominates. In ontological psychoanalysis, the analyst's horizon is the field of becoming oneself—the ontological realm, the contact with the truth of being at each single moment. In epistemological psychoanalysis, the vertex of the knowledge of the self predominates. In other words, we can think of a continuous oscillation between knowing (transformations in K) and being (transformations in "O"), in which the analyst, attentive to the intersubjective movement of the analytic field, can make one of the vertices figure, with the other remaining as background, and vice-versa. It involves states of predominance between the ontological and the epistemological, an oscillation between figure and background, always connected and coexistent, oscillating vertices, an experience of binocular vision.

In the book *Transformations* (1965a/2014), Bion proposes a reflection about psychoanalytic efficacy, overcoming usual discussions on the truths of psychoanalytic knowledge. Here, Bion revisits the purpose of interpretation in psychoanalysis, arguing that the phenomenon is known, but reality is made. As such, interpretation must go beyond the expansion of the patient's knowledge of themselves, favoring becoming.

In other words, interpretation needs to favor a transformation in the sense of becoming oneself, not just in terms of self-knowledge. Here, we return to Ogden's (2015) testimony when he says that Bion's (1967a/2014) text, "Notes on memory and desire", transformed him, making him more the analyst he is at each moment, with each patient. A simple phrase that holds a vast theoretical complexity, the transition between Bion's theory of thinking (1962) and the theory of transformations (1965a/2014). The horizon of ontological psychoanalysis is to favor the patient's movement toward becoming oneself, becoming truth, and intuitive thinking is fundamental in this process of continuous becoming, inherent to human existence.

Ogden (2015) states that Bion's text, so unique and condensed, is a landmark for psychoanalysis as it proposes an expansion of the psychoanalytic method: the analyst's task is to intuit the psychic reality, becoming one with the patient. Let's make an analogy to bring the reader closer to this complex proposition: it is as if analyst and patient were together in the same oneiric reality, experiencing, each from their singularity, the same emotional experience, or, in Bion's thinking, at-one-ment.[21] Memory and desire do not favor this unprecedented experience lived with the analysand, as they confine the analyst to what he already knows, in the past (memory), and/or in desire (future),[22] rather than in the present moment, the only time of lived experience that generates a genuine thinking (dream thinking and transforming thinking).

Within its spectral nature, a theoretical element naturally evokes a set of other concepts, so that intuitive capacity is directly linked to the conception of Truth, of emotional experience, of O:

> The experience of the analyst's getting to know the patient is unique to each analytic encounter, and yet is unavoidably shaped by the particular ways that the analyst has of perceiving and organizing his experience of what is happening, i.e., it is experience viewed through a multifaceted, ever-changing lens informed by one's psychoanalytic ideas and experience. As Wallace Stevens put it, "Things seen are things as seen" (quoted by Vendler, 1997, p. ix). The analyst's experience of getting to know who the patient is becoming is inseparable from the patient's experience of getting to know who the analyst is and is becoming.
>
> (Ogden, 2004a/2005, p. 8)

Ogden (2015) writes, from his reading of Bion's text, that a psychoanalytic process is conducted solely in the present, and that the reality of psychoanalysis is the reality of the unconscious. The author offers a close and creative reading of Bion's text:

> [...] he is saying that the analyst must refrain not only from memory and desire, but also from "sense impressions and objects of sense." He is separating emotions such as depression, anxiety, and fear from the sense impressions (the physical "accompaniments" [p. 136]) of emotions.
>   [...]
> The realm of the unconscious, Bion vehemently insists, is the realm of the psychoanalyst—no one knows the unconscious in the way that the psychoanalyst does, and he must protect it from being "confounded" [p. 137] with the conscious realm of experience. The unconscious is the realm of thinking and feeling that together form the psychic reality (psychoanalytic truth) of an individual at any given moment. The unconscious is not a realm of physical sensation. Physical sensation resides in the domain of conscious experience.
>
> (Ogden, 2015, pp. 291–292)

Ogden also writes:

> In other words, if the psychoanalyst is to be genuinely analytic in the way he observes, he must be able to abjure conscious, sensory-based modes

of perceiving, which draw the analyst's mind to conscious experience and to modes of thinking (for example, memory and desire) that are fearful/evasive of the perception of the unconscious psychic reality (the truth) of what is occurring in the session. Instead, the analyst must rely on a wholly different form of perceiving and thinking. That form of thinking, which Bion calls intuition, has its roots in the unconscious mind. Receptivity to sense impressions, "awareness," and "understanding" are the domain of conscious thought processes.

(Ogden, 2015, p. 293)

Returning to Ogden's (2019) ideas on epistemological and ontological psychoanalysis described above, we can consider that the analyst needs these oscillating vertices of mental states, epistemological and ontological, between knowing and being, conscious and unconscious. There are no delineated boundaries between one state and the other, since they are co-created, coexisting and affecting each other in complex dialectical tensions:

This passage is something of an announcement that the task of the analyst is not that of understanding or figuring out the nature of the psychic reality of the moment in the analytic session; rather, the analyst's work is to intuit that unconscious psychic reality by becoming at one with it. Bion does not define the concept of intuition, nor does he offer a clinical illustration of it, but the term itself strongly suggests the predominance of unconscious mental processes in analytic thinking.

(Ogden, 2015, pp. 293–294)

The horizon of the psychoanalyst is the transformation into "O", becoming truth or the truth that is made. Ogden writes that Bion's proposition may evolve a kind of mysticism and reminds the reader of the everyday and human experience of dreaming:

When we dream—both when we are asleep and when we are awake (Bion 1962a)—we have the experience of sensing (intuiting) the reality of an aspect of our unconscious life, and are at one with it. Dreaming, in the way I am using the term, is a transitive verb. In dreaming, we are not dreaming about something, we are dreaming something, "dreaming up" an aspect of ourselves. In dreaming, we are at one with the reality of the dream; we are the dream. While dreaming, we are intuiting (dreaming up) an element of our unconscious emotional lives, and are at one with it in a way that differs from any other experience. In dreaming, we are most real to ourselves; we are most ourselves.

(Ogden, 2015, p. 294)

The same logic applies to the analytic pair, in the exercise of dreaming the undreamt and interrupted dreams of the analysand. The undreamt experience manifests for both in the analysis room. Becoming truth, that is, living the transformation into O, implies precisely living this reality that precedes both, independent of any act of knowing, perceiving, and apprehending (Ogden, 2012, p. 152). For Ogden, O is a state of "being-at-one-with" (2015, p. 294).

What Ogden emphasizes, in line with Bion's thinking, is that if there is something undeniably true in an analytic encounter, it is precisely the emotional experience of each moment of each session, and this experience is independent of the interpretations that the analyst and the analysand may make. Ogden ventures, with originality, to find an invariance in several concepts that point precisely to this unattainable, but intuitable reality that always escapes the possibility of symbolization. Thus, O, for Bion, would roughly correspond to the concepts of thing-in-itself (Kant), ideal forms (Plato), and the register of the Real (Lacan) (Ogden, 2003, p. 397).

Returning to the 2015 text, Ogden writes that the experience of reverie is paradigmatic of the experience of intuiting the psychic reality and implies a renunciation of the analyst's ego, a radical hospitality, as we wrote in another text.[23]

> [...] By self-renunciation, I mean the act of allowing oneself to become less definitively oneself in order to create a psychological space in which analyst and patient may enter into a shared state of intuiting and being-at- one-with a disturbing psychic reality that the patient, on his own, is un- able to bear. The analyst does not seek reverie, any more than he seeks intuition. Reverie and intuition come, if they come at all, without effort, "unbidden".
> (Ogden, 2015, p. 294)

Ogden (2015) concludes the theoretical part of this text by bringing a final intuition from Bion, where he says that when the interpretation is formulated, all the work has already been done. When we are able to formulate an interpretation based on the representability of words, all the unconscious work (the essence of analysis) has already happened, entering the realm of knowledge and the already-known; in other words, it has already become the past, as the experience of at-one-ment has already occurred.

We conclude this section by returning to the necessary and continuous oscillation between the vertices of epistemological and ontological psychoanalysis: the word is a container for an experience that has already happened, and also a way of actualizing what has been lived. When it is expressed well, successfully accomplished, a genuine thought (dream and transformative) gives rise to new experiences in a circular process of expanding intimacy and psychic space.

The fundamental idea sustained throughout the conception of intuition, associated with transformations into O and being at one with emotional reality (at-one-ment), is that there is always something real, non-metaphorical, that we seek to apprehend. Once an interpretation is formulated, that is, once a psychic apprehension of an emotional phenomenon lived in the analytic pair is achieved, O will spontaneously re-manifest in its incognoscibility. In other words, the analytic pair should not conceive itself saturated in its thinking exercise, in the sense that one thought, upon finding a thinker, would interrupt the process of the emotional experience. At the moment a thought finds a thinker, there are evidently many other thoughts without a thinker to be thought. In Ogden's words (Ogden, 2003):

> As a starting point for thinking about what we mean when we say an idea is true, let us return to the idea that there are things that are true about the universe (including the emotional life of human beings) that pre-exist and are independent of the thinking of any individual thinker. In other words, thinkers do not create truth, they describe it. Thinkers from this perspective are not inventors, they are participant observers and scribes.
>
> (Ogden, 2003, p. 596)

We consider this moment opportune to recall Bion's analogy revisited by Ogden, that waking life resembles the experience of the blue sky, illuminated by sunlight, thereby obscuring the stars that, even though we don't see them, we know are there throughout the day. This passage leads us to a digression that we consider valuable and, dare we say, we might be engaging in an oneiric reading of the authors—truth to be told, we cannot precisely define where our waking reading ends and our oneiric reading begins. The light of waking life, which covers and offers elements to intuit what is beyond this perception, led us directly to a passage by Bion (1977a/2014):

> [...] taking the cue from dreams that I have had, colours like the blue of the sky, the red of blood, and the yellow of ochre, the colour that is made out of earth. They are primitive colours, these primary colours, and they might be very useful. When it comes to this sort of thing which I have called a beta-element, it gets more difficult; I don't know what to call that. Perhaps, provisionally it would do to say, 'gross darkness', which is different from darkness which has a certain amount of light in it; this would be with absolutely no light whatsoever, the sort of light verbalized by Victor Hugo as "le néant", or by Shakespeare [Macbeth, V. iii] when he talks about "a tale told by an idiot, full of sound and fury, signifying nothing" – zero, 0.
>
> (Bion, 1977a/2014, pp. 42–43)

Interestingly, when we revisit Ogden's first published book, *The Matrix of the Mind* (1986/2004), we see a similar discussion arising in his text, only on a different theoretical route. It is as if, metaphorically, we are seeing Ogden arriving, by another road, to the same town in which Bion decided to stay years before. Ogden, in the text, found associations to the concept of unconscious fantasy (phantasy) in Melanie Klein, appealing to Chomsky's notion of deep structure, as well as recalling other authors such as Jakobson and Saussure, all capable of shedding light, from their theoretical perspectives, on the conception of pre-existing systems of perception (which in Bion will be an important element of apprehension of psychic life, as in the passage above, concerning primary colors). Thus, Ogden (1986/2004) also arrives at the question of colors:

> To begin with a basic example of an inherent system of organizing percep-
> tion, human color perception is not simply a matter of passively receiving
> sensory data and converting those data into visual experience. The primary
> colors, perceived as discrete differentiated groupings, are the products of
> a preexisting schema by which one organizes into groups certain portions
> of the continuous range of wavelengths of light (Bornstein, 1975). The
> groupings of wavelengths that we call colors are both arbitrary and universal
> among human beings and are the product of the way in which we organize
> the continuous spectrum of wavelengths, each wavelength differing from
> the next one by a fixed quantity of energy. We all divide the spectrum in
> precisely the same way (in the absence of color blindness) because of a
> preexisting biological schema that we use to organize our perceptions.
>
> (Ogden, 1986/2004, p. 14)

We all divide the spectrum in the same way, we see the same colors, yet each emotional experience lived under the same sky requires the exercise of thinking and becoming. Interestingly, Bion and Ogden encountered the same clinical phenomenon, but they came through different theoretical paths. In Borges' words, in Ogden's text, reminding us of Bion's voice:

> [...] though there are hundreds and indeed thousands of metaphors to be
> found, they may all be traced back to a few simple patterns. But this need
> not trouble us since each metaphor is different: every time the pattern is
> used, the variations are different.
>
> (Borges, 1967/2000, p. 40 apud Ogden, 2003, p. 599)

Here, once again, presented in a different way, is the conception that regard-less of the number of theories, models, and metaphors for mental functioning, ideas will always have a distinct and therefore singular, idiosyncratic use. In this text, we are discussing Bion's concepts that, when illuminated by Ogden's mind, gain new nuances. The presumption of ending the movement of continuous thinking, of continuous becoming, was the target of criticism from both Bion and Ogden: there was " [...] little that Bion more deplored in ana-lytic interpretations than the analyst's explicit or implicit claim that the inter-pretation reflected the unique qualities 'of his knowledge, his experience, his character'" (Ogden, 2003, p. 598).

The very idea of possessively claiming authorship results in the valoriza-tion of the content above the container, that is, that what has been discovered is worth more than the process of thinking. Or, from another perspective, that the origin of thought is more important than the uses made of it. We believe that Ogden has much to contribute on this point, in line with Bion's thinking. After all, in the pursuit of the truth of emotional experience within the tradition of intersubjectivity, is it possible to define who was the author who had an idea? Is it more appropriate within the theory of thinking to say that an idea occurred to someone rather than someone had an idea? We will try to answer these questions methodologically based on Ogden.

Reading people, reading books

Let us return, finally, to the initial provocation we presented when Bion suggests that the analytic encounter is a privileged place to "read people, not books" and laments that we spend our time reading books, when we could read people. At this point, after going through some passages of Ogden's work in which we identify, whether manifest or latent, Bion's thinking, we believe that this idea can be illuminated from new vertices. Bion, in our view, is precisely making a provocation against devitalized knowledge production, or a psychoanalysis that prioritizes books (epistemology) instead of emotional experience (ontology).

In Ogden's work, we notice a recurrent effort to interpolate these vertices, dedicating himself ontologically to his readings. His inspiration comes, precisely, from Bion. On the very first page of the chapter "Reading Bion" in the book *Creative Readings*, Ogden says:

> Perhaps most important to the way I read his work is the state of mind I try to bring to it – a state of mind in which I fully accept what I believe to be Bion's view of his own writing: he strives not to be understood, but to serve as a catalyst for the reader's own thinking.
>
> (Ogden, 2012, p. 112)

What we see here is the application of the theory of thinking for the act of reading, giving it a value of experience and expanding the reader's continent for their emotional experiences. Referring to the article "Notes on memory and desire" (Bion, 1967a/2014), Ogden points out that, by revisiting it numerous times in an attempt to decipher the mystery of the text, he discovered that the key to reading and apprehending the text was precisely this. It was about doing something *with* the text, in the realm of experience, instead of extracting something *of* the text, in the field of knowledge (Ogden, 2015). Or, again, it was about "being in" rather than "speaking about" (Ogden, 2012, p. 121). From Bion's proposition, an experience of reading unfolds: once we run the risk of resorting to memories and desires, sensory clues that disorient psychic apprehension to the past or the future, we can include, here, the use made of readings, so that they do not serve as a fear of the truth, as an escape from emotional experience: "In this endeavor, I am not attempting to arrive at what Bion "really meant"; rather, I am interested in seeing what use – clinically and theoretically – I am able to make of my own experiences of reading early and late Bion" (Ogden, 2012, p. 113).

Here, we identify a methodological tradition that spans the fields of research and clinical work, found in Bion's style and propositions, revisited by Ogden in his own style.[24] Ogden calls it "transitive reading", in the sense of taking the text as a dynamic element interacting with the reader, words that will gain expression from the reader's subjectivity and the present moment of reading. When we examine the concept of emotional truth, we find the reason for this proposition: if truth is always transitive, so should readings be. This proposition is in line with the Bionian universe presented here, in the sense that emotional experience, Truth, is always transitive, dynamic, and always a glimpse. In this sense, a text is not "something" in itself, but manifests itself to the reader in a particular form, apprehended by their mind.

The very suggestion of "how to read" a book, typical of Bion's books introductions, is also made by Ogden (2012), indicating that the reading experience is not presupposed and involves the living presence of the reader in its act. It is not a matter of "absorbing" the text, but of becoming the author read and seeing "the world through the eyes" of this one (Ogden, 2012, p. 10). Ogden proposes that we, as readers, transform reading into an emotional experience, intersubjective in nature, in which we allow that:

[...] "foreigners" (words and sentences that are not one's own) into oneself, one is also permitting oneself to be read by that foreigner (the writing) [...] in being read well by what one is reading (in using the experience of reading to read oneself), the reader may feel that he is becoming alive to a way of being that he has always felt to comprise an essential aspect of himself or herself, but has not known how to put into words, or how to more fully become the person who thinks and expresses himself in that way.

(Ogden, 2012, p. 10)

This conception offers a freedom of movement between ideas, consistent with Bion's conception that thoughts are in search of a thinker, that is, that Truth is there and we seek to approach it with our thinking apparatus. Since reading consists of an encounter between reader and text, in mutual affectation, we are faced with the principle of undecidability of the origin[25] of a thought (which is not in the text or the reader, but in the encounter). The same principle applies to the analytic encounter, based on Bion's conception of reverie as the evolution of projective identification, which consists on the impossibility of recognizing where a thought is: there is a pair (or a group) of work, in a collaborative effort to think the unthinkable. Here, paradoxically, there is an impossibility of recognizing authorship as a point of origin and, at the same time, we identify invariances in the texts that allow us to see many thinkers about something in common:

In considering the question of how one person's ideas concerning what is true influence those of others, we routinely adopt a diachronic (chronological, sequential) perspective in which the thinking of one person (for example,

Freud) is seen as influencing the thinking of contemporaries and those who follow temporally (for example, Klein, Fairbairn, Guntrip and Bion). Despite the seeming self-evidence of the merits of such an approach, I believe it may be of value to call into question this conception of authorship and influence.

(Ogden, 2003, p. 594)

While sequential, chronological logic is maintained, the ability to think becomes a captive of a temporal perspective, instead of allowing ideas to connect freely. In other words, there is a conception of temporality that can hinder links and connections. The idea of authorship presupposes that someone comes before and claims ownership of something that is in transit, whose birth, origin, is indeterminate. Let us take as an example Susan Isaacs' idea of "phantasy activity", and the subsequent notion of alpha-function in Bion. Even though Bion's concept came chronologically later, Ogden's dynamic and transitive reading allows him to recognize that alpha-function is already there, presented by Isaacs under another name and from a different vertex, years before. In Ogden's words: "Bion, I believe, held similar views on the question of the temporal bi-directionality of influence of ideas on one another [...] ". And also: "The future, for Bion, is as much a part of the present as is the past. The shadow of the future is cast forward from the present and is cast backward from the future on to the present — 'it depends on which direction you are travelling in'" (Ogden, 2003, p. 595):

You can look at this as you like, say as memory traces, but these same memory traces can also be considered as a shadow which the future casts before.

[...] but it can also be regarded as showing the shadow of a future we don't know any more than we know the past, a shadow which it projects or casts before. The caesura[26] that would have us believe; the future that would have us believe; or the past that would have us believe – it depends on which direction you are travelling in, and what you see.

(Bion, 1976/2014, pp. 125–126)

In this sense, Ogden demonstrates how his mind, in his readings, engages in a lively conversation with the authors, embarks on various "journeys" in his readings, offering distinct views at each moment. Therefore, we agree with Ogden when he says that it is very difficult to grasp at what point Bion's thinking ends and his own begins. Throughout his texts, we see multiple authors in dialogue, diverse temporal transits (as proposed in this text with Ogden's articles), and ideas identified in different authors. The result is, simultaneously and paradoxically, a free erudition in which there is a meticulous work with concepts (and numerous citations) associated with a free flow of ideas.

In Ogden's words: "Every piece of analytic writing requires a reader who assists the author in conveying something of what is true, something that the author knew, but did not know that he knew. In so doing, the reader becomes a silent co-author of the text" (Ogden, 2003, p. 594). Working pairs, whether they are author and reader, or analyst and analysand, seek a Truth without an author, a thought without a thinker. For both Bion and Ogden, and echoed by Borges,[27] Truth was not invented and does not require a thinker to create it (Ogden, 2003, p. 400).

Thus, for Bion, evoked by the voice of Ogden, psychoanalysis was, prior to Freud, a thought without a thinker (Bion, 1966/2014, p.38;[28] Ogden, 2003, p. 400). Within this perspective, Ogden embraced the freedom to vigorously engage, through his authorship, with a plurality of psychoanalytic authors. With this freedom offered by the notion of Truth in Bion, Ogden was able to create his writing style and find associations (links) between concepts, theorists, poets, and fragments from his own clinical practice.

Ogden is an author in search of authors, a thinker in search of thinkers. Reading Ogden is undoubtedly a transformative experience.

Notes

1 Due to this complexity, we will elucidate some of Bion's concepts in footnotes and recommend to the interested reader the dictionary of Paulo Sandler, *The Language of Bion. A Dictionary of Concepts* (2005), for further reference.

2 We suggest that readers appreciate the original texts of Thomas Ogden.

3 This article was originally published in 2008 (Fort Da, 14B: 11–35); in 2009, it was republished in *Rediscovering Psychoanalysis. Thinking and Dreaming, Learning and Forgetting*.

4 It is noteworthy that Ogden frequently evokes Jorge Luís Borges in his dialogues with Bion's work, precisely due to Borges being a poet whose ideas shed light on the intertextuality between the authors.

5 Concept from the philosophy of mathematics, applicable to various practical sciences such as physics, psychoanalysis, chemistry, music theory, among others. The idea of invariance involves recognizing that something remains unaltered, a peculiar mark that allows the recognition of something, regardless of the transformations it may undergo. In Bion's work, the notion of invariance is applied to the idea that, through intuitive glimpses, we access something that transcends time, space and individuality (Sandler, 2005, p. 474–475)

6 There are three basic assumptions: dependency, pairing, and fight-flight. Succinctly, when the dependency assumption predominates, the group believes that a leader or messiah will come to save and solve all problems. The pairing assumption holds the belief that two people in the group will produce a messiah, which may be an idea or a utopia. The fight-flight assumption entails the belief that all problems will be solved by fighting or fleeing from the enemy.

7 In this part of the text, Ogden quotes Keats' phrase as an inspiring element for Bion (1965a/2014, 1967a/2015) to propose an expansion of the psychoanalytic method with the insignia "without memory, without desire, and without prior understanding," so we consider (although Ogden does not make this association directly). We can approximate the genuine thinking referred to by Ogden in this text (2008/2009) and the intuitive thinking discussed in Ogden's later text (2015), in which he creatively interprets Bion's 1967a text, "Notes on memory and desire".

8 We emphasize that, as an addition to Kleinian theory, Ogden postulated a position preceding the paranoid-schizoid position, called the autistic-contiguous position (Ogden, 1989).

9 Ogden's understanding of projective identification will be discussed in Chapter 7, "From projective identification to the concept of the analytic third. A thought in search of a thinker".

10 The text (Ogden, 2004b/2005) was originally published in 2004: Ogden, T. H. (2004) On holding and containing, being and dreaming. International Journal of Psychoanalysis, v. 85, pp. 1349–1364, 2004.

11 The understanding of projective identification as an unconscious communication, and not just as a defense mechanism, represents a Bionian increment to Melanie Klein's concept.

12 Regarding the concept of reverie, refer to Chapter 10, "From limbo to light: reverie in Thomas H. Ogden" in this book.

13 The term "unlinkable", that is, incapable of generating links, bonds, connections, means, in other words, that they are outside the scope of thinking, as presented above when referring to the text "Attacks on linking" (Bion, 1959/2014).

14 "The conception of the part-object as analogous to an anatomical structure, encouraged by the patient's employment of concrete images as units of thought, is misleading because the part-object relationship is not with the anatomical structures only but with function, not with anatomy but with physiology, not with the breast but with feeding, poisoning, loving, hating" (Bion, 1959/2014, p. 146).

15 The spectral understanding of Bion's concepts is emphasized in several texts by the Brazilian psychoanalyst Arnaldo Chuster, a contemporary of Thomas Ogden.

16 The contact barrier that creates the conscious and unconscious mind is constantly modified by the alpha-elements. If a person is unable to dream/think the emotional experience, they neither sleep nor wake, lose capacity for dreaming and contact with shared reality, essentially existing in a psychotic state of mind.

17 The term denotes a sudden change or disruption of the previous state, which can be real or hallucinated. It involves a change capable of destroying a prior organization and, at the same time, indicates invariance, in the sense that it allows the observer to notice that, despite being a catastrophic event, something is preserved. The greater the fear of change, the greater the catastrophic event, indicating resistance to recognize the natural transformation of a phenomenon (Sandler, 2005, pp. 102–103)

18 In Bion's work, "knowing" is an activity indicated by the K link, a symbol for knowledge, which occurs through the emotions of love (L – love link) and hate (H – hate link). Knowledge is possible through the transit of emotions or, in other words, the human capacity to dream/think/represent lived experience.

19 The construction "becoming the truth" is intentional, as it is associates with becoming "O". In our understanding, truth is connected to becoming, to the transformation into being.

20 The presentation of these ideas about epistemological and ontological psychoanalysis is also featured in the article "Palavras aladas guiando o encontro analítico" – "Winged words guiding the analytical encounter" (Florido Cesar et al. 2022).

21 At-one-ment, or "to be at-one," indicates a state of presence in an event characterized as alive, truthful, uncontaminated by lies. It is a condition for being in contact with a person or apprehending an immaterialized event, in a transitory

and partial way, from intuition. It is not a matter of knowing something, since we are dealing with phenomena of the realm of "being" rather than "knowing": being-one-with would be the equivalent of being with, becoming something (Sandler, 2005, p. 62)

22 The desire to "cure" the patient is a motivating factor for almost all analysts; for the interested reader we suggest the text by Figueiredo (2021), "Ser psicanalista: um ofício meio doido" – ("Being a psychoanalyst: a somewhat crazy profession").

23 In the text "The psychoanalytical intuition and reverie: capturing facts not yet dreamed" (Ribeiro, 2022), the interaction between reverie and intuition is addressed, as well as the analyst's necessary hospitality for the experience of reverie.

24 Under the inspiration of the psychoanalytic approach to reading and writing proposed by Bion and further developed by Ogden, we indicate the text entitled "A pesca do fragmento intersubjetivo na pesquisa psicanalítica" ("Fishing for the inter-subjective fragment in psychoanalytic research") (Ribeiro et al., 2022), in which a methodology for academic research based on this perspective is proposed and grounded.

25 The principle of the undecidability of the origin, originally presented by the math-ematician Kurt Gödel and employed in quantum physics, concerns a methodology for researching phenomena that abandons the idea of a single correct answer for a given observation. It is applied in cases where the object of study is unstable. Bion implicitly turns to this principle, pointing out that in the analytic bond there is always a moment of undecidability about the origin of a mental phenomenon in the analytic pair, which by its inherently unprovable nature, remains under indeci-sion (Chuster, 2003, p. 50)

26 Caesura, another concept from Bion's framework, indicates an event that at the same time connects and separates others, simultaneously and paradoxically. It implies both continuity and rupture. This is a concept of abstract quality that can be applied to various mental phenomena (Sandler, 2005. p. 97). The notion of cesura is inspired by a phrase from Freud: "There is much more continuity between intra-uterine life than the impressive caesura of the act of birth would have us believe" (Freud, 1926, p. 162).

27 Se nas páginas seguintes houver um ou outro verso que deu certo, perdoe-me o leitor pela audácia de tê-lo escrito antes dele. Somos todos iguais; nossas mentes inconsequentes são muito parecidas, e as circunstâncias nos influenciam de modo que há algo de acidental que faz você ser o leitor e eu o escritor – o escritor inseguro e ardente – dos meus versos [que ocasionalmente capturam algo de verdadeiro da experiência humana] (Borges, 1923/1972, p. 269 apud Ogden, 2003, p. 400).

28 "[...] psychoanalysis, the thing-in-itself, existed. It remained for Freud to reveal the formulation embed-ded in it. Conversely, once formulated by Freud it remains for others (including Freud himself) to discover the meaning of the conjunction bound by his formulation. It is necessary to postulate 'thinking' without supposing a thinker to be essential" (Bion, 1966/2014, p. 38).

References

BION, W. R. (1959). Attacks on linking. In: *The Complete Works of W. R. Bion*. London: Karnac Books, 2014, v. 6, pp. 308–315.

BION, W. R. (1961/2014). *Experiences in Groups and Other Papers*. In: The Complete Works of W. R. Bion. London: Karnac Books, 2014, v. 4, pp. 95–246.

BION, W. R. (1962/2014). A theory of thinking. In: The Complete Works of W. R. Bion. London: Karnac Books, 2014, v. 6, pp. 153–161.

BION, W. R. (1965a/2014). *Transformations: Change from Learning to Growth*. In: The Complete Works of W. R. Bion. London: Karnac Books, v. 5, pp. 115–280.

BION, W. R. (1965b/2014). Memory and desire. In: *The Complete Works of W. R. Bion*. London: Karnac Books, 2014, v. 6, pp. 7–18.

BION, W. R. (1966/2014). Catastrophic change. In: *The Complete Works of W. R. Bion*. London: Karnac Books, 2014, v. VI, pp. 19–44.

BION, W. R. (1967a/2014). Notes on memory and desire. In: *The Complete Works of W. R. Bion*. London: Karnac Books, 2014, v. 6, pp. 203–210.

BION, W. R. (1967b/2014). *Second Thoughts: Selected Papers on Psycho-analysis*. In: The Complete Works of W. R. Bion. London: Karnac Books, 2014, v. 6, pp. 45–202.

BION, W. R. (1973/2014). *Brazilian Lectures*. In: The Complete Works of W. R. Bion. London: Karnac Books, 2014, v. VII, pp. 1–197.

BION, W. R. (1975/2014). *A Memoir of the Future – Book One: The Dream*. In: The Complete Works of W. R. Bion. London: Karnac Books, 2014, v. 12.

BION, W. R. (1976/2014). On a quotation from Freud. In: The Complete Works of W. R. Bion. London: Karnac Books, 2014, v. X, pp. 123–127.

BION, W. R. (1977a/2014). *Taming Wild Thoughts*. In: The Complete Works of W. R. Bion. London: Karnac Books, 2014, v. V, pp. 87–114.

BION, W. R. (1977b/2014). *A Memoir of the Future – Book Two: The Past Presented*. In: The Complete Works of W. R. Bion. London: Karnac Books, 2014, v. 13.

BION, W. R. (1979/2014). *A Memoir of the Future – Book Three: The Dawn of Oblivion*. In: The Complete Works of W. R. Bion. London: Karnac Books, 2014, v. 14, pp. 3–138.

BORGES, J. L. (1967/2000). *This Craft of Verse*, ed. C.-A. Mihailescu. Cambridge, MA: Harvard University Press.

BORGES, J. L. (1923/1972). *Jorge Luis Borges – Selected Poems 1923–1967*. London: Allen Lane/The Penguin Press.

BORNSTEIN, M. (1975). Qualities of color vision in infancy. *Journal of Experimental Child Psychology* 19: 401–419.

CHUSTER, A. (2003). *Novas leituras: a psicanálise dos princípios ético-estéticos à clínica*. Vol. II: parte prática. Rio de Janeiro: Companhia de Freud.

CINTRA, E. M. U. & RIBEIRO, M. F. R. *Por que Klein?* São Paulo, SP: Zagodoni, 2018.

FIGUEIREDO, L. C. (2021). *A mente do analista*. São Paulo: Escuta.

FLÓRIDO CESAR, F.; RIBEIRO; M. F. R. & PERROTTA, C. (2022). Palavras aladas guiando o encontro analítico. *Revista De Psicanálise Da SPPA*, v. 29, n. 2), pp. 297–314. Recuperado de https://revista.sppa.org.br/RPdaSPPA/article/view/1049

FREUD, S. (1911). Formulações sobre os dois princípios do funcionamento psíquico. In: *Observações psicanalíticas sobre um caso de paranoia relatado em autobiografia: ("O caso Schreber"): artigos sobre técnica e outros textos (1911–1913)*. Traduzido por Paulo César de Souza. São Paulo, SP, Brasil: Companhia das Letras, 2010, v. 10, pp. 108–121.

FREUD, S. (1926). Inibições, sintomas e angústia. In: *Obras psicológicas completas de Sigmund Freud: edição standard brasileira*. Rio de Janeiro: Imago, 1969, v. 20, pp. 95–204.

OGDEN, T. H. (1986). *The Matrix of the Mind – Object Relations and the Psychoanalytic Dialogue*. USA: Rowman & Littlefield Publishers, 2004.

OGDEN, T. H. (1989). *The Primitive Edge of Experience*. Northvale, NJ: Jason Aronson.

OGDEN, T. H. (2003). What's true and whose idea was it? *Int. J. Psychoanal,* v. 84, pp. 593–606.

OGDEN, T. H. (2004a). This art of psychoanalysis: dreaming undreamt dreams and interrupted cries. In: *This Art of Psychoanalysis: Dreaming Undreamt Dreams and Interrupted Cries.* London and New York: Routledge, 2005.

OGDEN, T. H. (2004b). On holding and containing. In: *This Art of Psychoanalysis: Dreaming Undreamt Dreams and Interrupted Cries.* London and New York: Routledge, 2005.

OGDEN, T. H. (2008/2009). Bion's four principles of mental functioning. In: *Rediscovering Psychoanalysis: Thinking and Dreaming, Learning and Forgetting.* USA and Canada: Routledge, 2009.

OGDEN, T. H. (2010). On three forms of thinking: magical thinking, dream thinking, and transformative thinking. In: *The Psychoanalytic Quarterly,* v. 79, n. 2, pp. 317–347.

OGDEN, T. H. (2011/2012). Reading Susan Isaacs: Toward a radically revised theory of thinking. In: *Creative Readings: Essays on Seminal Analytic Works.* USA and Canada: Routledge, 2012.

OGDEN, T. H. (2012). *Creative Readings: Essays on Seminal Analytic Works.* USA and Canada: Routledge.

OGDEN, T. H. (2015). Intuiting the truth of what's happening in Bion's "Notes on memory and desire". In: *The Psychoanalytic Quarterly,* v. 84, n. 2, pp. 285–306.

OGDEN, T. H. (2019). Ontological Psychoanalysis or "What do you want to be when you grow up?". In: *The Psychoanalytic Quarterly,* v. 88, n. 4, pp. 681–684.

RIBEIRO, M. F. R., FLORES, D. B. & RAMOS, J. F. (2022). A pesca do fragmento subjetivo na pesquisa psicanalítica. In: *Pesquisas acadêmicas em psicanálise: reflexões teóricas e ilustrações práticas.* São Carlos: Pedro & João Editores. https://pedroej oaoeditores.com.br/2022/wp-content/ uploads/2022/05/Pesquisas-academicas-em-Psicanalise.pdf (Último acesso 14 de janeiro de 2023).

SANDLER, P. C. (2005). *The Language of Bion: A Dictionary of Concepts.* London: Karnac.

6 Thomas H. Ogden, Reader of Winnicott

Epistemological, Clinical Theoretical and Aesthetic Dialogues

Pedro Hikiji Neves and Daniel Kupermann

Introduction

Thomas Ogden is a contemporary theorist who approaches psychoanalysis from different matrices, articulating Freudian, Kleinian, Bionian and Winnicottian contributions in a cohesive way. His work is therefore situated in a transmatricial field (Figueiredo & Junior, 2018), that is, it articulates different matrices of thought from the psychoanalytic substrate. In this chapter, we propose a three-fold understanding of Ogden's work and present Winnicott's influence on each of them. To this end, we characterize some of Ogden's fundamental concepts, such as the analytic third (Ogden, 1994) and his use of the notion of the trinity between symbol, symbolized and interpreting self.

Ogden develops his own reading of various psychoanalytic themes. Thus, he dialogues creatively with a variety of authors and their concepts, such as projective identification (Klein, 1946), regression to dependence (Winnicott, 1982) and play in the potential space (Winnicott, 2020), and *reverie* (Bion, 1959, 1962). Our focus, however, will be on his use of Donald W. Winnicott's thinking. To this end, we will first try to answer the question "Who is Ogden's Winnicott?"; in other words, how does Ogden appropriate and relate to Winnicott's understanding of the clinical? We then set out to understand Ogden's points of convergence, divergence and innovation in relation to Winnicott along three axes. Our reading is therefore interested in considering the space left by Winnicott's theory in which Ogden was able to "play".

We recognize the contributions of Ogden's reading along three axes: a first epistemological, relating to the understanding of what the intersubjectively constituted subject is; a second theoretical-clinical, relating to the conceptual description of what happens between the analysand and analyst in the psychoanalytic setting; and a third aesthetic, emphasizing the phenomenological description of how the analyst is affected by the clinical encounter. These three axes are directly related to each other, as the notion of the intersubjective subject (epistemological axis) is the basis for an understanding of clinical theory (theoretical-clinical axis) which, in turn, is used to interpret the specific experiences of the analyst in the session (aesthetic axis). This distinction is also useful because Ogden starts from Winnicott's language and

DOI: 10.4324/9781003423188-6

proceeds to interpret it according to his references, notably the dialectic and the trinity between symbol, symbolized and interpreting self.

From an epistemological point of view, Ogden presents Winnicott as the founder of a theory of the psyche that includes an intersubjectively constituted subject, formed in the dialectic between mother and infant. There is a third term in the relationship, the "mother-infant", which exists even before mother and infant can be considered separate subjects. The same happens in analysis, where there is an analyst, an analysand and an analytic third, product of the dialectic established between the two.

Considering the existence of this analytical third implies the formulation of a clinical theory consistent with this epistemology. On the theoretical-clinical axis, Ogden conceptualizes transference and countertransference based on the analytic third. The Winnicottian potential space, which arises between the analysand and the analyst, is pervaded by the dialectical tensions of the encounter. In play, the rigid boundaries between self and other become malleable, and there is a movement of intersubjective co-creation. To describe this area of creation and characterize what is "in the middle" of the interaction, Ogden investigates the matrix of transferential-countertransferential movements, and argues that there are specific ways in which the analytical pair generates experience.

Finally, there is the aesthetic axis, which considers the sensory experiences specifically undergone by the psychoanalyst. During the session, through contact with the patient, the analyst experiences bodily sensations, images, thoughts, somatic hallucinations and daydreams. The epistemology and clinical theory employed point to the importance of these affections: they are not experienced by the clinician in isolation, but indicate something experienced in interaction, in the analytic third. Therefore, the articulation of the last two axes is relevant to clinical thinking: the analysis of the transference-countertransference contextualizes the analyst's particular experiences and influences his clinical management, as it specifies the dialectical relationship he establishes with the patient.

Who is Ogden's Winnicott?

Donald Winnicott is an author of great importance for psychoanalytic thinking. In *Playing and Reality* (2005/1971), he uses metaphors and paradoxes to describe the unique experience of becoming a subject in a shared space. The child who plays with their first objects can intertwine the information and stimuli of their external environment (their first favorite objects and toys, which occupy this transitional area) with the fantasies of their internal world (giving life and appreciation to that object), creating an area of play in which these two worlds can overlap.

The subject then emerges from contact with the other, precisely in this potential space between the child and the caregiver. Early on in his work, Winnicott states that the baby does not exist apart from maternal care (2017/

1988), because the newborn cannot exist separately from a caregiver, since it is not yet autonomous or independent. Therefore, at birth, the child is intimately linked to the mother (or substitute), who provides, through her care, a psychological matrix on which the child can develop. This is a relationship of absolute dependence, whose bond is strong enough to justify the use of the unitary expression "mother-infant" to describe this situation.

This matrix, as the place for the baby's initial biological and psychological maturation, is part of the foundation of the subjective constitution. In *Subjects of analysis* (Ogden, 1994), Ogden argues that by defending that there is no such thing as an infant – as it is always accompanied by a mother – Winnicott is elaborating a theory whose subject is constituted in an intersubjective matrix. Therefore, children, in the first period of life, are inseparable from their mothers (or substitutes), who provide them with physical and psychological support. Consequently, the first psychological "entity" that can be named in the development of the newborn is not the infant, but the infant with its mother: in short, the mother-infant. At this early stage, there is no child as a subject, nor is there any psychological capacity for the infant to differentiate itself from its mother. This is achieved later, and never completely.

Differentiation is always incomplete, and the intersubjective field is always present. Just as there is a need to recognize this mother-infant entity in the maternal relationship, there is also a third subject that emerges from/in the encounter in the relationship between analyst and analysand. The name given by Ogden (1994, p. 60) to this subject is the analytic third, which is the "product of a unique dialectic produced between the separate subjectivities of the analyst and the analysand within the analytic setting". To support this conception, Ogden approaches the Winnicottian text from other references. He therefore uses dialectics to reinterpret Winnicott's notion of paradox, and understands potential space through the trinity of symbol, symbolized and interpreting self. A rigid division between these concepts is artificial, since Ogden's work builds both concepts together.

The Hegelian dialectic reread by Kojève is referred to in Ogden's work as "a process in which each of two opposing concepts creates, informs, preserves, and negates the other, each standing in a dynamic (ever-changing) relationship with the other" (Ogden, 1993, p. 208). Winnicott's writing, especially in the chapter "transitional objects and transitional phenomena" in *Playing and reality* (2005/1971), implies some paradoxes that are formulated by the baby in its initial relationship with the world. The transitional object, for example, simultaneously created and encountered by the infant, can be considered part of the external and internal world at the same time, and this paradox must be accepted and not questioned by the mother and other caregivers. By transforming the paradox into a dialectic, the pairs – external-internal, oneness and duality, and creation and discovery (of the object) – are placed in dynamic tension, and the consequences of the English author's innovations can be understood in a different way.

Following Ogden's discussion (1993), dialectics is a key to understanding the psychological activity of generating potential space. Two definitions of potential space are given: in a generic way, potential space is the area Winnicott conceptualizes as "giving rise to play" (2020, p. 74); and, in a more precise way, the author describes potential space as a "hypothetical area that exists (but cannot exist) between the baby and the object (mother or part of the mother) during the phase of repudiation of the object as not-me, that is, at the end of being merged in with the object" (p. 204).

Ogden addresses the paradox in question (the hypothetical area that exists but cannot exist) by describing space in a triangular way. For him, the potential space is configured in the dialectic between symbol and symbolized, mediated by the interpreting self. In order to clarify the relationship between these terms, we will examine the infant's development process, particularly the moment when they begin to perceive a separation between their internal and external worlds and, through play, start to symbolize.

For Winnicott (2020), potential space is the area of play. According to Ogden (1993), what is essential for play is the child's ability to generate personal meanings, that is, to separate symbol (thought), symbolized (what is being thought) and interpreting self (the thinker generating their own thoughts and interpreting their own symbols). From this separation, there is the possibility of triangulation, and so the potential space arises, between symbol and symbolized, mediated by an interpreting self. This is the area of individual creation about the world, which Ogden calls the dialectic between reality and fantasy.

The dialectical way of working present in Thomas Ogden's thinking supports his contribution on the analytical third. Just as there is the mother, the child and the mother-child, there is, in the analytical setting, the analyst, the analysand and the third intersubjective subject that appears in them/through them. The experience of analysis involves a dialectical movement between subjectivity and intersubjectivity that needs to be considered.

The analytic third is a concept that explores and advances the clinical consequences of an intersubjective subject. Even before constituting their own subjectivity, Winnicott's child would be born from an intersubjective matrix, a mother-baby experiencing an "invisible oneness" (Ogden, 1993, p. 231), without clear separations between subjects. In this sense, just as the child does not exist apart from maternal care, neither does the analysand if we disregard the presence of the analyst.

The existence of a third subjectivity in the maternal relationship, the mother-child, raises the question of what reflection this condition has on the clinical setting. Ogden finds – or, more appropriately, both creates and discovers – this third subjectivity in the form of the analytic third. Therefore, the clinical parallel of the three terms "mother", "infant" and " mother-infant" is: "analyst", "analysand" and "analytic third". The latter is, according to Ogden (1994, p. 64), "the product of a unique dialectic generated by/between the separate subjectivities of the analyst and the analysand within the analytic setting".

Epistemological Axis: The Intersubjective Subject

Thomas Ogden's epistemological view is coherent with his reading of the Winnicottian intersubjective subject. This axis presents Ogden's object of study, and specifically the subject of his theory. This perspective is the basis for his theoretical, clinical and aesthetic readings. In *Subjects of analysis* (Ogden, 1994), Ogden uses dialectics to explore Winnicott's contributions to the concept of subject in psychoanalysis. He emphasizes that a central factor in his definition is the dialectic between the pairs oneness and twoness.

The oneness/twoness relationship refers to the initial moment of the child's life, when maternal identification is extreme with the infant. Ogden states:

> The mother engages simultaneously in the psychological process of allowing her subjectivity to give way to that of the infant (in her experiencing his needs as her own) and at the same time maintaining sufficient sense of her own distinct subjectivity to allow herself to serve as interpreter of the infant's experience, thereby making her otherness felt, but not noticed. The intersubjectivity underlying primary maternal preoccupation involves an early form of dialectic of oneness and two-ness: the mother is an invisible presence (invisible and yet a felt presence).
>
> (Ogden, 1994, p. 50)

In Winnicott's view, the constitution of one (subject) can only happen from two: there is no such thing as a baby outside of maternal care. The "basic unit" (Winnicott, 1958, p. 99), therefore, does not lie in the individual, but in the baby/mother environment as a whole: "The center of gravity of being does not arise in the individual, it lies in the global situation." It is this inseparability between subject and environment that leads Ogden (1994) to describe this process of emergence of the subject as intersubjective.

The epistemological axis, then, is based on this understanding of intersubjectivity. The subject emerges in tension, simultaneously experiencing oneness (being-in-one) and duality (being separate). Therefore, just as it is not possible to talk about the infant without talking about his mother, it is not possible to talk about the analysand without talking about his analyst. This subject constituted by the encounter is always affected by the other, and a major contribution of this concept to the clinic is the recognition that it is impossible to distinguish a rigid barrier between an internal world (inside) and an external one (outside).

In *Transitional objects and transitional phenomena* (1975), Winnicott addresses the issue of the internal and external worlds, emphasizing that the characteristic of the child's transitional object is that it is paradoxically created and found. Winnicott is notable for not resolving these paradoxes, and thus opens up space for the reader to decode the meanings of this enigma, as Ogden (2001) points out. The creative use of language is one of the elements that establishes Winnicott as a relevant and influential author. The space left open by the paradoxical language is filled by the reader with his own baggage, so that he can "play along".

To expand the understanding of this phenomenon, Ogden creates his own language, with a different system of concepts, based on distinct references. Instead of sustaining two opposing statements simultaneously ("the baby created the object" and "the baby found the object"), for example, Ogden (1993) proposes that we imagine this problem as a tension between two poles, creating and finding, which are dialectically related, that is, based on creation, negation and preservation between two opposing terms. The reading of paradoxes from the perspective of dialectics and the importance given to intersubjectivity are the fundamental marks of the epistemological axis of Ogden's reading of Winnicottian thought, and have direct consequences for the following two axes.

Theoretical-Clinical Axis: Regression to Dependence and Play in the Analytic Third

From the epistemological foundation of Ogden's thinking, a clinical theory consistent with his intersubjective perspective is constructed. In this segment, we present Ogden's developments on regression to dependence and shared play, upon which he draws to develop the concept of the analytic third. His epistemological perspective presents him with the problem of conceptualizing transference and countertransference from an intersubjective point of view, and to this end he also draws on Melanie Klein's thinking on the paranoid-schizoid and depressive positions.

Since Winnicott, there has been the view that psychoanalysis is nothing more than a "highly specialized form of playing" (2005/1971, p. 56). Analyst and analysand therefore play together, in a shared activity situated in the third area of experience (2005/1971), that is, in the interweaving of the creative possibilities of the two. It is important for the therapist to be able to create a safe environment in which patients, especially those who have been traumatized and whose subjectivation processes are compromised, can regress to a state of absolute dependence.

Following the schema of the split personality presented by Winnicott (2017/1988), the adaptation to the environment driven by the way of submission results in a lasting false self through which the subject presents himself to the world and also through which he expresses himself in analysis – protecting a hidden true self. If the analytic conversation were to be restricted to what is verbalized by the analysand's false self, as was the case for decades when the "interpretative style" predominated in psychoanalysis (cf. Kupermann, 2024), the process would become both interminable and innocuous. It is therefore necessary for the analyst to find some means of accessing the sensible core of the analysand, represented by their true self.

According to Winnicott, the *sine qua non* for access to the patient is the reliability provided by the setting, which allows them a regression to dependence in the presence of the analyst. The regression to dependence – a competence preserved by the analysand in their process of subjective constitution – recovers the experience of the "illusion of omnipotence" through which the relationship with the environment and the other begins to be constituted in a more spontaneous and creative way. There would thus be a kind of "unfreezing" of the maturing process and the analysand would have more authentic modes of expression (Winnicott, 1982). It will be up to the analyst, in this new situation, to use their entire empathetic sensitivity in order to reverberate the spontaneous gestures expressed by the analysand – whether with previously unheard words or through meaningful silence.

Ogden recognizes that the boundaries between self and other are always illusory, and that the subject is necessarily permeable to the other to some degree. He is therefore interested in studying the properties and qualities of the potential space that is constituted between the members of the analytic pair. What kind of interaction takes place in the third area of experience? What fills the space between two subjects? What does the regression to dependence of the analysand provoke in the mind of the analyst?

The product of the meeting of subjectivities is not a perfect synthesis, nor is it a harmonious field. Tension remains, and every tentative synthesis alters the two poles of the clinical experience – analysand and analyst – and reorganizes them into new arrangements. This field of tensions has been described as the analytic third: a third subject that emerges from the interaction between two subjectivities. Analytic interaction is therefore dialectical: it involves two poles and a creative tension between them. Thus, the two participate in this experience together. One of the psychoanalyst's roles is to describe the specific qualities of this relationship. According to Ogden:

> [...] the analyst attempts to recognize, understand, ana verbally symbolize for himself and the analysand the specific nature of the moment-to-moment interplay of the analyst's subjective experience, the subjective experience of the analysand, and the intersubjectively generated experience of the analytic pair (the experience of the analytic third).
>
> (Ogden, 1977, p. 94)

The analytic third is also a third subject in the relationship. This implies recognizing that transference and countertransference don't only happen on the therapist-patient axis, but there is also transference to the analytic third. This distinction becomes clear in the maternal situation, as we could say that the infant relates to "two mothers", the mother-as-object but also the mother-as-environment.

Understanding the specific dynamics of transference and countertransference provides the analyst with more resources to describe what happens in the potential space. However, every game has a background, and it would be possible to delimit the "emotional background" of analytical play. To this end, Ogden takes up Melanie Klein's concept of subjective positions to highlight the underlying way in which the pair produces experience, and names it the transference-countertransference matrix. For him, the experience of transference and countertransference:

> [...] is the result of the interplay of three modes of creating psychological meaning: the autistic-contiguous, the paranoid-schizoid and the depressive. The dynamic interplay of these modes of generating experience determines the nature of the background state of being (or psychological matrix) within which one is living and constructing personal meanings at any given moment. As a result, an understanding of these modes of generating experience [...] is essential for an understanding and interpretation of transference-countertransference.
>
> (Ogden, 1977, p. 138)

The transference-countertransference matrix is the analytic pair's particular way of creating experience and is the product of a dialectic of the three positions: schizo-paranoid and depressive, proposed classically by Klein; and the autistic-contiguous, developed in Ogden (1989). In this chapter, we will not develop the Klein positions, but instead deal with the autistic-contiguous position, which is Thomas Ogden's original contribution. He says:

> "The autistic-contiguous position is associated with the most primitive mode of attributing meaning to experience. It is a psychological organization in which the experience of the self is based upon the ordering of sensory experience, particularly sensation at the skin surface (cf. Bick, 1968, 1986).
>
> (Ogden, 1977, p. 140)

The Kleinian and Ogdenian subjective positions are ways of creating experience. They are also about the organization of the subject in relation to its signs, as Leiman (2000) points out. The analytical pair, likewise, has this dialectic as the backdrop for their work. We have chosen to highlight Ogden's contribution in order to show his efforts to create a theory of the clinic consistent with his epistemology. In order to deal with the concept of transference-countertransference, it is necessary to describe its matrix in order to include the intersubjective perspective coming from the analytic third.

By examining the matrix of transferential movements and the forms of experience of the pair, Ogden creates a theoretical support for contextualizing what is experienced affectively by each person, in what we call the aesthetic field. Epistemology provides a substrate for theory, which in turn contextualizes the experience of each analyst with each patient. These three axes of Thomas Ogden's reading of Winnicottian thought are obviously interrelated, especially in the exchanges between the theoretical-clinical and the aesthetic: the lived phenomenon is contextualized by theory, which in turn alters the way of living the sensitive experience.

Aesthetic axis: The psychoanalyst's sensitive presence

To describe the analyst's sensitive approach, we draw on the field of aesthetics. Among the multiplicity of notions of aesthetic present in the psychological field, we will initially present two definitions that are relevant to our study. The first is by Gilberto Safra, describing the term "aesthetics":

> [...] to address the phenomenon whereby the individual creates an imagetic, sensory form that conveys feelings of pleasure, enchantment, fear, horror, etc. These images, when actualized by the presence of a significant other, allow the person to constitute the foundations or aspects of their self, so that they can exist in the human world.
>
> (Safra, 1999, p. 20, footnote)

In this excerpt from *The aesthetic face of the self: Theory and clinic* (Safra, 1999), Safra brings the aesthetic tradition closer to the clinical field, emphasizing the human encounter. From this passage, we emphasize our interest in the dimension of what is felt, of the intersubjective field of affect.

In turn, Elkaim and Stengers (1994) draw our attention to the mutuality in the experience of affect that we have in the world. The authors highlight "the way in which, before we formulate meanings expressible in words, the world makes sense to us, according to the way in which it affects us and the way in which we affect it" (p. 48).

These definitions of aesthetics help us to underline the impact of the clinical situation on the analyst. We understand the aesthetic field, therefore, as the one that properly names the phenomena of the affective order, intersubjectively created. It is in the analytical third that the partners of the pair create images that are actualized by the sensitive presence of the other.

In *Playing and reality*, Winnicott (2017/1988) offers us two concepts that illustrate his understanding of the clinic as an aesthetic encounter. In the essays on the theory of play, the author indicates the need for there to be, in the setting, a "reverberation" between the gestures – and psychic creations – of the analysand and the analyst so that the former can abandon their withdrawal, face their unthinkable anxieties and discover the meaning of being alive. The concept of "reverberation" is, in turn, inspired by the mother's role as a "mirror", which, by reflecting her infant's gestures, fosters its processes of integration and emotional development.

Similarly, in the clinical encounter, the psychoanalyst must be able to exercise a function of mirroring the gestures of the analysand, which is expressed through a series of manifestations that we can call aesthetic, such as the rhythm, volume and timbre of the voice, the frequency of interventions, listening to silence and also bodily movements during the session (cf. Kupermann, 2008). It is this mirroring, above all, that allows the analysand to feel recognized in their singularity, and enables them to recover their playful-creative power, as well as allowing them to carry out the painful processes of elaborating traumatic nuclei.

Ogden advances the field of Winnicottian research into the way in which the aesthetic impact of the other is felt by the psychoanalyst, including producing psychic acts in the field traditionally called countertransference. To do this, he turns to the Bionian concept that, during sessions, the psychoanalyst experiences reveries, somatic illusions and sensory experiences (Ogden, 1994), which guide his clinical conduct. Part of the clinician's task is to elaborate and metabolize the aesthetic impression of the clinical encounter, in order to obtain further perspectives on the transferential-countertransferential movements of the encounter. So, while the second axis of description deals with a theory of the clinic that takes intersubjectivity into account, the third axis focuses on the analyst's sensitivity.

In *This art of psychoanalysis* (2007), Ogden argues that psychoanalytic practice fundamentally involves an "effort on the part of analyst and analysand to say something that feels both true to the emotional experience of any given moment of an analytic session and utilizable by the analytic pair for psychological work". These truths, however, are paradoxically "universal and exquisitely idiosyncratic to each individual, and are both timeless true and highly specific to a given moment of life" (p. 61). These paradoxes illustrate a theoretical problem: how to articulate the general and specific dimensions of the clinic in a theory?

Our reading of Ogden proposes that his strategy is to divide the clinical phenomenon into the three axes we have presented, and we find the relationship between the universal and the idiosyncratic between the theoretical-clinical and aesthetic axes. Ogden pays attention to the more subtle and personal reveries of the psychoanalyst. These thoughts and sensations, which at first seem meaningless, were experienced through the analytic third, in the relationship.

Reverie is a concept originally conceived by Bion (1959, 1962), but has gained prominence with contemporary authors. Ogden describes reverie as everyday, non-intrusive thoughts, feelings and sensations (Ogden, 1998). The level of description of this clinical phenomenon is quite specific, as analysts' ruminations are often left out. By making theoretical room for the most banal thoughts, the analyst can make use of this set of affectations to generate "specific, verbally symbolized" meanings that can be used in the process of interpretation. The aesthetic axis of analysis observes the analyst's particular affect.

The nuances of each interaction are taken into account, taken as source material and analyzed based on an understanding of the intersubjective field. The contextualization of the reverie is the step that transforms the "individual" feeling into an event thought up by the analytic third, in other words, it was produced by the dialectical creative tensions that take place between analyst and analysand. This is possible because the analytic third is experienced (asymmetrically) by both, in a shared field of interaction (Ogden, 1994).

The second and third axes are inseparable in psychoanalytic practice. The relationship between the theoretical-clinical and aesthetic spheres is complementary; it consists of the eternal interplay between theorizing about what is experienced and the experience itself. When describing his way of working with dreams, for example, Ogden advocates a "generative movement between dream and reverie, between reverie and interpretation, between interpretation and experience in (and of) the analytic third" (Ogden, 1998, p. 151). The coexistence and tension between the material spoken by the patient (the dream), the analyst's daydreams and the theoretical understanding of these phenomena is clear. Each element influences and changes the understanding of the next.

References

BION, W. R. Attacks on linking. *International Journal of Psychoanalysis*, v. 40, pp. 308–315, 1959.

BION, W. R. *Learning from experience*. London: Marisfield Library. Trabalho original publicado em 1962.

ELKAIM, M. and STENGERS, I. Do casamento dos heterogêneos. Boletim de Novidades Pulsional, n. 63. São Paulo: Livraria Pulsional, 1994.

FIGUEIREDO, L. C. and JUNIOR, N. E. C. *Adoecimentos psíquicos e estratégias de cura: matrizes e modelos em psicanálise*. Editora Blucher, 2018.

KLEIN, M. Notes on some schizoid mechanisms. *International Journal of Psycho-Analysis*, v. 27, p. 99–110, 1946.

KUPERMANN, D. *Presença sensível: cuidado e criação na clínica psicanalítica*. Civilização Brasileira, 2008.

KUPERMANN, D. *Why Ferenczi? The empathic style in psychoanalysis*. São Paulo: Blucher, 2024.

LEIMAN, M. Ogden's matrix of transference and the concept of sign. *British Journal of Medical Psychology*, v. 73, n. 3, pp. 385–397, 2000.

OGDEN, T. H. Projective identification and psychotherapeutic technique. *Contemporary Psychoanalysis*, v. 13, 517–538, 1977.

OGDEN, T. H. On the concept of an autistic-contiguous position. *International Journal of Psycho-Analysis*, v. 70, pp. 127–140, 1989.

OGDEN, T. H. *The matrix of the mind: Object relations and the psychoanalytic dialogue*. Jason Aronson, 1993.

OGDEN, T. H. *Subjects of analysis*. Northvale, NJ and London: Jason Aronson, 1994.

OGDEN, T. H. *Reverie and interpretation*. Northvale, NJ and London: Jason Aronson, 1998.

OGDEN, T. H. Reading Winnicott. *The Psychoanalytic Quarterly*, v. 70, n. 2, pp. 299–323, 2001.

OGDEN, T. H. *This art of psychoanalysis: Dreaming undreamt dreams and interrupted cries*. Routledge, 2007.

SAFRA, G. *The aesthetic face of the self: Theory and clinic*. São Paulo: Escuta, 1999 (original work published in Portuguese as *A face estética do self: teoria e clínica*).

WINNICOTT, D. W. *Collected papers: Through paediatrics to psycho-analysis*. London: Tavistock Publications, 1958.

WINNICOTT, D. W. Transitional objects and transitional phenomena, in idem, *Through Paediatrics to Psycho-Analysis: Collected Papers* (pp. 229–242). London: Hogarth Press, 1975.

WINNICOTT, D. W. Regression to dependence, in idem, *The Maturational Processes and the Facilitating Environment: Studies in the Theory of Emotional Development* (pp. 203–215). London: Hogarth Press, 1982.

WINNICOTT, D. W. *Playing and reality*. Routledge, 2005 (first published in 1971).

WINNICOTT, D. W. *Human nature*. Routledge, 2017 (originally published in 1988).

WINNICOTT, D. W. *O brincar e a realidade* (B. Longhi, trans.). São Paulo: Ubu Editora, 2020 (original work published 1971).

7 From Projective Identification to the Concept of Analytic Third by Thomas H. Ogden

A Psychoanalytic Thought in Search of an Author

Marina F. R. Ribeiro

In recent years, I have been researching the transformations that occur in psychoanalytic concepts, especially regarding projective identification[1] and its development into the idea of the analytic third. Just as the process of analysis is a probe that expands the field under investigation itself (Bion, 1970/2007), psychoanalytic theory is also constantly expanding, bringing new conceptual developments, the products of a living psychoanalysis, understood as an open work. We can think that while the invariant of psychoanalysis lies in recognizing the existence of the unconscious, there are now numerous variants, and it is up to the psychoanalyst to identify their own theoretical repertoire to construct a guiding thread within the vast universe of contemporary psychoanalysis.

The intention of this text is precisely that: to expose an Ariadne's thread,[2] in order to weave a theoretical plot of its own, within numerous possible cutouts, seeking to deepen the concept of Thomas Ogden's analytic third. To do so, I have used the understanding of the psychoanalytic matrices of Figueiredo and Coelho Junior (2018), in the book *Psychic illnesses and healing strategies: Matrices and models in psychoanalysis*. I have made this choice because I consider the authors' cutout of the psychoanalytic theoretical universe an organizer for reading and understanding the multiple theoretical and clinical intersections we find today.

Thomas Ogden's Transmatricial Thought

Figueiredo and Coelho Junior (2018) postulate two major matrices for psychoanalysis: the Freudian-Kleinian and the Ferenczian. The matrices are forms of illness,[3] and each one will correspond to a healing strategy. The first matrix, Freudian-Kleinian, is characterized by its focus on anxieties and the numerous defenses erected to cope with them, with falling ill occurring when the defenses are ineffective. The second matrix, Ferenczian, considers that there are psychic forms of pain and suffering that surpass the active capacities of the psyche, leaving it in a state of death or near death: death within.

DOI: 10.4324/9781003423188-7

From the Freudian-Kleinian matrix, we have illnesses due to activation, and from the Ferenczian matrix, illnesses due to passivation. The authors consider that Bion is a representative of the Freudian-Kleinian matrix, while Winnicott represents the Ferenczian matrix. Both are present in elaborations named as transmatricials. Highly prevalent in contemporary psychoanalysis, these are "paradigm crossings",[4] resulting in creative articulations.

Thomas Ogden's though is located precisely at the intersection between Bion and Winnicott, making this author one of the psychoanalysts representing contemporary transmatricial psychoanalysis, among others such as André Green, Antonino Ferro, René Roussillon, Christopher Bollas and Anne Alvarez (Figueiredo & Coelho Junior, 2018).

I emphasize that matrices are theoretical and clinical organizers, fitting within these always partial delimitations, intersections, such as the fact that Melanie Klein was a patient of Ferenczi. I think it is unavoidable to be interested in the theories that inhabit the minds of our analysts, both consciously and, most importantly, unconsciously. In this sense, there is a theoretical construction in psychoanalysis marked by the intensity of transferences and countertransferences, which can only be conjectured.

I highlight a comment from Freud to Ferenczi (1908–1911) in one of the several letters exchanged between them, in which Freud considers that theories should not be made, but they should fall into your house unexpectedly, like uninvited guests, while you are busy examining details. I think this is an excellent state of mind suggested by Freud: to walk around a little distracted, in a state of floating attention, and find what we were not looking for: a psychoanalytic thought in search of an author?[5] Perhaps extreme conceptual cohesion does not fit this researcher in a state of floating attention, who is also immersed in the issues and demands of daily clinical practice. The theory, as I conceive it, is only a possible approximation of the clinical experience; it does not encompass the totality of the experience, and is always partial, provisional and historical.

At various moments in his work, Bion (1962, 1965, 1970/2007) warns that the experience itself is unknowable and we only have contact with its transformations. Each psychoanalytic theorist illuminates and narrates a facet of the clinical experience within a certain theoretical paradigm; in this sense, dialogue and resonances between authors are fundamental in the vast universe of contemporary psychoanalysis.

Taking dialogue and resonances as a guide, Coelho Junior (2019) writes an article with the meaningful title "From Ogden to Ferenczi: The constitution of a contemporary clinical thought". The author inverts the temporality to which we are accustomed, suggesting that, in the a posteriori of psychoanalytic theoretical constructions, we can find connections and resignifications, both in the sense of temporal progression and in the other way round, within the numerous possible intertextualities (Paz, 1984). He then makes a kind of revitalization of possible connections with Ferenczi's work legacy, from which Ogden seems to have benefited in the construction of his thought, probably through the texts of Balint and Winnicott.

We can say that Ferenczi remained in the latency of the history of psy-choanalysis for decades, but produced effects on his successors, the most evident being Balint and Winnicott. But there are also silent and unexplained effects in Melanie Klein's work.[6] I think it is relevant to note the presence of Ferenczian thought in contemporary psychoanalysis, the *enfant terrible* of psychoanalysis, whose ideas have begun to be understood and resumed in recent years. He was indeed a brilliant and daring clinician who had the courage to write about the reciprocal and unconscious affectation between analyst and patient. In the vicinity of the thought expressed above, we find the text by Rocha Barros and Rocha Barros:

> It is important to take into account that even texts considered classic ones acquire new connotations as they are read over the years. It is common for a recent text to shed new light on classic articles. Texts undergo transform-ations through what Octavio Paz called intertextuality. Texts from different eras interact with each other, producing new meanings or, simultaneously, erasing meanings that have become anachronistic.
>
> (Rocha Barros & Rocha Barros, 2018, p. 15)

Corroborating the same thought, Ogden (2004) writes that not only do pre-vious contributions affect the subsequent ones, following a chronological order, but also that reading contemporary authors alters our reading of classic texts in psychoanalysis. When revisiting Ferenczi, we can find what was there, but also what was not: ideas that could not yet be thought of, but that, even so, were still present in the text for a reader in the future, in the time of the a posteriori, finding new meanings and resignifying classic texts.[7]

If we understand the unconscious, our field of observation, as immanence and not as an oracle (Ogden, 2004), we can think that theories are ways of capturing a meaning, a conceptual metaphor, as expressed by Ogden (2016). In conducting an analysis process, the meanings we capture are always momentary and partial, and should be abandoned so that new ones can emerge in each session. After all, why would psychoanalytic theories be different from their object of study, the unconscious? After this brief con-textualization of Ogden's transmatricial matrix of thought, I present the con-cept of projective identification based on the author's texts. It is important to remember that the concept of projective identification belongs to the Freudian-Kleinian matrix and has interesting developments in Ogden's work, some of which I highlight in this text.

From Projective Identification to Ogden's Analytical Third

In an interview with Luca Di Donna in 2013 (published in 2016), Ogden talks about a possible line of development throughout his work,[8] a difficult question for an author who has written about so many different themes.

Ogden had already wondered about this line of development in his texts; the answer given to the interviewer guides the investigation of this article.

In 2013/2016, Ogden reports that what initially intrigued him was how two people think, a question that already appears in his initial articles: "On projective identification" (Ogden, 1979), republished in 2012 in the book *Projective identification: The fate of a concept*. In his first book, entitled *Projective identification and psychotherapeutic technique* (Ogden, 1982), he more extensively develops the ideas that are condensed in the article, bringing several clinical vignettes. His work has been remarkable for his ability to narrate, in an imagetic way, the details of the emotional experience lived in the analytical session, in particular how two minds think together. Ogden leads the reader to the intimacy of the analysis room, making reading itself a transformative experience.[9]

In the 2013 interview, Ogden says that he rarely uses the term "projective identification" because everyone has their own definition and understanding of the concept. He then prefers to describe the phenomenon: it is about the mother and her baby creating a third mind, where the emotional experience is transformed into the experience of the third. Here, we have the transition from the concept of projective identification to the concept of the third; that is, the way two people think from a third mind that is formed in their encounter. Ogden states that:

> I view Klein's concept of projective identification [...] as a monumental step in the expansion of the analytic understanding of the nature and forms of dialectical tension underlying the creation of the subject.
>
> (Ogden, 1994, p. 8)

Ogden begins the 1979 article by highlighting that projective identification is a phenomenon that occurs both in the intrapsychic sphere and in the sphere of interpersonal relationships; that is, in the first sentence of the text, he makes his intersubjective understanding of the concept clear. From the author's perspective, it is a type of defense, a mode of communication, a primitive form of object relation, and a path to psychological change.

In Klein's classical texts, projective identification is understood as a defense and as a primitive form of object relation. Bion, on the other hand, conceives it as a mode of communication and a path to psychological change; we can say that, from this expression, Ogden's[10] authorial mark begins to appear. The conceptual transformations lie in these small shifts in meaning, in the subtleties of the text, and in the use of expressions

I emphasize that this text was written over forty years ago (Ogden, 1979/ 2012), a time when understanding intersubjectivity between analyst and analysand was not a well-explored theme, perhaps difficult to approach, as it still is today. The author's freedom of thought allows him to make his "paradigm crossings" at a time when this rarely happened. Moved by his clinical experiences with schizophrenics, Ogden seeks an interlocution with texts and authors[11] in which he finds meaning[12] for what he experienced with these patients. His first two books testify to this trajectory of appropriation and presentation of little-known English authors in the United States: Klein, Winnicott, Bion, Balint, among others.[13]

Resuming, I highlight some ideas presented in the 1979 article, in which there are several interesting connections, brought about in a condensed form. Ogden makes articulations of projective identification with both Winnicott's concepts and Bion's concepts. From Winnicott, even though this author refers little to the concept of projective identification, Ogden writes that it is a transitional form of relationship, constituting a primitive type of object relationship, a basic way of being with the object not yet separated. In other words, he surprisingly allocates the Kleinian concept in Winnicott's theory.

As for Bion, Ogden (1979/2012) emphasizes that the author understands the concept as an interpersonal interaction, bringing the experience of projective identification closer to the idea of a thought without a thinker, a thought in search of a thinker: being a continent is, therefore, thinking an unthought thought. He also states that, from the Bionian perspective, when there is no continent mind for projective identification, this causes a disorganizing impact, both in the mother-baby relationship and between analyst-patient.

In addition to Klein, Winnicott, and Bion, in the 1979 article, Ogden quotes Rosenfeld, Balint, Searles, Grotstein, and Robert Langs, among others, reflecting his investigative attitude and commitment to the clinical phenomena he was investigating. Ogden places the concept of projective identification outside the limits of Kleinian authors and goes further when talking about the technical implications of the concept.

Ogden (1979/2012) addresses a still delicate topic today: the analyst is a human being, with a past experience, repressions, conflicts, fears and his own psychological difficulties.[14] In his conception, the analyst's main tool is his ability to understand his own feelings and also what is happening between him and the patient. For this, he needs to have the competence to formulate his understanding clearly and precisely, using words that have a therapeutic effect, in tune with the patient's time, the timing of interpretation. Future texts by Ogden delve into the issue of interpretation[15] or as he names it, analytical dialogue.[16].

Still in the 1979 text, Ogden highlights that technical failures are often difficulties in processing the patient's projective identifications. In his book on the subject, *Projective identification and psychotherapeutic technique* (1982), three years after the publication of the article, when describing one of the ways in which projective identification can present itself, he uses the English word "enactment" several times. It is about a clinical phenomenon that, in the 1980s, became a new concept. In another article (Ribiero, 2017), I reflect on how the description of enactment is present in Ogden's understanding of projective identification, although at that time he used the word and not the concept, as it had not yet been named.[17]

If we imagine for a moment that the patient is both the director and one of the principal actors in the interpersonal enactment of an internal object relationship, and that the therapist is an unwitting actor in the same drama, then projective identification is the process whereby the therapist is given stage directions for a particular role. In this analogy, it must be borne in mind that the therapist has not volunteered to play a part and only retrospectively comes to understand that he has been playing a role in the patient's enactment of an aspect of, his inner world.

(Ogden, 1982, p. 4)

Ogden (1982) then suggests that the later concept of enactment may be amalgamated with projective identification; they are interpersonal psychic phenomena in the analytic situation that merge, making it difficult to delineate a clear boundary between them. But as far as I could ascertain, he does not use enactment as a concept in his later publications. What I intend to highlight in this discussion is the difficulty and complexity in defining conceptual boundaries; perhaps it is a continuous, necessary, partial, and always unfinished effort.

Going on, the aim is to clarify some formulations present in the 1979 article, in the first book published in 1982, and in the text in which he formulates the concept of the analytic third, from 1994, having as a guiding thread the conceptual transformation that occurred. That is, how the initial texts present, in an early stage, ideas that are being transformed and named as concepts in later articles. I highlight Ogden's understanding that projective identification is an interpersonal event, paving the way for the construction of the concept of the analytic third. This evidently intersubjective way of understanding projective identification is already present in other authors, mainly in Bion.

In the book *Subjects of Analysis* (1994), which includes the article "The analytic third", Ogden begins Chapter 6 as follows:

In this chapter, I shall offer some reflections on the process of projective identification as a form of intersubjective thirdness. In particular, I shall describe the interplay of mutual subjugation and mutual recognition that I view as fundamental to this psychological-interpersonal event.

(Ogden, 1994, p. 94)

Nearly twenty years have gone by since the 1979 article, and, as a psychoanalytic and clinical author, with much more experience and ease in relation to the originality of his thought, Ogden postulates what appeared in the initial texts as potentiality, also describing the phenomenon from a new perspective: the one of the subjugating third, pointing to the transformation of the analytic pair in the process that goes from subjugation to recognition.

Ogden understands that the two people involved, both the one who projects and the one who receives the projection, suffer distortion and denial of their subjectivities. The subjugating analytic third, therefore, alters the subjectivities involved if the analytic process is successful, and there will be a transformation of both, leading to the creation of something that is greater than the sum of the two participants: "In projective identification, analyst and analysand are each limited and enriched; each is stifled and vitalized" (Ogden, 1994, p. 101). It is through the recognition of the other that we become self-reflexively human. When vitalization and recognition are not possible, a form of imprisonment to the subjugating third, and the analytic process paralyzes.

The article (1994) in which Ogden postulates the concept of the analytic third was written in celebration of the 75th anniversary of *The International Journal of Psychoanalysis*. Perhaps due to this historical milestone, Ogden began the text by stating that it is no longer possible to think of the analyst and analysand as separate subjects, with the dialectical movement between the two subjectivities being an important clinical fact. Starting from Winnicott's postulation that there is no baby without a mother, Ogden considers that analyst-analysand also form a unit that coexists in dialectical tension. The author understands the dialectic as follows:

> Dialectic is a process in which opposing elements each create, preserve, and negate the other; each stands in a dynamic, ever-changing relationship to the other. Dialectical movement tends toward integrations that are never achieved.
>
> (Ogden, 1994, p.12)

M. C. Escher's engraving (1946), "Bond of union",[18] seems to be a successful image of the dialectical unity of analyst-analysand. The engraving points out the permeability between minds; we can think that the third is the engraving in its entirety, the scene of the analytic encounter. The balls that circulate the pair seem to be a good representation of the analytic objects, which are described by Ogden, in the 1994 text, by means of the detailed presentation of a clinical situation: the stolen letter.[19] The analytic object[20] is precisely the letter that represents the psychic reality of the analytic third; that is, the analytic object is in the potential space between analyst and analysand, apprehended and created by the analyst's reverie.[21]

The concept of reverie, originally from Bion (1962/1991), becomes the way in which the analyst apprehends the analytical objects, a creation, a manifestation of the waking dream[22] of the analytical third. Ogden (1994) writes that the intersubjective experience of the third is apprehended through reveries. If we are inspired by Winnicott's paradoxical expression, that the mother is discovered and found by the baby, we can think that the reverie is created and found by the analytical third.

Explaining the concept of reverie in a more thorough way, I have come back to some ideas expressed in a previously written article (Ribiero 2017): reverie, as the very sense of the word reveals, is daydreaming. The imaginative capacity of the mind is reverie; it implies mental and emotional permeability and availability to the communication of the other. Much of the psychic movement of a session implies the analyst's capacity for reverie and the possibility of its use in interpretations. However, this experience is often disorganizing, as it is experienced as something extremely personal and intimate, initially under- stood more as a technical failure than as something that emerges from the encounter between the two minds which are present in the room. If we can make use of it, reverie functions as a true compass, indicating directions of the emotional field generated by the encounter of two minds, of analyst and analysand (Ogden, 1997). In other words, reverie is how the analytical object is created and found during the session, a creation of the analytical third.

But, after all, how can we understand the concept of projective identifica- tion today? Ogden considers "projective identification as a dimension of all intersubjectivity, at times the predominant quality of the experience, at other times only a subtle background." (Ogden, 1994, p. 97). After the postulation of the analytical third, we find few references to projective identification in Ogden's texts after 1994.

The Third and the Analytical Field: Some Notes

Returning to the interview with Luca Di Donna (2013/2016), we find another answer from Ogden, in addition to the one mentioned at the beginning, clari- fying a significant issue regarding two related contemporary intersubjective concepts: the analytical third and the concept of the analytical field. After all, how do they differ or resemble each other?

It is worth remembering that the concept of the analytical field was postulated by Baranger and Baranger (1961–1962/2010)[23] in the 1960s, and internationalized in psychoanalysis by Antonino Ferro in the 1990s and 2000s. It is about considering the encounter of two subjectivities, analyst and analysand, in constant interaction, thus generating both new thoughts and also erecting unconscious defenses, the so-called "bulwarks", formed as from an unconscious fantasy of the pair. Everything that happens in the ana- lytical field is the result of both the functioning of the analyst's mind and the analysand's mind in complex interaction.

Scholars of Melanie Klein's work, the Barangers were immersed in the con- cept of projective identification, which leads us to think that the understanding of the analytic situation as a bi-personal field is also a development of the extensive knowledge that these authors had of Klein's work, making it difficult to dimension these theoretical intersections.

Katz (2017) presents the development of the field concept in three waves: the first based on the Barangers' work, called the "mythopoeic model"; the second, from Antonino Ferro's work, the "oneiric model"; and the third, based on the work of American psychoanalysts, the "plasmic model".[24]

The author emphasizes that the idea of a field emerged on different continents at similar times and in a relatively independent way, which reminds us of the idea of a psychoanalytic thought in search of authors.[25]

In the 1990s, Antonino Ferro combined the mythopoetic model of the Barangers' psychoanalytic field with Bion's model of mental functioning, initiating the second conceptual wave: the dream model. Added to this second wave are the works of Civitarese, who, in addition to understanding the analytic session as having dreamlike qualities, considers the session as a playing field (Katz, 2017).

Returning to Ogden's answer regarding the differences between the third analyst and the analytic field (Ogden, 2016, p. 176), we observe that he uses both concepts, depending on which aspect of the analytic situation he is referring to. He considers that the concepts are metaphors that name and highlight different aspects of mental functioning. The metaphor of the third analyst emphasizes the creation of a third mind, irreducible to the sum of two minds. The analytic field emphasizes the pair's forces created by the conscious and unconscious experience; we can say that it has a spatial character. Both overlap, with no clear distinction between them; that is, we must allow for some imprecision in the concepts, according to our author.

Ogden (2016) tends to use the concept of the analytic field linked to issues that involve the *setting*; and that of the third analyst linked to *reverie*; that is, the way this phenomenon expresses a production of the third, and not an exclusive creation of the analyst or the patient, as already mentioned. However, he states that, in a short time, both metaphors – third analyst and analytic field – tend to become obsolete, and others will have to be invented.

Conclusion

Returning to the beginning of this chapter, psychoanalytic theory, like analysis, is a probe that expands its own field of investigation (Bion, 1970/2007), and is an open work. Following this idea, psychoanalytic theories tend to expand, leaving the analyst with the increasingly complex task of constructing their own conceptual framework, which makes sense and supports their clinical experience at every moment. Always considering the circularity that exists between theory and clinic, in other words, concepts arise from clinical experience and return to the clinic, in a transformational and dialectical process.

Considering the idea that thoughts do not have an owner, but arise precisely from the continuous interaction between people, and are referred to from their authors, we can conjecture that concepts are created, discovered and named by different authors, at different times, and in the a posteriori of various texts, in complex intertextuality (Paz, 1984). An author, in the field of psychoanalysis, may be one who has the ability to capture, conceptualize and narrate clinical phenomena and, in addition, articulate them with existing theoretical paradigms, creating new conceptual plots, new paradigm crossings.

In this chapter, I focused on analyzing in some texts by Thomas Ogden the transformation of the concept of projective identification into the analytic third. As already mentioned, it is in the subtleties of the text that we can find these slippages of meaning that favor the construction of new concepts with clinical pregnancy.[26]

Ogden (2004; 1997; 2016) writes at various occasions that psychoanalysis needs to be invented for each patient; that is, as analysts, we are reconstructing our theoretical framework, our Ariadne's thread, in a lively way at each session. As psychoanalysis's scholars and researchers, it is up to us to historicize and articulate the concepts, crossing paradigms with rigor and ethics, in this creative transmatrix universe of contemporary psychoanalysis.

Notes

1 According to Rocha Barros and Rocha Barros (2018), the concepts of projective identification and containment are among the five considered most important ones for contemporary psychoanalytic practice.
2 The well-known myth of the Ariadne's Thread or better known as the Labyrinth of the Minotaur narrates the trajectory of Theseus, a hero who saved the city of Crete from the terrible Minotaur, a creature born from the union of Zeus and the wife of the city's king, Minos. Thus, the king builds a labyrinth to imprison the creature, but he could only do so through the sacrifice of seven girls and seven boys every seven years. Ariadne, the daughter of King Minos, fell in love with Theseus, son of Aegeus, king of Athens, and decided to help him kill the monster. So, on his journey into the labyrinth, she hands Theseus a ball of golden thread that would help him enter the labyrinth without getting lost. And so it was done: Theseus finds and confronts the creature, defeating it with a magical sword given to him by Ariadne and returning to the beginning of the labyrinth. While escaping from the labyrinth's doom, Theseus sees the truth when he discovers that through the thread, the starting point was also his arrival! (Available at: https://vidapsiquicab log.wordpress.com. Accessed October 30, 2018.)
3 " [...] Psychic illnesses can be universally thought of as interruptions in 'health processes [...]" (Figueiredo & Coelho Junior, 2018, p. 9).
4 Expression used by Figueiredo (2009).
5 Arnaldo Chuster writes about serendipity: 'The term Serendipidade (Serendipity, in English) was created in 1754 by the English writer Horace Walpole, in the book Travels and adventures of three princes of Serendip, to mean something found in a pleasantly unexpected way, and that adds substance to our wisdom. For the author, it is a transformative experience. We are different, after the finding'. https://www. arnaldochuster.com/. Accessed in: October 24, 2023.
6 The influence of Ferenczi's thought on Melanie Klein's work is a field of research that has recently been opening up. Klein was his patient, however, due to institutional political problems at the time, it was not recommended to quote him. Unlike Karl Abraham, her second analyst, who can be freely referred to.
7 Ogden published a book with several articles that are creative readings of classic texts, *Creative Readings: Essays on Seminal Analytic Works* (2012).
8 The work of Thomas Ogden covers articles published from 1974 to 2018.
9 The idea of the third subject created in the reading experience is present in the first chapter of the book *Subjects of Analysis* (Ogden, 1994).
10 One characteristic of Ogden's texts is that he uses the psychological term quite frequently, specifically in the mentioned passage: psychological change.

11 We can conjecture that the fact that Hartman's ego psychology predominates in American psychoanalysis led Ogden to seek the English horizons of psychoanalysis, continuing his studies at the Tavistock Clinic in London.

12 We can think of meaning as a truth; truth understood from Bion (emotional truth as the primordial food of the mind); that is, we also seek, in the texts we choose to read, a meaning for the clinical experience.

13 Ogden appropriates and presents these authors to Americans, especially in his first books *Projective identification and psychotherapeutic technique* (Ogden, 1982) and *The matrix of the mind: Object relations and psychoanalytic dialogue* (Ogden, 1986).

14 Given that the analysts' analysis and supervision enable them, but do not exempt them, from their humanity; on the contrary, it is the humanity of the analysts that makes them analysts.

15 "The transference is a topic of conversation, which at times is very helpful in understanding something of what it is that is preventing the patient from 'speaking his mind'. I don't find that the term interpretation well describes how I speak to patients. I think the phrase 'talking with the patient' better captures the feeling of the conversations I have with patients than does the phrase 'making an interpretation'" (Ogden, 2016, p. 171).

16 The author creates sophisticated technical formulations, such as the expression "falar-como-se-estivesse-sonhando" (Ogden, 2007).

17 The enactment was postulated in the 1980s, with Theodore Jacobs' article being considered a milestone in the appearance of the concept: "On counter-transference enactments" (1986).

18 https://mcescher.com/gallery/most-popular/. Accessed October 23, 2023.

19 Due to the extent of the clinical situation described by Ogden, I refer the interested reader to the text.

20 Analytical object is a concept that appears in the work of Bion (1962/1991, 1963/2014) and in the work of Green (1974/1986). In this text, I only present Ogden's understanding (1994, p. 71): "[…]I understand the event as a reflection of the fact that a new subject (the analytic third) was being generated by (between) Mr L. and myself, which resulted in the creation of the envelope as an "analytic object" (Bion 1962/1991, Green 1974/1986). And also: "This third subjectivity, the intersubjective analytic third (Green's [1974/1986] "analytic object"), is a product of a unique dialectic generated by/between the separate subjectivities of analyst and analysand within the analytic setting." (Ogden, 1994, p. 64).

21 The reverie can also be verbalized by the patient; the reverie is created and discovered by the analytical third.

22 Bion (1962/1991) believes that there is the dream of the night and the waking dream, which is the waking state of mind oneiric thought.

23 The influence of Kurt Lewin (1951) and Merleau-Ponty (1945) was fundamental to the Baranger couple (Churcher, 2008). In a later work, Madeleine Baranger (2005) refers to the influence that Bion's work had on the basic assumptions of group functioning, contemporary to the Barangers' seminal article of 1961–1962/2010.

24 The third wave is structured from the American Ego Psychology. I refer the interested reader to the text of S. Montana Katz (2017) for further clarification on the third wave.

25 This idea is also present in the text of Tamburrino (2016, p. 41).
26 Concepts that have great clinical utility.

References

BARANGER, M. (2005). La teoría del campo. In: Lewkowicz, S. & Flechner, S. (orgs.). *Verdad, realidad y el psicoanalista: Contribuciones latinoamericanas al psicoanálisis.* (pp. 49–71). London: IPA.

BARANGER, M. & BARANGER, W. (1961–1962). A situação analítica como um campo dinâmico. *Controvérsias a respeito de enactment. Livro Annual de Psicanálise XXIV.* São Paulo: Escuta, 2010.

BION, W. R. (1962/1991). *Learning from experience.* London: Karnac.

BION, W. R. (1963/2014). *Elements of Psychoanalysis.* In The complete works of W. R. Bion (v. 4, pp. 1–86). London: Karnac.

BION, W. R. (1965/2014). *Transformation.* In The complete works of W. R. Bion, Vol. 5. London: Karnac.

BION, W. R. (1970/2007). *Attention and interpretation.* London and New York: Karnac.

CHURCHER, J. (2008). Some notes on the English translation of The analytic situation as a dynamic field by Willy and Madeleine Baranger. *International Journal of Psychoanalysis. 89,* pp. 785–793.

COELHO JUNIOR, N. E. (2019). From Ogden to Ferenczi: the constitution of a contemporary clinical thought. USA: *American Journal of Psychoanalysis. 79*(4), pp. 468–483.

DI DONNA, L. (2013). A conversation with Thomas H. Ogden. In: *Reclaiming unlived life: Experiences in psychoanalysis.* London and New York: Routledge, 2016.

ESCHER, M. C. (1946). Bond of union. In: *M. C. Escher: gravuras e desenhos.* São Paulo: Paisagem.

FIGUEIREDO, L. C. (2009). *As diversas faces do cuidar.* São Paulo: Escuta.

FIGUEIREDO, L. C. & Coelho Junior, N. E. (2018). *Psychic illnesses and healing srategies: Matrices and models in psychoanalysis [Adoecimentos psíquicos e estratégias de cura].* São Paulo: Blucher.

FREUD, S. & FERENCZI, S. (1908/1911). *Correspondência Freud e Ferenczi.* Rio de Janeiro: Imago, 1994.

GREEN, A. (1974/1986). The analyst, symbolization and absence in the analytic setting. In idem, *On Private Madness.* Madison, CT: International Universities Press.

JACOBS, T. (1986). On counter-transference enactments. In: *Enactment: toward a new approach to the therapeutic relationship.* London: Jason Aronson.

KATZ, S. M. (2017). The third model of contemporary psychoanalytic field. In: Katz, S.; Cassorla, R., & Civitarese, G. (eds.). *Advances in contemporary psychoanalytic field theory.* (pp. 139–160). London and New York: Routledge.

OGDEN, T. H. (1979). On projective identification. In: Spillius, E. B.; O'Shaughnessy, E. (eds.). *Projective identification: the fate of a concept.* (pp. 275–300). London and New York: Routledge, 2012.

OGDEN, T. H. (1982). *Projective identification and psychotherapeutic technique.* London: Karnac.

OGDEN, T. H. (1986). *The matrix of the mind: object relations and the psychoanalytic dialogue.* New York: Jason Aronson.

OGDEN, T. H. (1994). *Subjects of analysis.* Northvale, NJ and London: Jason Aronson Inc.

OGDEN, T. (2004). *This art of psychoanalysis: Dreaming undreamt dreams and interrupted cries*. London: International Journal of Psychoanalysis.

OGDEN, T. H. (2007). On talking-as-dreaming. *International Journal of Psychoanalysis, 88*(3): 575–589.

OGDEN, T. H. (2012). *Creative readings*. London and New York: Routledge.

OGDEN, T. H. (2016). *Reclaiming unlived life: Experiences in psychoanalysis*. London and New York: Routledge.

PAZ, O. (1984). *Os filhos de barro*. Rio de Janeiro: Nova Fronteira.

RIBEIRO, M. F. R. (2017). Uma reflexão conceitual entre identificação projetiva e enactment. In: Cintra, E., Tamburrino, G., & Ribeiro, M. F. R. (orgs.) *Para além da contratransferência: o analista implicado*. (pp. 41–54). São Paulo: Zagodoni.

ROCHA BARROS, E. L. & ROCHA BARROS, E. M.. (2018). Melanie Klein ontem, hoje e amanhã. In: Cintra, E.; Ribeiro, M. F. R. *Por que Klein?* (pp. 13–22). São Paulo, SP: Zagodoni.

TAMBURRINO, G. (2016). *Enactments e transformações no campo analisante*. São Paulo: Escuta.

8 An Encounter with Thomas H. Ogden in the Analytic Third

Gina Tamburrino

Of the numerous rewarding experiences I had throughout the development and maturation of my psychoanalytic clinic, one of great value was meeting Thomas Ogden. With him, I was able to deepen the clinical thought that the greatest importance of the events in the analysis room lies in the moments when the experience in and of the intersubjective analytic third is generated. It is in this experience that we can, in fact, meet what we have become at that moment, with that patient. I consider this experience, if not the most important, then certainly one of the most crucial in an analysis because it is through this experience and from it that transformation can happen.

In his book, *Subjects of Analysis* , Ogden begins the first chapter with the following statement:

> It is too late to turn back. Having read the opening words of this book you have already begun to enter into the unsettling experience of finding yourself becoming a subject whom you have not yet met, but nonetheless recognize.
>
> (Ogden, 1994a, p. 1)

I see no happier way to open the door and introduce us to the depth of his thought, and especially to put us in contact with the concept of the intersubjective analytic third, clinically and theoretically; it is on this concept that I want to delve into in this brief chapter. This initial placement of the author is an expression of what each analysis can become/becomes each time, not only with each patient, but at each meeting with each of them. The encounter is not reducible to the analyst or the analysand as separate subjects, but the essence of the encounter lies in what is produced "in tension" *between* the third subject of analysis and the separate subjects (analyst and analysand) (Ogden, 1994a, p. 2).

It is important to say that his article dedicated to the intersubjective analytic third was written in commemoration of the 75th anniversary of *The International Journal of Psychoanalysis*. This same work was also published in the collection of articles from his book: *Subjects of Analysis*, from 1994,

DOI: 10.4324/9781003423188-8

having been titled: "The analytic third: Working with intersubjective clinical facts" (Ogden, 1994b, p. 61). Ogden observes that from the elaborations of Klein and Winnicott, the conception of the analytic subject emphasizes the interdependence between subject and object in psychoanalysis. He refers to the intersubjective analytic third as "Green's 'analytic object' (1975)" (p. 57).

> This third subjectivity, the intersubjective analytic third (Green's [1975] "analytic object"), is a product of a unique dialectic generated by/between the separate subjectivities of analyst and analysand within the analytic setting.
>
> (Ogden, 1994b, p. 64)

In his article "The intuition of the negative in *Playing and Reality*" (Green, 1997) – presented at the International Congress "The Psycho-Soma, from Pediatrics to Psychoanalysis", to celebrate the 25th anniversary of the publication of Winnicott's book: *Playing and Reality* (1971), André Green mentions the presence of the negative in Winnicott's work. In this article, Green explains what he means by *third* object – related to the negative (one of the meanings) – which "implies the idea of something that is not present" (Green, 1997, p. 240):

> This notion of a 'third' object has its application in the analytical situation. I proposed that we understand the exchanges between patient and analyst or, in other terms, between transferential and countertransferential processes as the creation of an 'analytical third', a specific result of the analysis (Green, 1975). This idea was also developed by Ogden (1994) and Gabbard (1997).[1]
>
> (Green, 1997, p. 240)

In this sequence of quotes, we have the recognition of A. Green by T. Ogden, and vice versa; both recognize the third that emerges in the analytic relationship, the exchanges *between* analyst and analysand, or, more specifically, the processes that occur *between* transference and countertransference. In addition, it is interesting to observe that a third emerges between these: the subjectivities of both authors. We remember Bion when he says that psychoanalysis is a probe that expands the field it investigates (Bion, 1970/2014).

Thomas Ogden presents the idea of interrelation between subjectivity and intersubjectivity in the analytic *setting*, linking to this what I understand as an important modification in the way the analyst's subjectivity is implicated in the analytic encounter. Ogden asserts that it is impossible to think of "analyst and the analysand as separate subjects who take one another as objects", as the analyst no longer occupies the position of a blank screen to receive the projections of the analysand (Ogden, 1994b, p. 62). The author revisits O'Shaughnessy (1983) and corroborates his statement: "Instead of being about the patient's intrapsychic dynamics, it is now widely held that interpretation should be made about the interaction of patient and analyst at an intrapsychic level" (O'Shaughnessy, 1983, as cited in Ogden, 1994b, p. 58).

The analyst and the analysand create and are created *by* and *in* the analytic process, so that the analyst is not just an investigator and observer in the analytic situation, as he participates with his subjective experience of the analytic relationship. The analysand, in turn, is not just "the subject of analytic inquiry", but is also "the subject in that inquiry", as he participates with his self-reflection, with his subjective experience of the encounter (Ogden, 1994a, p. 4):

> [...] analyst and analysand come into being in the process of the creation of the analytic subject. The analytic third, although created jointly by (what is becoming) the analyst and analysand, *is not experienced identically by analyst and analysand* since each remains a separate subject in dialectical tension with the other. Moreover, although the analytic third is constituted in the process of the mutual negation/recognition of analyst and analysand, it does not reflect each of its creators *in the same way* [...] The transference and countertransference reflect one another, but are not mirror images of one another.
>
> (Ogden, 1994a, p. 5; the italics are mine)

With the concept of the analytic third, Ogden (1994b) emphasizes the dialectical dimension between uniqueness and duality, between subjectivities and intersubjectivities that are *being* generated by the analytic pair, in the analytic *setting*.

The analyst and analysand as separate individuals (subjectivities), who have their own feelings, thoughts, bodily reality, etc., coexist with the *intersubjective analytic third* that emerges from the collision of individual subjectivities (Ogden, 1994b). Thus, it is not about identifying what belongs to the analyst or to the analysand, but rather an attempt to describe as much as possible "*the specific nature of the experience of the interplay of individual subjectivity and intersubjectivity*"; this is the analytic task (Ogden, 1994b, p. 64; italics are mine):

> [...] the intersubjectivity of the analyst-analysand coexists in dynamic tension with the analyst and the analysand as separate individuals.
> [...] the intersubjectivity of the analyst-analysand coexists in dynamic tension with the analyst and the analysand as separate individuals.
>
> (Ogden, 1994b, pp. 63–64)

The clinical vignette, presented below (Tamburrino, 2016, pp. 59–61), expresses the particularity of an experience in which the analytic third is structured, based on the coexistence of subjectivities and intersubjectivities of the analytic field:

> Helena arrived, settled on the couch, and began to talk excitedly about the apartment renovation that she and her husband had been working on

in recent days. She continued to talk about how busy she was with the arrangement of the new apartment; that she and her husband had bought several items and were anxiously awaiting some furniture that had not yet arrived. She was happy and excited with all the things she needed to resolve. She said she was already thinking about the next phase; with the end of the renovation, she would need to decorate the house and buy all the utensils, and that this was tiring, but also enjoyable. Helena spoke non-stop, leading me to know every detail of the preparations, the colors of the walls, the textures, the objects that would match the environments, the paintings, extending herself in an endless description of her tasks. I listened interestedly to it, but I began to feel tired and taken by a kind of vertigo and, amid the list of colors, decorative objects, texture of the walls, I began to struggle with sleep that took me. Unknowingly, I began to think about my grandmother and saw myself in a conversation with an aunt of mine. I asked her not to touch my recently deceased grandmother's things because I feared that she (my aunt) would dispose of all belongings too prematurely. So, I catch myself with these thoughts, and I return frightened to the patient's listening, feeling guilty for leaving her talking alone and for thinking about the death of my grandmother who was alive! I consume myself in shame thinking that I had distanced myself, and maybe slept, and maybe dreamed, and the more I think, the more absurd it seemed what had happened. I am confused and worried, and I do not see how to get a grip on the situation, how to understand what Helena was talking about. With some relief, I realize that she was still talking about the reform. Then, suddenly, Helena stops for a brief minute, breathes, as if taking a breath, and says she needed to tell me something else that had happened. She talks about her visit to her parents, in the city where she was born: *My mother asked for my help to clean my grandmother's house because my father does not encourage himself, as always.* The grandmother had recently passed away (a few months before) and the mother wanted to give a destination to "her" belongings, from the grandmother. I am surprised by her speech (a meeting with my daydreams) and I ask Helena if it was already possible to do this (I refer to the pain of touching the grandmother's belongings). At the same time, I think that this was the concern minutes before while I was talking hallucinatorily with my aunt. Helena explained about the mother's rush, because the house where the grandmother lived was very vulnerable, so that valuable things could disappear. It was then that Helena began to detail her feelings awakened during the cleaning and tidying up of her grandmother's house, referring to the sensation of seeing things deteriorated, broken and ugly; things that had already been so well cared for were now very damaged (I think, dead!). At this point, I remind Helena that her grandmother had been declining since cancer, added to Alzheimer's, and that she possibly had not realized the precariousness, limitations and losses that accompanied her grandmother in the last years of her life. Now everything appeared clearly and raw: the deterioration of the house, furniture and belongings. Helena agrees and begins to speak sadly *"I think I have never lived something like this before; I have not lost many loved ones and even when I lost them, I was much younger to think or understand these things that I am thinking now. I think I realized that things end up ending ... life ends ... and very quickly ...* (then her voice regains vigor again to continue speaking) *that's why I'm in such a hurry ... hurry to live ... hurry to do things."* The voice loses its lively tone again as Helena adds: *"But I had never felt like this before."*

Helena had been narrating her experience of encountering finitude in a completely new way, closer to the reality of human living and dying. I could understand what she was saying very closely; and at that moment, it was not "just" about my most recent experience with my grandmother, who despite her advanced age was alive, nor about the most recent experience that Helena had with the death of her grandmother, but about our shared emotional experience, which unfolded into deep feelings of human existence and finitude. Between me and Helena was happening an emotional experience in and of the intersubjective analytic third, "in the process of the mutual negation/recognition" (Ogden, 1994a, p. 5) between us (at an unconscious level). The analytic third, in this situation, "it does not reflect each of its creators in the *same way* [...] The transfer and countertransference [...] are not mirror images of one another" (Ogden, 1994a, p. 5 [italics are mine]). Helena's narration had taken me to my own undergrounds of experiences of finitude and death.

[...] the analytic experience occurs at the cusp of the past and the present and involves a "past" that is being created anew (for both analyst and analysand) by means of an experience generated between analyst and analysand (i.e., within the analytic third).

(Ogden, 1994b, p. 76)

In a poetic way, Ogden opens the chapter by quoting T. S. Eliot:

And he is not likely to know what is to be done unless he lives in what is not merely the present, but the present moment of the past, unless he is conscious, not of what is dead, but of what is already living.

(Eliot, 1919/1960, as cited in Thomas Ogden, 1994b, p. 61)

The analytic third is, therefore, always generated in "the present moment of the past" (Ogden, 1994b, p. 61). It is with this aspect that Thomas Ogden opens his chapter exclusively dedicated to the intersubjective analytic third, where he presents, as always, clinical experiences of great depth, sensitivity and beauty. Immersed in this clinical-theoretical contribution of Ogden, I understand that my *reverie* – of a conversation *happening* between me and my aunt – revealed above all, the unconscious elaborations that were unfolding in the deep relationship between me [Tamburrino] and Helena. This conversation with my aunt had never occurred before, but it occurred at that moment, within me, revealing itself in the process of *reverie*, fruit of the intersubjective analytic third that was happening/organizing itself *between* analyst and analysand. Therefore, it was not about the recovery of a memory. My grandmother with fragile health and advanced age did not occupy the center of my concerns at that moment, but there were aspects of my history and psychic construction (Tamburrino, 2016, pp. 59–61):

> The patient and analyst engage in an experiment within the terms of the psychoanalytic situation that is designed to generate conditions in which the analysand (with the analyst's participation) may become better able to dream his undreamt and interrupted dreams. The dreams dreamt by the patient and analyst are at the same time their own dreams (and reveries) and those of a third subject who is both and neither patient and analyst.
>
> (Ogden, 2005a, p. 2)

The experience of *reverie* with Helena "is contextualized by the intersubjective experience" created by analyst and analysand. In this sense, counter-transference should be considered in the *"dialectic of the analyst as a separate entity and the analyst as a creation of the analytic intersubjectivity"* (Ogden, 1994b, pp. 73–74; italics are mine).

The experience of the analytic third is not identical for analyst and analysand, although it is jointly created by both. It is an asymmetric construction, since "it is generated in the context of the analytic setting, which is powerfully defined by the relationship of roles of analyst and analysand". It is very important to consider what Ogden reminds us about "not (*being*) engaged in a democratic process of mutual analysis" between analyst and analysand (Ogden, 1994b, pp. 93–94); with Helena, the experience of the analytic third was experienced through the experience of awe in the face of life's finitude. "The analyst's experience in and of the analytic third is (primarily) utilized as a vehicle for the understanding of the conscious and unconscious experience of the analysand." (p. 94), although we cannot and should not deny that the analyst also undergoes a transformative experience, every time.

In the experience of creating the "analytic third", objects, dreams and situations reach "psychological meanings, that had not existed prior to that moment" (Ogden, 1994b, p. 75). The meaning that is created there at the moment of the analyzing situation surpasses the unipersonal meanings (of the analyst), however, it does not "suppress" them; these continue to coexist in tension with the new meaning created in the here-and-now of the analytic experience that is being created by the pair, by the intersubjective analytic third (Tamburrino, 2016).

My experience with Helena occurred "(in and through the analytic intersubjectivity)" (Ogden, 1994b, p. 76). This is a new experience, never happened before for me or for Helena, created between the analysand pair at that relational moment with a unique sense to that moment of the encounter. The analyst's *reverie* (in front of the belongings of the dead grandmother) is the way in which the experience of the third analytic could come to light. Ogden tells us that "[...] *a major dimension of the analyst's psychological life in the consulting room with the patient [...] takes the form of reveries related to details*" that belong to everyday life and the life of the analyst. The most intimate and personal aspects of the analyst's life are altered by his experience within and from the third analytic, and this needs to be recognized by the analyst, so that he can allow this modified aspect to participate in the analytic process (Ogden, 1994b, p. 82; italics are mine).

Note

1 Free translation of: Essa noção de um "terceiro" objeto tem sua aplicação na situação analítica. Propus que compreendêssemos as trocas entre paciente e analista ou, em outros termos, entre processos transferenciais e contratransferenciais como a criação de um "terceiro analítico", em resultado específico da análise (Green, 1975). Essa ideia foi desenvolvida também por Ogden (1994) e Gabbard (1997)

References

BION, R. WILFRED (1970/2014). Attention and interpretation. In The complete works of W. R. Bion , Vol. VI. London: Karnac Books.

ELIOT, T. S. (1919/1960). Tradition and individual talent. In *Selected essays*. New York: Harcourt Brace & World.

FIGUEIREDO, L. C., RIBEIRO, M. F. R. & TAMBURRINO, G. (2024, in press). *Reading Bion's transformation*. London and New York: Routledge.

GREEN, A. (1997) The intuition of the negative in playing and reality. In *International Journal of Psychoanalysis* 78(6): 1071–1084. London: International Journal of Psychoanalysis.

OGDEN, T. (1994a). On becoming a subject. In *Subjects of analysis*. Northvale, NJ & London: Jason Aronson Inc.

OGDEN, T. (1994b). The analytic third: working with intersubjective clinical facts. In *Subjects of analysis*. London: Jason Aronson Inc.

OGDEN, T. (2005a). *This art of psychoanalysis: Dreaming undreamt dreams and interrupted cries*. London: International Journal of Psychoanalysis.

OGDEN, T. (2005b). What's true and whose idea was it? In *This art of psychoanalysis: Dreaming undreamt dreams and interrupted cries*. London: International Journal of Psychoanalysis.

O'SHAUGHNESSY, E. (1983). *Words and working through*. London: International Journal of Psychoanalysis.

TAMBURRINO, G. (2016). *Enactments e transformações no campo analisante*. São Paulo: Escuta.

WINNICOTT, D. W. (1971). *Playing and reality*. Harmondsworth: Penguin.

9   Supervising with Thomas H. Ogden

Narratives from the Analytic Third

Idete Zimerman Bizzi

According to Thomas Ogden (2022a), the fiction that an analytic writer is able to write contains, in itself, truths that are more faithful to the analytic experience than any literal transcription of an analytic dialogue. This chapter on the supervisory experience with Dr. Ogden is a work of fiction, profoundly truthful to the author's experiential reality. Especially with regard to the descriptions of the dialogues in supervisory meetings, they are versions inescapably shaded by a subjective filter.

Prelude

On a typical sunny winter day in San Francisco, with clear skies and cold wind, I was about to meet Dr. Ogden in person, for the first time. The morning runs smoothly. I visit the San Francisco Center for Psychoanalysis (SFCP), as previously arranged, attend seminars, and, as our supervisory appointment time approaches, I can feel anxiety mounting. I stick to my initial plan of going back to the hotel where I was staying, before going to Dr. Ogden's office in the early afternoon. I have plenty of time. I review my writings, the clinical material for the supervisory session, and, by this time, the expectation of the encounter begins to take on large, unexpected proportions inside myself. Unexpected, for it is out of tune with my usual serenity in our previous meetings.

Two years prior, Dr. Ogden had made room in his schedule to supervise me, and our conversations, via Skype audio calls, had been taking place smoothly. From the beginning, the atmosphere of our meetings was one of receptivity, free thinking, and, amidst the exchange of ideas and reveries regarding the clinical material, there had always been room for spontaneous conversations on general subjects. Far from being strangers, I would say that we already knew each other reasonably well, and Dr. Ogden was quite familiar with my professional and personal background. It is true that we had never seen each other in person, but why would that matter as much as my agitated unconscious was telling me it did? I would just be meeting up with my supervisor again, right?

DOI: 10.4324/9781003423188-9

In spite of the facts of reality, what I feel in these hours that precede the onsite supervisory session is a mixture of joy, fear, and a growing need to share the imminence of this encounter with someone, as if something distinctly rare were about to happen. Intending to elaborate a little on the turbulence that plagues me, I start writing, thinking while I write, and the sentences come to me, free of any commitment to a logical coherence, just like the first fundamental analytic rule. And they emerge as follows: "I feel that I am about to enter a sacred library, such as the Library of Alexandria, and it feels like I will not be able to choose a book to read, as they are all of paramount importance." "I have too many questions. Would there be a question that might contain the essence of everything I would like to know? I wonder if anyone other than myself could give answers to my questions."

In this mental state, I remember Bion, the relevance he gives to curiosity, and to questioning, in all its unsaturated richness. (Bion, 2018; Tálamo, 2000). Within myself, I relativize the importance of answers. I play with the idea of asking questions to Dr. Ogden, and I group them, one after another, into a naive and sincere list of questions that occur to me. The first questions call for simple pragmatic answers: "Do you consider that therapy carried out in weekly appointments, based on theoretical and technical analytic premises, can be called psychoanalysis?" I realize that, like this one, other questions come up, and all of them are based on the idealization that someone holds the wisdom, and can provide the ultimate or truthful answer, which is in line with what Ogden (2016a) calls magical thinking. Two more questions: "Do you (a yes/no question, again!) perceive a countertransference pattern in yourself? Do you notice any difficulties with specific personality types, and ease with certain character or functional traits?" That's good, I think. I managed to advance to the next phase (Rezende, 2017), to be more abstract, and to formulate a question that includes a qualitative categorization, even if still quite rigid in its objectivity. In my intimate catharsis, I spontaneously play at asking questions. Or, to put it another way: the growing pressure of thoughts still without a thinker, in my psyche, attests, at the same time that it propels the intense reverie unfolding in my unconscious, motivated by the imminence of the encounter with someone whom I respect and cherish so much. Ahead of the mental exercise, a formulation occurs to me, and it is like a selected fact (Bion, 1962): "Have you ever felt like you are a thief of truths? As if they, the truths, would naturally come to you, for you are a skilled observer, and you ask the right questions, but they do not belong to you?"

Immediately, I understand: I think of Beatriz, a patient I had not talked with Dr. Ogden about, and about whom I had no clinical material on hand.

Encounter with Dr. Ogden

A few minutes before the appointment, while some people leave through the left door of the clay brick house, go down the stairs towards the sidewalk and greet me, Dr. Ogden comes out to the green-painted wooden door on the right, close to where I am standing, and greets me with a smile and a friendly look. He says it is a pleasure to see me, and I feel, in fact, very welcome. He shows me the way to the consulting room, "straight and to the left". Many books, wood, the smell of wood, cozy. I thank him for having me, I say it is a pleasure to be there, and I hand him the box of chocolates I had brought from Brazil, which he seems to appreciate. He asks me how my stay in San Francisco has been, if everything is going well. He seems, in fact, interested in knowing that, and I share with him some incidents I had experienced since my arrival, such as the fire alarm going off at the hotel, no hot water due to renovations, and, finally, when I move to another hotel early in the morning, while I am at the lobby having a coffee, in the short period of half an hour, two distressed people, one after the other, enter the hotel in psychomotor agitation and are restrained by the security guards. Dr. Ogden listens to me attentively, then asks me a few questions, and says he is sorry I had to go through all that; that he should have recommended a hotel. He tells me a little about that hotel he had thought of and about relatives that have stayed there while visiting the city. The generosity, care and kindness that Dr. Ogden demonstrated on that day and on the following days in San Francisco, and in the following years in which we have maintained the supervisory meetings, are some of his qualities that never cease to amaze me as unique and profoundly natural.

I tell him about the seminars recently held at SFCP. We talk about Winnicott, Bion, prenatal mental life and about how teaching gets rough when the "whys" take precedence over the "hows" in psychoanalysis. I share with Dr. Ogden my mental path a few hours earlier as I prepared for the supervisory session.

IZB   I was thinking about what I would like to discuss with you in person, then I remembered something you once told me, that when a patient is late, you like to start the session, while waiting, by writing what comes to your mind. I started, then, to take note of my thoughts, and the only questions that came to me were "yes/no questions"; little by little, more significant questions emerged, until I remembered a clinical case, in particular, which I think encapsulates many of the questions that were occurring to me.

Dr. Ogden follows my narrative with interest and prepares to listen to my clinical report with paper and pen in hand.

I say that Beatriz is a patient who abandoned treatment, to which Dr. Ogden reacts immediately by saying that, from his experience, talking about patients who are no longer under treatment is not that productive, as you cannot witness the patient's reactions to what the analyst says, and to the interaction, whereas with patients being treated, the process is more vivid. I understand that, and I say that I agree, but I explain a little more my internal reasons, which are undoubtedly quite vivid. I say that I wonder whether, in the case of this patient, there could have been something on my part that may have precipitated the end of treatment, even if I cannot consciously identify it. I remind him of a paper I wrote, which he had read some time ago and made some comments and suggestions on, where I propose a countertransference classification system (Bizzi, 2018a, 2018b):

IZB   I propose three subtypes of countertransference: The creative one, in which the analyst's subjectivity is permeable; the foreign one, when the analytic dyad falls ill from the patient's illness, and the analyst's subjectivity is temporarily saturated; and vicious countertransference, when there is an inversion of the natural flow between patient and analyst, and the analyst inadvertently imposes an excessive personal impact on the analytic interaction.

Dr. Ogden kindly says that this is very interesting, asks me to keep on talking, and I explain that, in an attempt to formulate the theory of this classification system and to devise clinical illustrations for each subtype of countertransference, the examples of creative and foreign countertransference occur naturally to me, but the illustration of vicious countertransference seems to be very difficult. I wonder to what extent cases with a poor outcome can reveal vicious countertransference. Dr. Ogden tells me he now understands my reasons and asks me to tell him about Beatriz.

Beatriz: The entombed doll and the agonizing analytic bond

In our first meeting, Beatriz explains her motivation to seek treatment in general terms: "I want to do psychoanalysis," "I want to grow as a person." She is a young woman, and looks like a doll: red-haired, delicate, small. She moves little and carefully, and gives the impression of a lack of spontaneity and a certain self-sufficiency. She wears high heels. She nearly dodges, when she passes by me, while coming in through the door to the consulting room, as if it were too narrow, or she were too wide, which seems strange.

Beatriz seems, in our first meetings, to be "getting things off her chest", speaking freely about her turbulent childhood surrounded by cousins, to whom she was constantly comparing herself and who seemed capable of achieving everything she wanted, but could not get: toys, good grades in school, awards. She considered herself sluggish, and excessively dependent on her mother's presence, often feeling deep separation anxiety. She speaks freely of her "long-standing low self-esteem", of her obsession with an aesthetic ideal of thinness, which led her to periods of excessive and worrying weight loss, shaking up her whole family. Contrasting with the transparency of her account, however, an affective atmosphere builds up in our interaction, which is at odds with the content of her associations. As if, somehow, she felt haughty, self-satisfied. She tells me about how she feels incapable of taking on professional commitments compatible with her skills. For example, her boyfriend, a well-established attorney, invites her to work in his office, but she feels insecure and false. The conversation unfolds with other examples of how Beatriz perceives herself to be performing below her capabilities in life, but the impact on me of the word "false" persists. Intrigued, and trusting my intuition that some primitive frailty was being covered up by Beatriz's orderly ways, I say: "The word you used, 'false', called my attention. Do you sometimes feel you are giving the impression of being something you are not?"

Beatriz's reaction is surprising: as if in a movie put on pause, she, who was playing with her hair, stands with her hand froze in the air, in a bizarre position, her eyes looking at nothing, motionless, and it crosses my mind that she is having an absence seizure. But she is not. After many seemingly endless seconds, she communicates again, and says, "Yes." That she fakes. As a teenager, she faked being fine when she was not. With her friends, she faked being something she was not, being happy when she was not.

This moment of deep intimacy and revelation in our initial encounter does not continue as the analytic process unfolds. In the first year of therapy, Beatriz is habitually smiling and appropriate, while a feeling grows within me that she is wearing a disguise. In her associations, the theme of simulation and insincerity is current, and Beatriz, in fact, keeps her boyfriend oblivious to her serious crises of jealousy and anger, and simulates a content, happy-go-lucky persona. Even though we talk about it, these aspects are as if devitalized in the analytic encounter. My attempts to address the subject from the point of view of emptiness, of a minus link,[1] result in long periods of silence that seem retaliatory to me. After those periods, Beatriz returns to her usual mood of cooperation and good fulfillment of the analytic contract, while I find myself the recipient of an uncomfortable feeling of a simulacrum, even more uncomfortable because of the impenetrable wall erected by Beatriz, leaving me with the feeling of knowing privileged information, as if received from an outsider.

Beatriz expresses an interest in controlling her impulsiveness, her aggressiveness, in order to preserve her relationship with her boyfriend, and I repeatedly fantasize that this is the main and perhaps only objective that she has with continuing the therapy. My growing discomfort contrasts with the patient's satisfaction as she gains greater control and better disguises her anxieties on various levels of her life. It seems that I carry the burden of knowing and perceiving her most fragile and destructive aspects, while she herself avoids experiencing them. Besides, I live with the uncomfortable impression that Beatriz seeks useful, pragmatic learning from analysis, which I feel as a misuse. Under these circumstances, the patient decides to interrupt treatment.

The analytic third in the supervision about Beatriz

Dr. Ogden and I discussed at great length the situation with Beatriz. He shares his impression that, with regard to the vicious countertransference, which I have tried to illustrate, and its potential influence on the patient's decision to interrupt analysis, it would have been the case had I been aggressive, had I verbalized that she was in therapy for the sole purpose of safeguarding her relationship. He sticks to this line of thought, and further argues that I did not act out my countertransference, until, later in our conversation, he asks, uncertain, but wanting to disagree, why I had thought it would be suitable to classify my countertransference as vicious. I say:

IZB   Because I had an objective, an obviously noble objective, of addressing Beatriz's simulacra, but perhaps I had been incapable of respecting her objectives more, and her need to forge stability in her life, even if with half-lies. Perhaps my therapeutic focus was out of sync with hers. It is the disproportion between what she was pursuing and what I was pursuing, in addition to my irritation, that catches my attention.

Dr. Ogden then responds with arguments that follow one another rapidly, with elation and a certain restlessness. He says there is, generally, a huge mistake with the use of the term "countertransference". That countertransference is not what the analyst perceives that he feels in relation to the patient. That when someone asks, "What is your countertransference?" and the analyst responds, "I felt irritated", that is not the countertransference. Countertransference, he continues, with a mixture of fervor and parsimony, is the unconscious homosexual attraction that the analyst feels, directed towards the patient, which is what makes the analyst get irritated, without having the slightest consciousness of it.[2]

Something in his voice suddenly changes, and now, Dr. Ogden is peaceful when he slowly and gently verbalizes that my countertransference is not the feeling that the patient is seeking treatment to maintain her relationship, and it is not my irritation either. He says:

From what you've told me about your father, during the time we've known each other, and the deep affection that connects you to him, I believe that, for you, your analytic work is a way of being with him, of making him alive; that is the profound significance of your work, and this patient, Beatriz, refuses to work analytically; she denies what you need.

I get emotional. We talked at length, about what Dr. Ogden tells me, and that brings a sense of conviction for each of us. Putting our understanding into words, we came to the conclusion that Beatriz, with her resistance and perverse use of the analytic setting, unconsciously and massively placed at the service of her false self, found in me, at that delicate moment in my life – when I had recently lost my father, also a psychoanalyst – an analyst who felt her most cherished purposes attacked, which perhaps, as I suspected, had an excessive impact on my countertransference.

I believe that the analytic third that Dr. Ogden (1994) and I established in this supervisory meeting was, in fact, what allowed us to dream my countertransference together and allowed the two of us to develop a "dream-thinking" (Ogden, 2016a), which was asking to come to light and which would hardly arise from a lonely pursuit. I believe that this moment illustrates a transform-ation in "O" (Bion, 1970), a mental experience born *from* and *in* the inter-subjective encounter, which Ogden (2022a, p. xiv) refers to in his latest book as "states of mind in which patient and analyst more fully come to life in the analytic process", anchored in a delicate synergy woven between the epis-temological and ontological dimensions of psychoanalysis (Ogden, 2019).

Mauro's analysis: A shared non-existence

A few years later, some days prior to a supervision session by Skype audio call, which is the format we kept to our meetings following my visit to San Francisco, I send clinical material to Dr. Ogden and add an unusual request to the email. I anticipate that he might feel awkward and will kindly disen-tangle himself from my proposal, which I would readily understand. I ask if he would be willing to help me to identify the *analytic third* in the clinical material I am sending, or evidence of its absence. I explain that, although I do not usually ask him theoretical questions, in a few days I will be discussing his "Analytic Third: Working with Intersubjective Clinical Facts" (Ogden, 1994) with a study group from the city of Passo Fundo, and that his specific impressions in this case would be very welcome.

About Mauro

Mauro is slender, has black hair pulled into a ponytail, and very fair skin. He is obviously handsome. He contacts me, seeking treatment, during the Covid pandemic, and in our first meetings via video call, a pattern of communica-tion is soon established. His face is smiley, friendly, and he has a slurring and slurred way of speaking. He stares at me with his big eyes, and begins his smooth unraveling of stories and facts and ways … and it's endless, seamless, without distinction between us:

Mauro   Where did we stop in the last session … we stopped … let me see …

I feel disconcerted by his recurrent requests that I remember what we were talking about in the previous session, and I find, to my astonishment, that recollections do not often come to my mind. In the sessions, I start to do unusually long interventions, and I realize that the pressure to be more active partly stems from the feeling of not having any data and not being able to connect with Mauro.

Mauro   My problem was that I started to question hero parents, you know, that illusion that they are perfect, then I started to doubt everything, to doubt that things were possible. You go to the dentist, for example, and he's just an individual, he doesn't know everything, he can spend his whole life doing what he knows, without missing what he doesn't know, but maybe he needs to do something, some procedure, I don't know, and he can't. It takes several errors for a disaster to occur. Several people have to make mistakes, the dentist, his assistant, not just one.

Associations succeed each other. Mesmerized, I listen to the narrative, which sounds like a siren song, filled with broad promising smiles and "amused laughs", leading to a lowered voice, whispered words, which make me turn my ear to the camera so I can better capture what escapes me and understand the empty, desolate look that appears every now and then. During the session, I have the distressing feeling of not knowing Mauro's story. Differently from what is usually me, I consciously try to recollect important events in his life, and I find a terrible emptiness, as if I had never talked to him. Vague memories occur to me: parents separated, close mother, lives alone:

Mauro   I feel that sometimes I have great ideas, then everything goes backwards. Then I encounter a problem. Another problem. I don't do anything. As time goes by, I feel I'm getting dumber. I can't use my reasoning capabilities like I used to.

I feel anxiety mounting sharply, and a frantic search for parameters and facts takes shape inside me. I know that Mauro narrated a profoundly traumatic event in childhood, which had a great impact on me, but which now eludes me completely. Once the session is finished and the forces of the analytic field are relaxed, that memory naturally gains ground. I remember his account, filled with emotion and tears, of the circumstances of his father's death, when Mauro was six years old, and how he spent hours hovering near the inert body, not realizing that something was wrong, obviously incapable of taking action and seeking help. He feels deeply responsible for his father's passing away.

A session with Mauro

Due to a holiday, I offer an alternative session time:

Mauro   I decided to accept this appointment so we don't have to go so many days without a session, but I don't have anything bothering me. I feel relatively well. Flattened, perhaps. I don't have much on my mind. I'm not sure if that is good or bad. Yesterday, I got very irritated. I would also like to talk about the topic we were discussing in the last session: my friends. I suppose I can share what I'm thinking, then we'll go from there. I also want to tell you about my mother. I don't think she's doing well.

Listing the topics to be addressed is like a meeting agenda that Mauro proposes; this is very clear to me as I listen to what he says. I can feel some level of artificiality, which I assume I must tolerate and keep trying to connect more deeply with him. I find myself conscious of my own thoughts for a long time, maybe twenty minutes, and suddenly I think "here the session begins", and I stop thinking about what I was thinking:

Mauro	– I made a dentist appointment. When my mother found out I was going to the dentist, she made an appointment too, right after mine. We went together. Cool. But then, in the waiting room, I started to get annoyed. We waited for an hour and a half. An hour and a half. And I'm really picky about appointments. I hate when they make me wait. And the waiting room started to fill up. It was infuriating.
IZB	– Especially in times of Covid.
Mauro	– Yes!

I feel like this is where we tune in; Mauro starts to speak vividly, as if he wanted me to understand him:

Mauro	– There was no gap between the chairs, and someone said, "We are all vaccinated. It's all right." No! It is not all right. This is against the health rules! I couldn't stay quiet, and I had to vent my anger. So, I said, "This is outrageous … unbelievable." I said it quietly, as if I were talking to myself, but loud enough for everyone to hear. If you're looking from the outside, you'd probably think I didn't want to be heard, but that's exactly what I wanted. I must admit that it gave me great pleasure.
IZB	– As a revenge?
Mauro	– Yes. Like a little revenge. They screwed me. I'll screw them too. Just wait and I'll give it right back at you. I think I took this from my paternal grandfather. He used to tease our dog, pulling his tail to see his reaction. He still does this at the nursing home, when he is feeling better.
IZB	– This seems be deeply rooted in your grandfather, because even today, after losing so many skills, he hasn't lost that habit.
Mauro	– Yes.

Mauro gets emotional and cries. I think of the myth of Tantalus. My associations draw a cruel grandfather, who perhaps was cruel to Mauro in his childhood; but the atmosphere of affection emanating from the patient's associations is one of elation, emotion and nostalgia:

Mauro	– My maternal grandparents are completely different. When we told them what Grandpa did to our dog, they said "poor little

doggy", and they didn't think it was funny when Grandpa took the dog to the sea, and left him on top of a Styrofoam board. The dog just stood there, stiff.

Mauro laughs, takes pleasure in sharing the story, while I still feel a mixture of discomfort, impacted by the sadistic violence embedded in the story, and a paradoxical sense of connection as I see him laugh spontaneously and invite me to share these memories:

Mauro   – Then, when we were seen by the dentist, Mom started talking about toothache, and that, because she can't chew, it's best to eat soft things, like ice cream. Damn it. She was inducing the dentist to say that she could have ice cream, and she knows she has to go on a diet, so I became rather indignant.

Pondering the analytic third in the supervision of Mauro

Usually, supervisory meetings with Dr. Ogden occur like a spontaneous conversation, where we exchange impressions; he asks questions about how I feel, what I think, listens with curiosity, and shares with me what comes to his mind, so each supervisory meeting is absolutely unique and different from the others. Occasionally, as is the case with this supervision of Mauro's analysis, Dr. Ogden skims through the material in sequence, commenting on each passage like a wise and skillful master constructing a master class. Without any commitment to literal facts, I try to reproduce here the impressions that Dr. Ogden shares with me. I choose to describe this moment in the first person, aware that I am writing a work of fiction, as I said earlier, in the terms that Ogden (2005) conceives (a dreamlike elaboration that brings to life what is essentially true to the experience), because it seems to be the best and perhaps only way to convey the strength, presence and liveliness of what he says:

THO   – You asked me to talk about the analytic third, so I went back to look at the first notes you sent me. Things seem clear there. You were immediately struck by him as someone whose beauty is a wall rather than something inviting. Theatrical. The grimacing, the volume of his voice going up and down. He used grimaces to try to be there, but not being there. He is hiding behind the grimaces. This was all very clear to you while this was happening. He asked you where you stopped last time. He is trying to be active. As if you don't know.

   The feeling of not knowing, not remembering his history: you are not knowing who you are talking to. You don't know who he is. And at that moment you didn't know who you were. Were you alive in this situation? You were lost, just as he was lost.

This self-understanding you were able to bring is an example of the analytic third. The two of you were together in this analytic death. He never came into being. He is showing this to you. It is not as if you feel you are looking to a strange person, someone you don't know. You are participating in this non-existence. You feel the blank. The blank is a hole, an absence. What Andre Green would call "the negative". He was not there. You were not there. This is an unconscious formation whose quality is an experience of the third.

Mauro keeps talking, you feel disconnected, and he says his problem is that he has started to question hero parents. He was doubting himself. How to create something out of nothing? He acknowledges he is nothing. He does not affect people. It takes many people to construct an error. One is not enough, one does not matter.

About lies: people say something, and it is just not true. There is no vitality to it. The mother lies to the dentist; the dentist lies to patients about the appointment time. This is not just an attack on reality. This is a substitution of reality. Here, imagination has no voice or power, no substance. Imaginary holds no power.

When he says he is flattened, he is saying that the hole cannot be filled. The experience that you both go through, with this feeling that you must feel that "we need to fill this hole, but this hole cannot be filled" is the analytic third. Fifteen times, in the session, he said the word "no". Your heart must have shrunk, with so many "no's", you are in the same hole.

He proposes something concrete to fill the void: the meeting agenda. He tries to act as if there were something that could hold him together. When he asks you to remember what you were talking about in the last session, there is no vitality in it, and the hole prevails, once again. Normally, when a patient asks me what we were talking about in the previous session, I do not remember, I always feel I have no memory, because there is nothing alive to that. It is like a desert.

I listen, attentively and deeply touched by his analytic sensitivity and generosity. We exchange ideas, and I tell him how I often feel the need to say something in sessions with Mauro to provide a third element, even a word, to place between us, as if we depended on that to stay alive. We converse, Dr. Ogden and I:

IZB   – Like when you have a nightmare you cannot wake up from, and you want to scream, but you cannot. The sensation of these moments is claustrophobic, as if I feel that I am there with Mauro, I know that Mauro knows that I am there with him, but I do not exist.

THO   – What did you mean by being conscious of your own thoughts in the first twenty minutes of the session, and then having the feeling that the session has just started?

IZB   – An excess of secondary process, as if I were trying to grasp something, an understanding that is not occurring naturally.

THO   – There's nothing to grasp here. That feeling you described, of being aware of the secondary process, reflects the unconscious formation of the analytic third. You both know there is nothing to grasp, even though you must grasp something. This is a paradox that you have to feel. Because you were able to feel it, to experience it, you were able relinquish the illusion that there was something, an understanding that you both could hold on to. Here, you learned from the experience of the third. You managed to do something with that experience, then you managed to give up that feeling and move forward, open to what will come. The analytic third is not something for the analyst to be trapped in.

I understand, at this point, that it was not just my surviving the first non-analytic, non-therapeutic twenty minutes of the session, in which I was massively and disconcertingly conscious of my thoughts as I sought to tune in with Mauro, that allowed the analytic work. My thoughts about my thoughts were, properly, the intersubjective "third object" that Mauro and I originated, the co-created element that allowed learning from experience, and the transformation in the analytic field.

Our conversation goes on. I say I would like to ask two questions:

IZB   – What you say makes a lot of sense. By hearing what you say about not having anything to grasp, and that I have to experience this reality, I ask you: do you think there is hope for this treatment?

THO   – Of course there is! You are sensitive to the experience of the third. The way you tune in with Mauro's experience is a very good analytic work.

The answer surprises me. It should be made clear that the supervisory experience through Dr. Ogden's speech, at moments like this, takes on a quality of inescapable reality, given its intrinsic intensity and depth; in that case, a void befalls me, relentlessly, hence my question. Dr. Ogden's narrative dream voice (reverie) is, at the same time, *descriptive*, like someone who clearly articulates in words what they observe, and *inscriptive*, guttural, impacting the senses and being somewhat scary, like someone who speaks from within the guts of the experience:

IZB   – My second question is of a technical nature. Do you think I should interpret or consider interpreting, expressing verbally to Mauro something about the absence, the void?

THO   – You know that I put less weight on the interpretation of the unconscious than I put on experiencing the feeling. I find that interpretations are important, and fundamental, in some circumstances, but,
in this situation with Mauro, I think that the important thing is you
to be able to live with that without trying to fill the void. I prefer to
wait until the patient himself can verbalize something understandable. A patient like Mauro, for example, might say "I feel like a robot;
I was there, but I was not there." It would not be this genuine if you
said that to him. Is it just my imagination, am I being delusional,
or … ? Your reverie of the myth of Tantalus certainly expresses the
reality of the experience of the third, but I had a reverie of Mauro
being in a place with doors, many rooms, moving from room to
room, trying to find a place. Something like … like you were looking
for somewhere you can breathe. Maybe it is just my imagination. But
you thought of Tantalus.

IZB   – Yes. I thought of the myth of Tantalus, but I did not feel it. Maybe it
was meant to be a reverie that never went through.

THO   – Good. It is a good thing that you can differentiate the two: something you think about, and something you dream about. The myth of
Tantalus was thought.

IZB   – Perhaps it was a stillborn reverie. [And, at this moment, I imagine
Mauro as a fossil, and someone is trying to measure his fetal heart
rate with a pinard horn.]

Echoes of the analytic third in the supervision of Mauro

In the session following this supervision, Mauro talks about an imminent
trip and the preparations he is making. To my astonishment, as if to reaffirm
Dr. Ogden's analytic sensitivity, forged by who knows what unfathomable
paths, Mauro says, right at the beginning of the session:

Mauro – As crazy as it may sound, this thought that comes to me from time
to time, that I don't have a place to go, to hide, a roof to protect me,
is a primitive thing, you know? I know that on the trip, I will not
be left without a place to stay, on the street, but … [Mauro cries,
emotional]

Sometimes I wonder if I'm not running away by accepting to go
on this trip, running away from … from … It is like … here, for
example, if I do not take a step forward, I just do not walk, I do not
move. But on the trip, I feel like I am going to be surrounded by
water, I must swim, and if I stop, I will sink. It is like my life was the
ocean; I swim, and from time to time, I find a place where I do not
sink, where I can breathe, an island. But an island is not a comfort-
able place to live.

Epilogue

Among the innumerable and significant aspects of the supervisory experience that deserved to be highlighted in this chapter, I chose two significant and fundamentally different episodes. The description of the encounter in San Francisco illustrates the emotional density, trust and intimacy that permeate the supervisory relationship with Dr. Ogden, built over time. Essential in the therapeutic relationship and in the analytic supervisory relationship, the experience of intellectual and affective collaboration based on these premises, has been, even more than a source of learning, an identifying model of *becoming* an analyst, in the arduous and permanent search for personal truths, in the patients and in oneself. The supervisory account focusing on understanding the analytic third, based on Mauro's analysis, is intended to offer a glimpse of both the form and content of Dr. Ogden's analytic thinking, under full and lively construction during the supervision. Both circumstances portray, *pari passu*, the dialectical interplay between the epistemological and ontological dimensions of psychoanalysis (Ogden, 2019), in the analytic supervisory relationship with Dr. Ogden, to the extent that, in our conversations, the pursuit of conceptual understanding naturally leads to reveries and transformations of *becoming*, which trigger, in a complementary way, the pursuit of analytic *whys*, and so on.

While choosing from a range of writing possibilities, I decided to provide a spontaneous description of some of my experiences as a supervisee of Thomas H. Ogden. Both the external circumstances surrounding each supervisory meeting and my own subjective perceptions and reveries, described in some detail, are intended to convey something that is inexpressible in words. In line with the essence of Ogden's work, in this report, I hope I have managed to: emphasize the *descriptions* of the supervisory interaction, complemented by *explanations*; highlight *experiences* while relativizing *determinations* (Ogden, 2018a, 2018b, 2019, 2022a, 2022b); underline the *hows* more than the *whys*, the *supervising* more than the supervisions, in their concrete format. Most importantly, I hope I have managed to illustrate the richness of this experience, in terms of the consistency, in the supervisory meetings, between the opus of this great thinker and his genuine way of working. In an attempt to describe the narrative voice that emanates from Dr. Ogden's dream (reverie) and thoughts, whose polysemic quality, I believe, can only be apprehended from interaction, I proposed the terms *descriptive quality* and *inscriptive quality* to portray the rare synergistic impact of the verbal and aesthetic dimension of his analytic speaking and telling. I keep trying to make sense of and find words that could translate this rare ability, which I find, also, in certain passages of the novels written by Ogden, in which the narrator establishes a *polyphonic and stereophonic voice*, as if he could be, at the same time, both inside and outside.[3] His voice sounds, at these moments, as perhaps it would sound to an outside observer, the conversation of Pinocchio and Geppetto from the entrails of the whale, defying water, darkness and the fear of the unknown with an improbable and powerful bonfire.

Dr. Ogden is a punctual, interested supervisor guided by a keen ethical sense since the beginning of our working together, seven years ago. He rejoices when I express questions and impressions, and invariably welcomes them in a patient and respectful manner. We laugh together occasionally. We disagree occasionally, and, at these times, I particularly admire him, as he grants me a space of fundamental individuality and helps me with the necessary and challenging "use of the object"[4] as a supervisor. Over time, the meaning and importance of these Skype meetings with Tom grow within me as, in these encounters, I have the freedom to think with, feel with, experience with, be with my supervisor, as I believe he also does. I could say that the honor of learning and, most importantly, of spending time in a spontaneous and creative way with the unique human figure and psychoanalyst that is Dr. Ogden is something of a dream come true. I feel, however, that I do more justice to the truth of my experience by saying that it has been, at each supervisory meeting, a reality that becomes a dream, and that paves the foundations for dreaming further.

Notes

1 According to Bion (1970), a minus link consists of a mental state that contrasts with the pursuit of essential human truths and often corresponds with the violent destruction of links connecting previously acquired mental elements and thoughts. Zimerman (1995, p. 67), in this regard, argues that the basic characteristics of the functioning of the psychotic part of the personality, according to Bion are "a permanent attack on every bond with the analyst; on the bonds between the different parts of the patient himself; and an attack on the knowledge of the painful truths that are found in both external and internal reality".

2 NB: Mentioning the unconscious sexual phantasy, at this point in our conversation, is one among other spontaneous illustrations that occur to Dr. Ogden when referring to the analyst's powerful unconscious premises within the intersubjective analytic third; in this report, it is more relevant in the association of ideas loaded with great emotional density, as intuitive bridges that Dr. Ogden builds in his reverie, *and less* in its literal content.

3 Novels by Thomas H. Ogden: *The parts left out* (2012), published in Portuguese, with the title *Meias verdades: Um romance* (2017), *The hands of gravity and chance* (2016b), and *This will do* (2021).

4 According to Winnicott (1971), the maturational growth of the human subject requires, from the caring objects, help in the sense of "using" the object; using, in this sense, relates to the ability to place the object beyond the area of object relations, and allow it to play a role in its dimension of actual nature.

References

BION, W. R. (1962). *Learning from experience*. London: William Heinemann Medical.
BION, W. R. (1970). *Attention and interpretation*. London and New York: Routledge.

BION, W. R. (2018). *Bion in New York and Sao Paulo and Three Tavistock Seminars*. London: The Harris Meltzer Trust.

BIZZI, I. Z. (2018a). On the analyst's personal equation. *International Journal of Psychoanalysis – Open*, *5*, 1–30. https://pep-web.org/search/document/IJPO PEN.005.0003A

BIZZI, I. Z. (2018b). Subjetividade do analista: a contratransferência revisitada. *Revista Multiverso*, *1*(1), 127–139.

OGDEN, T. H. (1994). The anaytic third: working with intersubjective clinical facts. *International Journal of Psychoanalysis*, *75*, 3–19.

OGDEN, T. H. (2005). On psychoanalytic supervision. *International Journal of Psychoanalysis*, *86*(5), 1265–80. www.tandfonline.com/doi/full/10.1516/ BEE8-C9E7-J7Q7-24BF

OGDEN, T. H. (2012). *The parts left out*. London: Karnac.

OGDEN, T. H. (2016a). On three forms of thinking: magical thinking, dream thinking, and transformative thinking. *In* T. H. Ogden. *Reclaiming Unlived Life: experiences in psychoanalysis* (pp. 17–45). London: Routledge.

OGDEN, T. H. (2016b). *The hands of gravity and chance*. London: Karnac.

OGDEN, T. H. (2017). *Meias verdades: um romance*. São Paulo: Blucher.

OGDEN, T. H. (2018a). The feeling of real: On Winnicott's 'communicating and not communicating leading to a study of certain opposites'. *International Journal of Psychoanalysis*, *99*(6), 1288–1304. www.tandfonline.com/doi/full/10.1080/00207 578.2018.1556071

OGDEN, T. H. (2018b). How I talk with my patients. *Psychoanalytic Quarterly*, *87*(3), 399–414. www.tandfonline.com/doi/full/10.1080/00332828.2018.1495513

OGDEN, T. H. (2019). Ontological psychoanalysis or 'What do you want to be when you grow up?'. *Psychaonalytic Quarterly*, *88*(4), 661–684. www.tandfonline.com/ doi/full/10.1080/00332828.2019.1656928

OGDEN, T. H. (2021). *This will do*. London: Sphinx.

OGDEN, T. H. (2022a). Preface. *In* T. H. Ogden. *Coming to life in the consulting room: toward a new analytic sensibility* (pp. xiv–xv). London: Routledge.

OGDEN, T. H. (2022b) Analytic writing as a form of fiction. In T. H. Ogden. *Coming to life in the consulting room: toward a new analytic sensibility* (pp. 163–165). London: Routledge.

REZENDE, A. M. (2017). *Pensando e repensando os mistérios da mente humana de K para O*. Belo Horizonte: O Lutador.

TÁLAMO, P. B. (2000). Laying low and saying (almost) nothing. *In* P. B. Tálamo, S. A. Merciai & F. Borgogno. *W.R. Bion: Between past and future* (pp. 20–26). London and New York: Karnac.

WINNICOTT, D. W. (1971). The use of an object and relating through identifications. *In* D. W. Winnicott. *Playing and reality* (pp. 86–94). New York: Basic Books.

ZIMERMAN, D. E. (1995). *Bion: da teoria à prática: uma leitura didática*. Porto Alegre: Artes Médicas, Porto Alegre.

10 From Limbo to Light

The Concept of *Reverie* in the Work of Thomas H. Ogden

Ana Fátima Aguiar, Marina F. R. Ribeiro, and Pedro Hikiji Neves

From limbo to light: *Reverie* in Ogden[1]

Thomas Ogden has his own style. His original concept of "analytical writing" (2005) allows the reader to be involved in an unique experience with the words. Words that make it possible for the reader to head for ideas, feelings, images and memories. They allow for changes in paradigms to happen without denying the legacy and originality of the classic psychoanalytic authors. This North American author presents us with a dialectic form of thought which surpasses the stagnant conflicts between different psychoanalytic schools. Using his original and creative views, he does that by articulating concepts from different theoretical frameworks.

As from the initial pages of his book *Reverie and interpretation: sensing something human* (1997), the author brings up a puzzling statement: he says that words and phrases come with a potential for a type of slippage, just like people. This comment points to what the author intends to encourage by his writing: freedom to slide between words and ideas, allowing a certain amount of imprecision. Ogden warns us that an effort to make ideas definite, precise, or fixed can have an asphyxiating effect. Therefore, he suggests that the reader allows himself to wander between words and to walk through terms and senses.in order to create new arrangements at each different experience with reading, so that it sounds like freedom in the minds of the one who reads it. It also creates a process of joint authorship which makes meanings that can be changed and affected available at each new context.

The use of words, just like their understanding when we hear or read them, needs to be alive. To Ogden (1997, p.4), when "living and breathing", words are like musical chords that resonate melodically. This resonance must be captured in all its extensive and imprecise polyphony.

The author also highlights that something similar must happen in psychoanalysis. The analytical hearing must overpass the act of only interpreting words or "loose" ideas (which are equivalent to a simple playing/hearing isolated musical notes), and open up to an amplified composition, in which the chords gain the range of a symphony.

DOI: 10.4324/9781003423188-10

Each note played by the analytic pair is submerged in a particular emotional context related to the specific ways of its transferential-counter-transferential dynamics. Based on that, one can conclude that a certain amount of imprecision should be attributed to both words and people, since both are alive and in constant movement. Fixating and stigmatizing them would change them into devitalized effigies. The analyst who does that loses his capacity to capture the human aspect of the experience. Because of that, the analytical work comprehends this "musical" form of listening, paying attention to the unplayed notes and to the unsaid words, amplifying possibilities so that musicality of undreamed dreams could reach the analytical duet and be played by it.

According to the author, here lies the main goal of the analytical writing: to create a form of language that grasps human vitality. In this particular form of writing psychoanalytically, Ogden, in a fluid dialogue, reaches (and also allows us to reach) the human, the emotional experience. Respecting the foundation concepts of each (re)created thought, he slides between and by words, ideas and concepts, cultivating his own recommendation: imprecision.[2]

By transiting in a fruitful way between different theoretical frameworks, Thomas Ogden is considered a transmatrix author, according to a distinction offered by Coelho Junior and Figueiredo (2018). These authors describe the existence of two great matrices for psychoanalysis: the Freudian-Kleinian one, and the Ferenczian one. The matrices are forms of psychic illness (and their defenses), and to each one there should be a different healing strategy. Bion's ideas circulate mainly through the Freudian-Kleinian matrix, while Winnicott's ideas circulate through the Ferenczian matrix. These core concepts of the development of the history of psychoanalysis support a contemporary form of thought which dialogues with both matrices, articulating their ideas. That explains the use of the term "transmatricial",[3] because it keeps the theoretical strictness but also formulates new conjectures by a creative intertextual tension.

It could be noticed that the Ogdenian thought process contemplates a form of circulation between what has already been produced, and the creation of new important formulations for the psychoanalytic movement. Therefore, the author allows us to feel the freshness of a pleasant encounter with the conception of a living, creative form of psychoanalysis and that should be, above all, an interesting one. Ogden says: "To be interesting, the analysis must be free to 'exercise,' to shape itself and be given shape in any way that the participants are able to invent" (1997, p. 8). Based on that, when it comes to the form of psychoanalysis that keeps itself attached to theory, he presents his criticism postulating that:

When the analysis is alive, it unselfconsciously manages for periods of time to be an experiment that has left the well-charted waters of prescribed form; it is a discussion fueled by curiosity and by variety of attempt; it is an endeavor that depends upon genuine exchange of views and comparison of standpoints. Analysis that has become a routinized form in which "knowledge" is conveyed from analyst to analysand is uninteresting; it is no longer an experiment since the answers, at least in broad outline, are known from the outset.

(1997, p. 8)

We believe that Thomas Ogden's ideas deserve their earned highlight in the contemporary psychoanalytic context largely because of the perspective he presents that claims psychoanalysis must be a living, interesting and human experience. In this type of analytical space, which is free and contingent, as the author presents it to us so well, intersubjectivity[4] can make itself present: in the encounter.

Ogdenian intersubjectivity is related to dialectical tensions in the analytical encounter. In this sense, the solid borders between the separate subjectivities of analyst and analysand become flexible. The analytic pair creates and is created by intersubjective dynamics submerged in tension between, simultaneously, oneness (at-one-ment) and twoness (being separate).

With that in mind, Ogden understands that the intersubjective experiences are always filled with projective identifications, which compose the most important content of the analysis. Ribeiro (2016, p. 46) explains that projective identification is seen by Bion as a basic activity of the human mind, an elementary form of communication. This means that the Bionian perspective considers projective identification in the field of intersubjectivity. Besides communicating emotion, projective identification is then comprehended as the origins of the capacity to think. Ogden considers projective identification as "a dimension of all intersubjectivity, at times the predominant quality of the experience, at other times only a subtle background" (Ogden, 1994, p. 99).

Based on the Bionian work, Ogden (1994, p. 24) highlights the idea that the analyst (as the mother, in Bion) keeps alive and, more than that, in a certain way brings to life such aspects projected by the analysand (as well as by the baby, in Bion), by means of successful containment.

Therefore, the experience of *reverie* becomes an important element for the analytic work, since it is by *reverie* that analysis may happen. We suggest here to think of *reverie* as an example of the concept of "created and found" by Ogden, while at the same time, when the author brings back this enigmatic concept from Bion's work, he also "makes it up" by presenting it with new clothes tailored with threads intertwined with Winnicottian concepts. Articulating different theories, the author circulates freely between the different matrices of thought, avoiding eclecticisms and keeping the dialectic tension between different perspectives.

Ogden's work on the concept of *reverie* is extensive. We manage to locate, among 44 articles[5] in which the author mentions the term, sketches of the first attempts of dialogue with the concept in two of his texts, one of them dated from 1988 and the other from 1992. However, in these first quotations, Ogden presents *reverie* in a way still very close to the original meaning postulated by Bion (1962) – as a state of receptiveness to the unconscious experience of the patient, similar to the receptiveness of the mother to the still unsymbolized experiences of the baby (Ogden, 1988). In 1992, he points to the condition of *reverie* in the mother, which may name and give shape to the experiences of the baby, from her interpretation of its internal states (Ogden, 1992).

However, as we understand it, the most original moment of his comprehension of *reverie* happens in 1994 with the texts *The Concept of Interpretative Action* (Ogden, 1994a) and *The Analytic Third: Working with Intersubjective Clinical Facts* (Ogden, 2013) in which it reaches higher and more creative flights, coming from the Bionion ground. In these texts, he narrates in a dense and vivid way a few *reveries* in the analytical encounter, presenting in the first person his immersion in the experience and offering handling of the situation in a consistent way, made possible as from the *reveries*.

This original and creative Ogdenian path is intensified in the following texts of his work – we may mention 1994, 1996 and 1997 as examples – in which we can see the origins of *reverie* as a concept, in a fluid continuity with Bionian ideas.

Based on that, we may think that Ogden "finds" in Bion a foundation that describes a way of nonverbal communication between minds, in which the analyst/mother metabolizes the primitive elements they receive from the analysand/baby. Therefore, daydreaming and somatic feelings are created from the alpha function, which is responsible for processing the still unsymbolized contents of the other, in themselves. On the other hand, mainly based on Winnicott, Ogden "creates" a type of *reverie* which is recontextualized. No longer limited to the infancy setting, according to Ogden, the analysis itself develops in the playing space between analysand's and analyst's the capacities of *reverie* (1997). Daydreaming originates and is contextualized in the dialectical movement that happens between therapist and patient.

Another important dialogue that Ogden weaves with the Bionian concept of *reverie* is its closeness with the idea of dream. Ogden brings back and gives a new context to dreaming in Bion as a way of processing emotional experiences. Freud (2019/1900) established the dream as an access to the unconscious and the symbolic contents, which are present in the oneiric images. Nonetheless, Bion points to the need to consider our own capacity to dream, that is, to create symbols from the living experience, as an acquired condition (and which could be lost). The essential process of the dream is not its content, but its "shape". Just like, in his work, Winnicott brings backthe importance of playing related to games, giving less importance to the content than to the process itself, Bion highlights the dreaming related to the dream (Coelho Junior and Figueiredo, 2018).

The essential part of dreaming, according to "Ogden's Bion", is the possibility of the subject to elaborate what was lived in representative elements: to transform beta elements into alpha elements. With that said, dreaming is no longer only about the activity that we do when we are asleep, because it happens during the sleep just as much as in the awakened life. While awake, we are only in touch with this activity in its "derivative form, for example, in reverie states occurring in an analytic session" (Ogden, 2005, p. 46). This sentence makes it evident that Ogden makes a connection between *reverie*, dreaming and alpha function, as supplementary processes related to the metabolization by the subject of their experiences in the world.

Clinical experience involves, in a great part, the act of shared dreaming. The analyst must "sustain over long periods of time a psychological state of receptivity to the patient's undreamt and interrupted dreams as they are lived out in the transference–countertransference" (Ogden, 2005, p. 5). According to this perspective, we may say that, just like Winnicott advocates viewing psychotherapy as two people playing together (Winnicott, 1991), Ogden may sustain, following Bion, that it is nothing but two people dreaming together.

In this context, "dreaming undreamed dreams" is an elaboration of the Bionian idea of *reverie* as the mother's condition to transform gross elements of experiences lived by the baby into others that are within the field of the "thinkable". A person who cannot dream is incapable of transforming their unprocessed experiences into chainable data, or "dream-thoughts" (Ogden, 2005, p. 47).

In an opening state, the subject experiences *reveries* that are created inside the relationship their subjectivity establishes with the other. Therefore, they are lived by them, but are also products of the dialectical tensions between the poles of this interaction, that is lived in/through them. This relational aspect of *reverie* justifies its clinical use by Thomas Ogden.

According to the author, the work of analysis is related to the experience of vitality. He realizes that vitalization and devitalization have a central and guiding role in the dialectics of the analytic situation, and he suggests that our psyche searches endlessly for experiences in which we may feel more fully human. The Ogdenian understanding of "being fully human" foresees being capable of genuinely being able of experiencing life with its pains, passions, fears and uncertainties.

In order to clarify what it means to be fully human, Ogden (1997) quotes a passage from Goethe's *The Faust* (1808), in which the leading figure made a pact with the devil and, in exchange for his soul, received from Mephistopheles an endless access to the forbidden pleasures and to the satisfaction of his phantasies. But Faust did not aspire to immortality or any other superhuman privileges. Instead, he sought to live exactly the human experience itself, submerged in floods of a world and a time full of happenings.

Just like this German masterpiece, we can think that what is done in analysis is to help the analysand to become more fully human. Therefore, Ogden goes on to bring up a passage in which Faust makes his desire explicit by saying:

> [...] and I'm resolved [that] my most inmost being shall share in what's the lot of all mankind that I shall understand their heights and depths, shall fill

my heart with all their joys and griefs, and so expand myself to theirs and, like them, suffer shipwreck too."

(Goethe, 1808, p. 46, apud Ogden, 1997, p. 32)

The analytic task, therefore, fundamentally involves "the effort of the analytic pair to help the analysand become human in a fuller sense than he has been able to achieve to this point" (Ogden, 1997, p. 15). In this sense, for the analyst to perform the important task of assisting their analysand to become more fully human, he must be implicated in the attempt of helping the analysand to expand the amount of emotions, feelings and thoughts generated from the relationships established not only in the present but also the past, with other humans, including their own analyst. From this perspective, Ogden sustains the idea that "in this effort to become more fully human that we are alive as analyst and analysand; it is in this experiment that the art of psychoanalysis lives" (1997, p. 19).

The Ogdenian thought conveys, therefore, the idea that the goal of analysis goes much further than solving intrapsychic problems or reducing emotional contents to symptomatology. Analysis favors the experience of being alive, which holds psychic forms of pain that we are commonly afraid of not being able to bear. The analyst must be available to assist his analysand in the difficult experience of living while being human, in all its complexity. We can see in Ogden's ideas an opening to endless possibilities related to the experiences lived in the analysis room. That is because, according to him, there are no limits in expansion, complexity, or intensity of feelings and thoughts, for what can be done in analysis, both for the analyst as well as for the analysand.

In this sense, Ogden postulates the importance of *reverie* as one of these phenomena lived in the analytic relationship, through which we put ourselves into a state of availability capable of keeping us, as analysts, receptive to access unconscious contents or, as Ogden (2005) says, dream the analysand's undreamed dreams.

Reverie in the sense it is perceived in the clinic is related by Ogden to Debussy's eponymous composition.[6] Ogden believes that music happens in the space between the musical notes, and, in psychoanalysis, the analytical dialogue happens between the spaces of the words said and the silence that resonates between analyst and analysand. It is in this interstice that *reveries* happen. According to the author (1997), *reveries* may be lived as rumination, daydreaming, sensations, perceptions, fantasies and images, which are built from the intersubjective encounter. Therefore, this experience is hardly discussed with others, since it is related to aspects not only of the patient, but also of the analyst himself. These contents are, many times, unsettling and even embarrassing. For this reason, the analyst may commonly face difficulties in making use of these *reverie* contents. Even though it is an intersubjective event, it is frequently associated with personal aspects of the analyst himself (Ogden, 1997).

According to Ogden, *reverie* is accompanied by sensorial and imagetic elements which take shape from the analytical encounter and he emphasizes that its use demands that the analyst tolerate feeling adrift of the contact with the unknown and the unknowable of the experience. The North American psychoanalyst also states that the use of *reverie* requires being cautious, so that there is no rush or eagerness to interpret such an unsettling experience.

Ogden (1997) claims that the experience of daydreaming is rarely "translatable", since any rushed attempts to translate it may easily implicate in a mistake, considering its unsettling aspects. According to him, the attempt to immediately interpret the analyst's daydreaming contents generally leads to shallow interpretations:

> The analyst's use of his reveries require a tolerance of the experience of being adrift. The fact that the "current" of reverie is carrying the analyst anywhere that is of any value at all to the analytic process is usually a retrospective discovery and is almost always unanticipated. The state of being adrift cannot be rushed to closure. The analyst must be able to end a session with a sense that the analysis is at a pause, at best, a comma in a sentence.
>
> (Ogden, 1997, pp. 160–161)

The session must be thought to be based on the emotions generated and not by the *reverie*'s contents themselves. Tolerating a state of not knowing keeps us open, awake and available, while facing the unpredictability of the analysis session and the disturbing feeling of being adrift. That said, Ogden makes an important point:

> Not knowing is a precondition for being able to imagine. The imaginative capacity in the analytic setting is nothing less than sacred. Imagination holds open multiple possibilities experimenting with them all in the form of thinking, playing, dreaming and in every other sort of creative activity.
>
> (Ogden, 2005, p. 26)

Even though *reveries* may look like daydreams exclusively from the analyst's internal world, they are intersubjective constructions, since they are created from the pairing of the analyst and the analysand. In the Ogdenian view, *reverie* includes mundane themes, bringing to the analytic setting elements of the analyst's personal and everyday life, but which come up from the imaginative capacity created in the analytic encounter.

Therefore, Ogden grants a dialectical conception[7] to the analytical situation, in which analyst and analysand create together an unconscious intersubjectivity. In this sense, intersubjectivity becomes the foundation and the center of the emotional experience between analyst and analysand, allowing for the transformation of psychic elements, not metabolized until then, into elements with the possibility of being thought by the analytic pair.

In a sort of limbo, analyst and analysand experience turbulence, indefinition, doubt. Moreover, even though it may cause such unsettling feelings, *reverie* is considered by Ogden (1997) an equivalent to an emotional compass, by which we are taken to experience an infinite amount of sensations and feelings, a flame that allows us to walk through still undiscovered paths.

Therefore, if the analyst can tolerate the unsettledness and make use of it, *reverie*, used as a compass in unknown territories, can guide us by indicating possible directions, destinies (or even traps) in the unpredictable and exclusive path created in the analytic encounter – from limbo to flame. As a result, even though *reverie* is almost always a disturbing experience, felt by the analyst to be a distraction, neglect, or flaw in his analytic function, it may be an important tool in the analysis room.

Reverie created and found, in and by the analytic third

Intersubjectivity is a central theme in the Ogdenian thought. In the book *Subjects of Analysis* (Ogden, 1994b), Thomas Ogden introduces the concept of the "intersubjective analytic third", which refers to the interaction of the subjectivities of analyst, analysand and of a third subjectivity: the analytic third. This would be a joint creation by the pair, while the analyst and analysand are created by the third. This analytic third (1998) sets the – potential – "space" in which analysis may happen.

Inspired by Winnicott and Bion, Ogden understands psychoanalysis as an exercise of two people that play and dream together, respectively. This middle ground created by analyst and analysand becomes the playground for the interaction of these two minds, which interact in overlapping *reverie* states (Ogden, 1997). The "shared dreaming" makes the session alive and indicates to both which is the emotional movement subjacent to the interaction.

Based on an interesting analogy inspired by the Winnicottian paradox that the mother is discovered and found by the baby, the *reverie* may be understood through the creation and encounter by the analytic third (Ribeiro, 2019). Winnicott's claim, that there cannot be a baby without the mother, may also be thought to correspond to the analyst and analysand, which together create a unity state that coexists in dialectical tension.

Therefore, in the Ogdenian perspective, *reverie* becomes, a creation and expression of the analytic third. As a mental imaginative capacity, *reverie* implicates mental and emotional permeability and availability to the psychic movement of the session's communication. From that, the analyst may think of its use in their interpretations. It is a way to grasp the analytic objects and also an expression of the awakened dream. To Ogden (1994), the intersubjective experience of the analytic third is captured by the *reveries* during the sessions.

Despite being a very intimate and interrelational construction, the analytic third is an asymmetrical,[8] ethical and creative construction between analyst and analysand. Psychoanalysis is made at each session, in the time and space of each intersubjective encounter. The analytic *setting* is the structure which favors the frame of all the elements and contents created there, jointly by analyst and analysand in a field which Ogden prefers to call "transferential-countertransferential". This is the field of the third subjectivity, which for the author is the most suitable term to elucidate the unconscious elements of the analyst in the session, since these are generated together, in an unconscious intersubjective construction of the analytic pair, in and by the analytic third.

Ogden supports the idea that one cannot consider transference and counter-transference as separate entities which only exist in response to one another. Other than that, they are aspects of an intersubjective totality which are experienced individually by both analyst and analysand. The analyst, immersed in the experience of the third, is capable of understanding more broadly the intersubjective facts that appear in the analytic situation. This understanding requires a sensitive, sophisticated and consistent type of attention from the analyst, so that the elements which are present in the analytic *setting* may be captured as contents generated intersubjectively by the analytic pair.

According to the author (Ogden, 1997), each encounter, and more precisely each instant, is experienced as a different aspect of the complex and intertwined group of emotions which constitute the analysand's internal world, and which make each of the analytical moments unique. This is because the analytical process constantly involves new creations of unconscious inter-subjective events that never existed before in the emotional life of either the analyst or the analysand.

Thomas Ogden also warns that, in analysis, it is necessary for us to be available as an object for the unconscious experiment of the analysand. We must also be open to the possibility of performing different roles in his unconscious life. This receptivity state (the origins of the creation of *reveries*) encompasses making the analyst's subjectivity available to a third analytical subjectivity which is neither the analyst's nor the analysand's.

Ogden (1997, p. 9) says "to consistently offer oneself in this way is no small matter: it represents an emotionally draining undertaking in which analyst and analysand each to a degree 'loses his mind' (his capacity to think and create experience as a distinctly separate individual)", and emphasizes that it is only after the end of the analytic process that both can "regain" their separate minds. Nonetheless, he stresses that these will not be the same as before, since people from a different time no longer exist after an analytical work is made. Analyst and analysand cannot be understood without each other. Therefore, new psychological entities are created and transformed by, in, and with the analytic third subject.

From "being with" to the shared dreaming

During a session, in a switching tone between surprise and astonishment, Paulo[9] interrupts me: "I just had the feeling that I dreamed you were telling me exactly that. What a weird feeling! I did not remember this before, but I do now … it must have been in some dream."

In the hiatus between words, the analyst's mind wanders: "We shall call it a dream then, Paulo." There was something there, before it was even said. A thought without a thinker, in Bionian terms. Something that is first dreamed and only later lived. They were no longer his dreams or my dreams. It was no longer possible to discern what was coming from the analyst or from the analysand. We dreamed together. We dreamed the session.

Surprise, astonishment, disclosure. A daydream, a dream. But whose was it? His, mine, ours. Yes, it was a dream dreamed by both. Shared, without being verbalized. Fluid communication that resonates, even without words. The unsayable, unthinkable being heard, metabolized … finally, captured.

In our first encounter, already in the waiting room while Paulo (dis) arranged himself to follow me, there was curiously a feeling of contemplation in myself … . As if I watched a baby trying to take its first steps, stumbling, unsettling. I kept myself there, contemplating that image: Paulo as a boy, the child in Paulo. For a fraction of a second, it came to my mind: "Where is his mother? Has the father come alone?" I immediately recall that this was not a child's analysis: "What a mess! Paulo is the new analysand, an adult!"

There I was, encapsulated by the intoxicating intensity of that daydream. I thought it best to avoid such strangely inviting thoughts and I decided to voluntarily return to Paulo, to the one presented materially in front of me – adult or as a child, it was no longer necessary to understand. It was only urgent that I could be capable of being available and receptive to a human being who was there.

Paulo starts the session by saying: "Someone recommended that the analysis was made with you … ." He shakes his head frantically and quickly corrects himself: " … I mean, that the analysis was made 'by you'!"

"With you" … those two words were echoing vibrantly in my mind. The image of the daydreamed child in the first minutes of my encounter with Paulo, whose mother was not present for the first session, rises up again. Does that mean Paulo was not the father, but actually the intuited child? A disorganized sketch of a scarce and disconnected thought was being created in the analyst's imagination. An unshaped unsymbolized thought, but which was wandering there, in that space between those minds … a thought trying to be found.

That child would come up in my mind and at the same time that he would make me confused and I would try to avoid him; he also seemed to become more and more vivid and captivating, arousing in myself a chain of affective emotions which were curious to me and, until then, incoherent.

The pictography captured in this clinical fragment is related to what Ogden defines as a new subjectivity created by the subjectivities of analyst and analysand: the intersubjective analytic third. This dynamic entity is lived as an experience in constant dialectical tension with the intersubjectivity generated in and by the analytic pair. According to Ogden, "it is through the (asymmetrical) experiencing of the analytic third by analyst and analysand that 'the drift' of the unconscious internal object world of the analysand is understood and (eventually) verbally symbolized" (1997, p. 154). The analyst's daydream is the capture of something unsaid, something that presented itself between the lines of the speech. It is exactly in the "in between" that the idea may be dreamed and, after that, thought by both.

Throughout Paulo's analytic process, by trying not to rush and by tolerating the non-immediate comprehension of ideas and images that are created in it by *reveries*, the analytic relationship started to be experienced as real and safe. From a route felt in a vitalized and containing space, it starts becoming possible to give meaning to Paulo's disturbance in pronouncing "with you", so soon, in such an initial relationship, still without any intimacy.

There are so many marks of unsymbolized emotional experiences lived by Paulo. Memories still not written in his psyche, thoughts still unthought, about experiences of helplessness, of an absent mother, lacking love. A lap that did not feel like home, that was not a container for his body, his feelings. Marks that caused him much trouble and resistance to, in fact, "be with", to allow himself to be in a different embrace and to be able to trust that there would be, in this one, contingence (until then, shallow). A new "lap" in which he would no longer slip in a liquid, unshaped way. Instead, one that could, finally, exist with shape and affection.

Even in fear and resistance, there was something "between" us from the very beginning. An opening to unconscious intersubjective communication, a mental state of receptivity which was prematurely experienced by Paulo, without him noticing. There was already a third, created (and simultaneously to be found) by analyst and analysand – a third element, in dialectical tension among the isolated subjectivities of analyst and analysand. And Paulo was, indeed, a child who presented himself to me in that first encounter. A scared infant, who was worried about what would happen in the encounter. Cornered and, at the same time, wishful, he let himself be in it. Paulo could then understand that I was there "with him" and "for him".

My availability for the encounter gradually created trust in our setting, establishing associations that arose. In Ogden's words:

> Analytic technique is guided by the effort to speak with the analysand about what it feels like for analyst and analysand to be with one another at that moment, it emphasizes the attempt to describe the most urgent fears that are shaping/constricting the analysand's capacity to experience that moment in a more fully human way.
>
> (Ogden, 1997, p. 217)

In this same work, Ogden presents his thoughts on the importance of dreaming our emotional experience. He also claims that dreaming our dreams is the way we can be capable of changing, growing, or transforming suffering. To the author, in the intersubjectivity created in analysis, both analyst and analysand engage with one another in the sense that they generate conditions so that both can become more capable of dreaming their undreamed dreams and interrupted dreams (or metaphorical nightmares). According to Ogden, these are the emotional experiences with which the patient is capable of performing a deeper unconscious analytic work about himself.

However, the patient's dreaming activity (their psychological elaboration of the unconscious) is interrupted in a moment where the capacity for dreaming is surpassed by the disturbing nature of what is being dreamed. At this point, the patient "wakes up", and "ceases to be able to continue doing unconscious psychological work" (Ogden, 2005, p. 24).

The dreams dreamed by the analysand and by the analyst during a session arise simultaneously from each subjectivity and the analytic third. This allows the analyst to have greater deepness related to the internal contents of his analysand and to tell him something that is true for the emotional experience (conscious and unconscious) in said moment. Therefore, this refers to a shared form of dreaming, by which one can exist more fully. As Ogden (2005, p. 23) claims, when we are capable of dreaming our experience, we are able to generate an emotional response to it, learn from it, and be changed by it.

With that said, by this intimate and trusting relationship found in the analytic experience, the conscious and unconscious contents from the mind of the analysand can be projected to the mind of the analyst (projective identification), so that they can be metabolized. This is how *reverie* happens, by being experienced by both, in the experience of the analytic third.

Ogden writes: "The generative movement between dream and reverie, between reverie and interpretation, between interpretation and experience in (and of) the analytic third, are for me the heart of that which is unique to the feeling of aliveness of analytic experience" (Ogden, 1997, p. 151). He claims that what happens in the analysis room has an important quality: the directionality that arises from the fact that psychoanalysis is, first and foremost, a therapeutic undertaking with the aim of increasing the analysand's ability to be alive to experience the human experience to the fullest.

Based on this view, it is clear how important the analytic space becomes for the experience of being and to be alive. The analytic work summons us to be sensitive and available, which allows for an opening of paths to a vitalizing experience. By means of a living and fluid psychoanalysis, Ogden puts us in contact with an implicated clinic, which takes shape from the presence of a receptive, human form of listening in the analytic experience. The biggest goal in it is to favor living while human, a process which foresees an expansion of the mind in a creative way.

Therefore, the sonority between the notes, the echoes between the words, the sayable and the unthinkable may be dreamed in the experience of, and in, the intersubjective analytic third, as well as in the opening and receptivity that the analyst makes available in their listening. And when one can dream, one can live their own emotional experience, learn from it, and transform it.

Notes

1 This chapter was written based on the research that is comprised in the Master's theses of authors Ana Fátima Aguiar and Pedro Hikiji Neves, in the Psychology Institute of the University São Paulo. Their advisor is Professor Marina F. R. Ribeiro.

2 Ogden expands this idea in his article "How I talk with my patients" (Ogden, 2018).

3 André Green, Antonino Ferro, Anne Alvarez, Christopher Bollas and René Roussillon are also considered transmatrix authors.

4 To Ogden (1994), the term "intersubjectivity" is also related to the idea of the analytic third (which we discuss further). This third comes from the interaction of the minds of analyst and analysand, as a product of the dialectics created by (and between) the subjectivities of each of them in the analytical encounter. Therefore, the Ogdenian intersubjectivity is the third subjectivity in the field, generated from both of them.

5 This number refers to the results, in English, of the search for the term "*reverie*" in the *Psychoanalytic Electronic Publishing* database (https://pep-web.org/, retrieved in December 20, 2022), which collates countless international psychoanalytical publications.

6 Claude Debussy (1862–1918) was an important French musician who, with his poetic and impressionist style, wrote a piano composition called "Reverie"; its soothing melody created a fluid musical dynamic which resonates to a dreaming, wandering state.

7 To Ogden (1994), dialectic is a process in which opposite elements create, preserve and deny one another, each in a dynamic and mutative relationship with the other. The dialectic movement is directed to integrations "that never fully happen" (p. 14).

8 The term "asymmetry" refers to the analysand's ethics in conducting the analysis, since they should be available and technically prepared to be in touch with the unknowable of the experience, as well as with regressed states of mind. They must also be capable of tolerating the turbulence and the feeling of not-knowing. Even in face of that, they must be able to keep themselves as a container for the contents of the analysand, being capable of performing the analytic work from this experience. Even though this asymmetrical aspect exists in this relationship, the minds of analyst and analysand in session work symmetrically because both are submersed in the same emotions in the analysis room. Therefore, we can understand that the mental functioning of the analytic pair is in constant interaction. The emotional experience lived in this context is an observation field for the analyst, which is an important technical tool for conducting the analysis (Ribeiro, 2020, p. 134).

9 The clinical material used here was taken from one of the author's analytic experience. In it, the analysand's name, as well as the other fragments of this clinical case will be described from a fictional dimension (Tanis, 2015). Ogden (2005, p. 110) suggests that "The analytic writer is continually bumping up against a paradoxical truth: analytic experience (which cannot be said or written) must be transformed into 'fiction' (an imaginative rendering of an experience in words), if what is true to the experience is to be conveyed to the reader."

References

BION, W. R. (1962). *O aprender com a experiência*. Rio de Janeiro, RJ: Imago, 1991.

COELHO JUNIOR, N. and FIGUEIREDO, L. C. (2018). *Matrizes do Adoecimento Psíquico e Estratégias de Cura*. São Paulo, SP: Blucher.

FREUD, S. (2019). *A interpretação dos sonhos*. L&PM Editores (originally published in 1900).

OGDEN, T. H. (1988). On the dialectical structure of experience—some clinical and theoretical implications. *Contemporary Psychoanalysis 24*: 17–45.

OGDEN, T. H. (1992) The dialectically constituted/decentred subject of psychoanalysis. II. The contributions of Klein and Winnicott. *International Journal of Psychoanalysis 73*: 613–626

OGDEN, T. H. (1994a). The concept of interpretive action. *The Psychoanalytic Quarterly 63*(2): 219–245.

OGDEN, T. H. (1994b). *Subjects of analysis*. Northvale, NJ and London: Jason Aronson Inc.

OGDEN, T. H. (1996). *Os sujeitos da psicanálise (C. Berliner, Trad.)*. São Paulo: Casa do psicólogo.

OGDEN, T. H. (1997). *Reverie and interpretation: Sensing something human*. Northvale, NJ: Jason Aronson.

OGDEN, T. H. (2005). *This art of psychoanalysis: Dreaming undreamt dreams and interrupted cries*. London and New York: Routledge.

OGDEN, T. H. (2010). *Esta Arte da Psicanálise: sonhando sonhos não sonhados e gritos interrompidos. Trad. Daniel Bueno*. Porto Alegre: Artmed.

OGDEN, T. H. (2013). The analytic third: Working with intersubjective clinical facts (1994). Relational Psychoanalysis, Volume 14: *The Emergence of a Tradition*, 459.

OGDEN, T. H. (2018). How I talk with my patients. *The Psychoanalytic Quarterly*, 87(3), 399–413.

RIBEIRO, M. F. R. (2016). Uma reflexão conceitual entre identificação projetiva e enactment. O analista implicado. *Caderno de psicanálise, 38*(35), Rio de Janeiro, RJ.

RIBEIRO, M. F. R. (2019). Alguns apontamentos acerca da função psicanalítica da personalidade no campo analítico. A narrativa do analista e a do escritor. *Caderno de Psicanálise* (CPRJ), *41*(40), 169–187.

RIBEIRO, M. F. R. (2020). Sobre reciprocidade e mutualidade no conceito de terceiro analítico de Thomas Ogden. In: *Ferenczi: Inquietações Clínico-políticas* (pp. 133–140). São Paulo, SP: Zagadoni.

TANIS, B. (2015). A escrita, o relato clínico e suas implicações éticas na cultura informatizada. *Revista Brasileira de Psicanálise* [online], *49*(1), 179–192.

WINNICOTT, D. W. (1991). *Playing and reality*. London: Routledge.

11 The Winged Words of Thomas H. Ogden[1]

Fátima Flórido Cesar and
Marina F. R. Ribeiro

This chapter discusses Thomas Ogden's thinking regarding the understanding of the ideas of vitality and devitalization in the analytical process, and primarily about the importance of the analyst's language, which in this text we call "winged words". We would like to introduce a first possibility of meaning to such winged words: the imprecision and uncertainty installed in what we often call winged *words* allow the vitality of the phenomenon to be maintained, with rips and slippages – that is, the experience of the analytical encounter. Words and silence that vivify by releasing the bonds of the desire to know everything. The verb that flies and escapes and that only in the refusal of certainties sustains the living experience. The wandering words that, in the poetic saying of Manoel de Barros,[2] promote inventions and escape from grammar, are the only ones capable of widening our limits, whether they are tall tales or nicknames. Widening our limits serves us as a translation into a *poiesis* of what Ogden emphasizes with significant consideration as the purpose of analysis: to help the patient become the most "fully human". Vitality is part of this horizon: to expand the ability to feel alive. We will transit through becoming alive and human, and through the discourse of language. Ogden (2016) writes that "language is not just a basket in which ideas are carried: the way in which language is used to state an idea is inseparable from the content of the idea" (p. 8). Not any language, but a certain one, the winged words, which we intend to present in such a way to allow the reach of this horizon. Alternatively, we could say in the plural form: the horizons of the human.

Before we specifically engage with the proposed theme, it is important to mention, based on the introduction of Ogden's book, *Creative readings* (2012), how he incorporates the ideas and readings he makes of other authors of psychoanalysis, or even of any reading. His reading is an experience: he writes what he lives when reading them. In this particular book, he offers a *creative reading* of important works by Freud, Fairbairn, Isaacs, Winnicott, Loewald, Searles and Bion.

Ogden states that creative reading constitutes an experience in which something is actively done with the text, "making it [the text] our own, interpreting it in a way that adds something to the text that had not been there before we

DOI: 10.4324/9781003423188-11

have read it" (Ogden, 2012, p. 2). Further on, he adds that when he reads, he tries to be taken by the writer's work: when reading a text by Melanie Klein, he becomes Kleinian. Similarly, when re-reading Winnicott's *"Fear of breakdown"* (2016), as we will also present in this chapter, he presents himself as Winnicottian and, from this point, develops his own ideas about the mentioned text.

Ogden made a creative reading of seminal concepts from the works of several psychoanalysts, and he advises the reader to decide who to give credit for their inferences:

> While the words on the page remain the same, what changes when I am successful in reading creatively are the meanings of the words and sentences, meanings that have been waiting to be found, but have never until the present moment found a reader to discover them, to be changed by them, and to change those potential meanings in the process of discovering them.
>
> (Ogden, 2012, p. 10)

We are left with the suggestion of reading and writing as an experience. When we wrote this text, we made a bet that our writing could be taking place in a creative way: that we have incorporated Ogden's ideas in our own way, as he did with several seminal authors of psychoanalysis. We hope that our readers will also make themselves available for a creative reading, and that it will be lived as an experience.

The living psychoanalytic language of Thomas Ogden

We now return to Thomas Ogden's view that the feeling of vitality and devitalization has great importance in the transference-countertransference, considering it the most important measure of what occurs during the analytic session. We would also like to address his emphasis and appreciation for the centrality of language in the therapeutic process: the vitality of words and vitality in words. We name the words with such power, within Ogden's clinical style, as "winged words". Already at the beginning of the book *Reverie and interpretation* (1997d), the adequacy of the choice of the term "winged" is announced:

> Words and sentences, like people, must be allowed a certain slippage. I do not mean to suggest that words, sentences (and human beings) can be said to mean (or be) anything we wish them to mean (or be). Rather, I am drawing attention to the stifling effect on imagination of our efforts to define, to specify with ever increasing precision, what we mean (who we are). Imagination depends on the play of possibilities. In this volume, words and sentences at their best will be only loosely "fastened to the page".
>
> (Ogden, 1997a, p. 5)

This looseness represents words with wings – winged – and to delve into Ogden's thoughts on language, we will make use of the following texts: "On the use of language" (1997b), "How I talk with my patients" (2018/2022), "On language and truth in psychoanalysis" (2022), "On talking-as-dreaming" (2007). References from the book *Reverie and interpretation* (1997d) are also present in this text, from which we will start to articulate the living word to the living analysis – the vertex present around which, the analytic process unfolds, as we mentioned above.

When was the last time an analyst and a patient felt the analysis alive? It is with this question that Ogden begins the chapter "Analyzing forms of aliveness and deadness" (1997c) in the book *Reverie and interpretation*. The author emphasizes the need for creative freedom and spontaneity in order to respond to the analysand from their own experiences. A living analysis and a living language enable the vitalization of the patient – in fact, of the analytic pair – constituting a counterpoint to dead language, to an analytic encounter plasticized by dogmas or paralysis of the pair. A living analysis requires that the analyst must be free to experiment, abandoning the stagnant path of prescribed forms: a variety of attempts must occur, driven by the curiosity that unites both participants in an active and mobile perspective of exercising themselves. Openness to the unprecedented ensures what Ogden highlights as the maintenance of experimentation, when paths are unpredictable, shifting, and monotony has no place. Therefore, we must avoid paralysis and a state of leading nowhere, when knowledge is transmitted from analyst to patient in an extremely sterile manner.

But what constitutes a living analysis? How can we guide the analytic process in this direction? In what way will we be able to track the movements of vitality and devitalization occurring in the session? These are crucial questions that awaken us both ethically and technically to the way we deal with periods of "limbo", "lukewarmness", deviations from necessary vitality, and seek to steer the encounter towards what Ogden points out as the main therapeutic purpose:

> I believe that every form of psychopathology represents a specific type of limitation of the individual's capacity to be fully alive as a human being. The goal of analysis from this point of view is larger than that of the resolution of unconscious intrapsychic conflict, the diminution of symptomatology, the enhancement of reflective subjectivity and self-understanding, and the increase of one's sense of personal agency. Although one's sense of being alive is intimately intertwined with each of the above-mentioned capacities, I believe that the experience of aliveness is a quality that is superordinate to these capacities and must be considered as an aspect of the analytic experience in its own terms.
>
> (Ogden, 1997c, p. 26)

Assisting the patients in expanding their experience of feeling alive (considering that some do not even achieve such a capacity) thus constitutes the main horizon of analysis, without disregarding other achievements. Complementing this goal in a unique way, Ogden highlights the work of the analytic pair to help the patient become more human than they have been until now – "it is a requirement of the species as basic as the need for food and air" (Ogden, 1997a, p. 15) – and goes beyond survival. Being alive is therefore linked to becoming human, which is very different from simply surviving.

The capacity to be alive, therefore, encompasses the possibility of experiencing the various ways of being in the world and accessing the various facets of our being – joys and sorrows – including knowing how to submerge and emerge from shipwrecks. It is what leads us to belonging to the human species: we link here the feeling of being alive with experiencing human emotions as widely as possible. Ogden emphasizes, however, that the inability to be fully human is part of all humanity; in desperation, we make "silent deals" (Ogden, 1997a, p. 17) – mostly unconscious – which would be pathological solutions. Thus, to a large extent, we stop becoming human, being able to sink into the inhuman – replacing life with modes of existence that are neither human nor alive. Plastic ways of living: this is the core of the psychopathology thought by the author, as we understand it. The result is not life, but an imitation of life and human experience: "a form of unconscious self-limitation of one's capacity to experience being alive as a human being" (Ogden, 1997a, p. 18).

We recognize in Ogden the fundamental importance he attributes to language as a pathway to grasp and convey the sense of vitality in the analytic setting. We suggest that the analyst must actively struggle with language in an effort to create ideas and phrases and find their own voice to articulate them. The struggle to convey one's own experience with words, and with one's own voice, is a significant part of what constitutes being alive in the analytic relationship (Ogden, 1997b). In order for the analysis to become a human event, it is necessary for both us, as analysts, and our analysands to make use of simple and living words – those that emerge from our own voice, not determined by dogmas, analytic prescriptions, techniques, or schools.

However, we do acknowledge, just like Ogden, that it is not easy to speak simply, with a voice that sounds spontaneous, human, not "therapeutic" (Ogden, 1997a, p. 12), so that we can encompass the countless ways of feeling and being, transiting between the ups and downs of human emotion, even reaching the edge of precipices.

But what constitutes a living communication? We understand that it is about inhabiting a field of imprecisions, of non-fixity of meanings (as we referred to at the beginning), of constant movement, so that the word presents itself differently in the course of encounters, showing itself, at every moment, as new and changeable, just like life. This is how therapeutic encounters should take place, free from paralysis and facilitated by a language of ever-changing uncertainties. This is the only way in which we can inhabit a state of lucidity, always precarious, as twilight – however, capable of constituting an offer of possible fertile shelter in the precariousness of existence. Paradoxically, in what does not close or conclude, in what little is known. On an opposite direction, stagnant language, linked to the ideology of analytical schools, loses its main task, which is to convey the sense of living human experience, highlighting the lack of vitality. In Ogden's words:

> Analytic language that is ideological is no longer alive because the answers to the questions being raised are known by the analyst from the outset and the function of language has been reduced to the conveying of that knowledge to the analysand.
>
> (Ogden, 1997b, p. 219)

In this type of theoretical interpretive speech, the analyst's imagination is missing, and it seems that he has lost his capacity for original thought, delegating his mind and his use of language to another one (real or imaginary), often without realizing it: "Such communications are indeed frightening ones that may lead the analysand to attempt to shield the analyst from awareness that the analyst has in a sense 'lost his mind'" (Ogden, 1997b, p. 221). Therefore, the author contrasts the living word with dead language, a dry therapeutic rhetoric: "The analyst's speech must be the creation of a person who is alive in that moment. Living human speech is as difficult to come by in the analyst's spoken use of language as it is in written prose or verse" (Ogden, 1997a, p. 12).

We are increasingly delving into Ogden's thinking about the importance of language as a means of bringing vitality to the analyst-analysand encounter: the occurrence of a human experience, as well as being in touch with the emotional truth: "language is not simply a package in which communications are wrapped, but the medium in which experience is brought to life in the process of being spoken or written" (Ogden, 1997b, p. 201).

It is necessary, therefore, to safeguard imprecision, not to give pre-packaged answers, not to arrive at the exact meaning, not to know too much. We are in the human field, of what is in constant motion – we, inexact and imprecise beings. To access this experience of unstable nature, it is necessary to develop a language that reveals it, that brings it to life:

> The analytic discourse requires of the analytic pair the development of metaphorical language adequate to the creation of sounds and meanings that reflect what it feels like to think, feel, and physically experience (in short to be alive as a human being to the extent that one is capable) at a given moment.
>
> (Ogden, 1997b, pp. 208–209)

The analyst, when creating metaphorical statements that constitute interpretations should not be invasive in order to try to demonstrate abilities with words. In short, we must develop the ability to "display of a 'feeling for words' and the capacity to create 'feeling through words'"[3] (Ogden,1997b, p. 209).

It is clear that what happens in the analytical setting, when it comes to vitality and devitalization, requires us to avoid the arid word "dismetaphorized", explanatory, causalistic. Instead, we should invest in cultivating words capable of creating and capturing human experience, which allow a wide range of emotions to come up: this is vitality/vitalization.

With that said, just like Ogden, we understand that language has a central importance in psychoanalysis; especially if our goal is to "help the analysand effect lasting psychological change that will enable him to become more fully human" (Ogden, 1997b, p. 216), describing even the most urgent fears (psychic pain) that prevent him from experiencing this encounter.

We acknowledge the close link between vitalization and vitality to living language, to maintaining the imaginative capacity of the analyst and his own mind, to creating his own speech and his own voice. This creation is seen by Ogden (1997b, p. 224) as an "act of freedom". Dead and stereotyped language, with speech being emitted only through commonplace: this is how interpretations lose vitality, "pre-packaged analytic theories being delivered by nobody in particular to nobody in particular" (Ogden, 1997b, p. 221).

Just as we speak of "imitation of life", we witness here the "imitation of analysis" (Ogden, 1997b, p. 223) – a coated, plasticized form of analysis that prioritizes certainty and knowledge instead of the provisional, the unstable sense. That is, paralysis and fixity in opposition to movement, to change, or to what surprises. We must not forget, therefore, that the speech with each patient is unique: different tones of voice, tunings, volume, cadences, syntax and choice of words resonate in the analysis room.

True and intimate conversation walks side by side: "the flow of conversation is a creation that only this patient and this analyst (the analyst I am becoming in the analysis) could bring to life in this particular way" (Ogden, 2016, p. 3). As opposed to a decoding type of language, the use of metaphorical and poetic language brings to life emotions not yet experienced. That is, it creates a new element between analyst and analysand, thus expanding the area of intimacy of the analytical pair. The points the author highlights bring up the novelty of each analytical conversation. If the analysis does not happen for this particular patient, it becomes generic and impersonal for both participants. This special way for the pair to meet is a condition for maintaining vitality in the analytical setting. Otherwise, boredom and aridity can dominate the scene.

What do we do with people who come to us for analysis?

Ogden (2014) asks this question and answers it: each patient brings to the analysis the feeling that in an important sense he "died" in childhood, or at a later stage, and he hopes that the analyst will help him restore "his unlived life". Winnicott also warns us that the source of psychic death is a series of events that occurred in childhood, which involved "primitive agonies" (Winnicott, 1960–1963), which the patient cannot bear. Threatened by such terrifying experiences, the "patient absents himself from his life", thus protecting himself from a psychic collapse and a psychosis. Paradoxically, when terrifying events cannot be experienced, they end up generating such a psychic state that an "unlived life" persists.

Ogden (2014) points out that we all have unlived aspects of our life that were very painful to be experienced. The "unlived" remains as forms of limitations in our personality. The author emphasizes that we are always involved in the unconscious work of dreaming – awake or sleeping, alone or with others – with the aim of integrating the unlived aspects of our life. Such ideas interest us to the extent that they give us the analytical task to develop a living language that enables the work of restoring the patient's unlived life.

In the text "Fear of breakdown and the unlived life", Ogden (2014) establishes a fertile dialogue with Winnicott's text, entitled "Fear of breakdown" (2016), highlighting that it is inherent to the human existence, as mentioned above, the persistence of portions of life that have not yet been lived, and that urge for integration in order for the individuals to complete themselves – to become what they are. Making his own interpretation of Winnicott's concept of breakdown, Ogden (2014) refers to the rupture of the mother-baby bond, with the baby being thrown into an extreme condition of helplessness and threatened with non-existence. However, he warns that this is not a psychotic outbreak, as psychosis is a defense against the experience of rupture. When isolated from the mother, the baby makes use of the psychotic defense of disintegration, as a paradoxical resource to free himself from the agony that arises from not being able to organize himself, thus producing a state of self-annihilation. As the baby did not have enough psychic constitution to experience the breaking of the mother-baby bond that occurred in childhood, the individual lives in fear of a collapse that has already happened, but which has not been experienced.

Ogden (2014) expands on Winnicott's thinking, assuming that what encourages the patient to find the source of the fear of breakdown is the feeling that parts of him are missing and that he needs to find them to become whole: what remains of the patient's life is mainly an unlived life. Here, we recognize what Ogden highlights as one of the most important tasks of analysis: the individual, not having experienced parts of what happened in early childhood, is urged to claim these parts, in order to complete himself through the integration of as much as possible of his unlived (unexperienced) life. This is a universal need – the need to have the opportunity to become the person with the potential to be, which is inherent to the individuals. We must emphasize that Winnicott's (2016) hypothesis is that the fear of breakdown is a fear of a collapse that has already happened, but was not experienced. Expanding this thought, Ogden (2014) highlights that, in different degrees, we all go through relevant breakdowns in the mother-baby bond and defend ourselves from them through the activation of psychotic defensive organizations.

We return here to the importance of the ability to be alive and, from this idea, the need for the analyst to help the analysand feel more fully alive through the integration of aspects of the unlived life; being central the use of language in a lively way, in such a way as to favor the processes of vitalization. Staying alive in our experiences constitutes the basis for the beginning of a full existence. However, at some moments, we all lose this capacity, becoming unable to feel that we are alive within ourselves or for the world around us. Limitations (of the ability to feel joy, to love one or all of our children, to be generous, to forgive someone) constitute aspects of our unlived life and refer to either what we could not experience or continue to be unable to do so. The search for the unlived is a universal condition: resuming lost parts of ourselves. Thus, the purpose of analysis, Ogden (2014) responds, is to help the patient live his unlived life in transference-countertransference.

However, feeling alive can be too painful for patients with acute forms of fear of a breakdown, as this points out to how much of their life they could not live: life was taken from them, which generates extreme pain. Here, we return to emphasize the importance of the living word to help the patient live his unlived life: always within a dimension in which the experiment and psychic creativity present themselves in a non-static way. Helping the patient live his unlived life, as mentioned before is the objective of the analysis. This is intertwined with the use of language, as long as it is structured in such a way that favors being in touch with the truth, allowing the word to reach the patient.

But what does a living language consist of?

We now move on to the question: what type of language is capable of reaching the patients in a way that helps them become what they are? We shall continue with the comprehension of what a living word is, one that can help the patients recover parts of their unlived life, a "winged word" with the power to lead them to become fully human;[4] paying more attention to how to speak than what to speak. For this, we will present the text "How I talk with my patients",[5] in which the author begins with the following communication:

Perhaps the most important clinical questions, and the most difficult ones for me as a practicing psychoanalyst, are those not so much concerned with what I say to my patients, as they are with how I talk with my patients. In other words, my focus over the years has moved from **what I mean to how I mean**. Of course, the two are inseparable, but in this chapter I place emphasis on the latter. I will discuss problems and possibilities spawned by the recognition that we can never know the patient's experience; the impossibility of generalizing about how we talk with patients given that it is incumbent upon the analyst to reinvent psychoanalysis with each patient; the analyst's approach to the patient's fear of psychic change; the way in which the analyst's "off-ness," his misunderstandings and misstatements may foster creative expression on the part of both patient and analyst; and the ways in which describing experience, as opposed to explaining it, better fosters discourse that addresses the unconscious level of what is occurring in the analysis.

(Ogden, 2022, p. 57, original emphasis)

The text seeks, therefore, to shed light on the use of words, as well as on the need for us to be silent, in such a way that we reach the patient, remembering the importance of avoiding the use of language that invites the patient to predominantly engage in conscious secondary-process thinking, when unconscious dimensions of thought are what is requested. To this end, he proposes that we use more *description* as opposed to *explanation*, in order to facilitate the analytical process. Similarly, certainty on the part of the analyst hinders both the analytical process and the patient's potential for psychic growth.

Just as the primary process is inseparable from the secondary process, what to say and how to say are equally linked. However, emphasis will be given to the latter, which the author names as the analyst's "out of self", his misunderstandings. He also emphasizes that, in the analytical encounter, describing the experience as opposed to explaining it facilitates the approach to what occurs in the unconscious. The way we speak with the patient takes precedence over what we want to say, Ogden (2022) emphasizes. It is therefore emphasized that, in the analytical encounter, describing the experience in opposition to the explanation facilitates the approach to what occurs in the unconscious. The paradoxical thinking continues when he states that:

Thus, in talking with patients, my own experience is incommunicable; the experience of the patient, inaccessible: I can never know the experience of the patient. Words and physical expression fall far short of communicating the patient's or my own lived experience. Nonetheless, the patient and I may be able to communicate something like our lived experiences by re-presenting the experience. This may involve using language that is particular to each of us and to the emotional event that is occurring, for example, by means of metaphor, irony, hyperbole, rhythm, rhyme, wit, slang, syntax, and so on, as well as bodily expression such as shifts in speaking tone, volume, and tempo, and quality of eye contact.

(Ogden, 2022, pp. 58–59)

Indeed, from this perspective, we immediately recognize something far from plasticized words and acts, a multiplicity of forms and possibilities of communication-words and acts with wings, in the sense of exchanges in the direction of unconscious freedom and the expansion of becoming human. The gap between minds, as the author names it, or the division between the subjectivity of the patient and that of the analyst, is not to be overcome, because

[…] it is a space in which a dialectic of separateness and intimacy may give rise to creative expression. In the analytic setting, if communicating individual experience were somehow possible, the patient and I would be robbed of the need/opportunity to creatively imagine the experiences of the other.

(Ogden, 2022, p. 58)

Another paradox is pointed out: the parts left out from communications open a gap where we may be able to fill this space between ourselves and the others. Ogden warns us that, once it is not possible to know the experience of our patients, everything will depend on what is happening at that moment between the individuals of the analytical pair. Now that we have addressed more deeply how the gap between the minds does not need to be overcome, we shall continue with the author:

This divide between the patient's subjectivity and my own is not an impediment to be overcome; it is a space in which a dialectic of separateness and intimacy may give rise to creative expression. In the analytic setting, if communicating individual experience were somehow possible, the patient and I would be robbed of the need/opportunity to creatively imagine the experiences of the other. Paradoxically, the parts that are missing, the parts left out of our communications open a space in which we may be able, in some way, to bridge the gap between ourselves and others. The patient's experience of being creative in the act of communicating is an essential part of the process of his "dreaming himself more fully into existence" (Ogden, 2004, p. 858), coming into being in a way that is uniquely his own.

(Ogden, 2022, p. 58)

The impossibility of knowing another person's experience leads to important ways to how Ogden talks with his patients: he suggests we avoid naming what they are feeling, limiting ourselves to saying what we are thinking and feeling. Thus, he clarifies:

When I do speak with a patient about what I sense is happening emotionally in the session, I might say something like: "While you were talking [or during the silence], this room felt like a very empty place [or peaceful place, or confusing place, and so on]." In phrasing things in this way, I leave open the question of who is feeling the emptiness (or other feelings). Was it the patient, or I, or something the two of us have unconsciously created together (the "analytic field" [Civitarese, 2008, 2016; Ferro, 2005, 2011] or the "analytic third" [Ogden, 1994])? Almost always, it is all three—the patient and I as separate individuals, and our unconscious co-creations.

(Ogden, 2022, pp. 58–59)

Asking questions like "Why were you absent yesterday?", for example, directs the patient to converse in a superficial, conscious manner, in terms of cause and effect, that is, according to the secondary process. When Ogden realizes he is asking this type of question, he questions himself about what might be happening in unconscious terms that might be scaring him. Certainty will also negatively interfere with the analytical process when parents are blamed – both by the patient and by the analyst – for the patient's current emotional situation. Although the patient may have been severely neglected, Ogden emphasizes the importance of not focusing his illness by linking it to parental guilt. If we proceed in this way, we take the risk of stealing from the patient the possibility of experiencing his life in a more complex and human way, which may even include an understanding of the sense of responsibility for the suffering experienced in childhood.

So, instead of thinking about a technique derived from ideas linked to particular schools of analytical thought, anchored in a feeling of certainty, Ogden thinks of clinical style as his own creation, a living process that originates from the analyst's experience and personality. Thus, we are outlining the vitalizing function of the analyst based on his personality, open to imprecision and uncertainty as a source of creativity. Instead of using the term "technique", let us think about developing a clinical style, as Ogden suggests:

> I think of "analytic style" as one's own personal creation that is loosely based on existing principles of analytic practice, but more importantly is a living process that has its origins in the personality and experience of the analyst.
>
> (Ogden, 2022, p. 59)

Once again, we emphasize here the necessity of simplicity in communication, rooted in rich veins of complexity. We are referring to succinct descriptions of states of feelings. However, we bring a paradox: simplicity is equally pregnant with wealth and requires psychic work from the pair, so that, from speech, an opening for psychic expansion can emerge, not only from the patient but also from the analyst. The scholar style can flirt with arrogance, which leads to destruction and rupture of the bond. Arrogance prevents the encounter. Here is an example of a description given by Ogden (2022): if a patient arrives at the session terrified, Ogden was used to asking: "What terrifies you?" In a recent experience in which a patient shared her fear of coming to see him, he said: "Of course you are" – a description exactly as it is, a way to welcome her fantasies instead of presenting reassurance or logical reasons typical of the secondary process. Welcoming the density of emotional experience requires that we are open to our own inner resources, a density that comes in the form of lightness, words with wings. In the example above, the backstage (Ogden's most stretched thought, but not dissociated from strolling through mutual unconscious communication between patient and analyst); that is, what comes in parentheses ("what you are feeling now seems just natural"), gained brief reaching words: "Of course you are." Thus, highlighting the importance of simplicity and humility:

I have also found that a shift from explaining to describing facilitates the analytic process by freeing both patient and me of the need to understand. "Merely" describing, as opposed to "discovering causes" for what is happening, reflects my sense of humility in the face of all that is "humanly understandable or humanly ununderstandable" (Jarrell, 1955, p. 62) in the lives of my patients and in the life of the analysis.

(Ogden, 2022, p. 61)

The author's statement, that "we all speak with a simultaneous wish to be understood and to be misunderstood, and that we listen to others both with the desire to understand and to misunderstand" (Ogden, 2022, p. 69), is very interesting. The desire not to be understood meets the need to maintain a facet of the self that remains isolated, as Winnicott (2016) states. According to Ogden, the desire to be understood carries a desire for closure. On the other hand, the desire to be misunderstood carries the desire to dream with oneself and not be seen by the analyst. The psychoanalyst states: "Respecting the patient's need for self-discovery places a demand on me not to 'know too much'" (Winnicott 1963, p. 189, quoted by Ogden 2022, p. 69). We are also enchanted by Ogden's following saying:

The work of understanding carries the danger of "killing" an experience that was once alive in an analytic session. Once an experience has been "figured out," it is dead. Once a person is "understood," he is no longer interesting, no longer a living, unfolding, mysterious person.

(Ogden, 2018/2022, p. 70)

Talking as dreaming

In the article, "On talking-as-dreaming" (Ogden, 2007), discusses how to guide language in cases where the patient is unable to dream. This challenge becomes the most urgent focus of the therapeutic process. He emphasizes that "The area of 'overlap' of the patient's dreaming and the analyst's dreaming is the place where analysis occurs" (Winnicott, 1971, p. 38, quoted by Ogden, 2007, p. 576) The patient who is dreaming manifests expressing himself through free associations. Meanwhile the analyst's awake-dreaming state presents itself in the form of daydreams.

But what constitutes a dream? We shall go on with the author:

I view dreaming as the most important psychoanalytic function of the mind: where there is unconscious 'dream-work,' there is also unconscious 'understanding-work' (Sandler, 1976, p. 40); where there is an unconscious 'dreamer who dreams the dream' (Grotstein, 2000, p. 5), there is also an unconscious 'dreamer who understands the dream' (p. 9). If this were not the case, only dreams that are remembered and interpreted in the analytic setting or in self-analysis would accomplish psychological work. Few analysts today would support the idea that only remembered and interpreted dreams facilitate psychological growth.

(Ogden, 2007, p. 576)

Ogden always emphasizes that psychoanalysis needs to be reinvented with each patient, like an experiment, when the analyst and patient create ways of speaking that are unique to the pair at a certain moment in the analysis.

When the analyst and patient cannot dream together, Ogden makes use of a form of speech that may seem "non-analytical", because both are dreaming about things like books, poems, movies, the taste of chocolate and so on:

> Despite appearances, it has been my experience that such 'unanalytic' talk often allows a patient and analyst who have been unable to dream together to begin to be able to do so. I will refer to talking of this sort as 'talking-as-dreaming.' Like free association (and unlike ordinary conversation), talking-as-dreaming tends to include considerable primary process thinking and what appear to be non sequiturs (from the perspective of secondary process thinking).
>
> (Ogden, 2007, pp. 575–576)

However, talking as dreaming is distinct from common conversations and requires the participation of the analyst which involves a certain analytical way of being with the patient; being the aim here to help the patient become more fully alive. Once again, we notice his concern to circumscribe the analytical task within the field of helping the patient to become as fully alive and human as possible. These meanings both overlap and guide the goal of Ogden's clinic. But what makes talking as dreaming different from a common conversation? Here is Ogden's answer:

> What makes talking-as-dreaming different is that the analyst engaged in this form of conversation is continually observing and talking with himself about two inextricably interwoven levels of this emotional experience: 1) talking-as-dreaming as an experience of the patient coming into being in the process of dreaming his lived emotional experience; and 2) the analyst and patient thinking about, and at times talking about, the experience of understanding (getting to know) something of the meanings of the emotional situation being faced in the process of dreaming.
>
> (Ogden, 2007, p. 576)

Here we have Ogden as a reader of Bion, the theoretical context of the text is based on Bion's transformation of the psychoanalytic conception of dreaming and of not being able to dream:

> Just as Winnicott shifted the focus of analytic theory and practice from play (as a symbolic representation of the child's internal world) to the

experience of playing, Bion shifted the focus from the symbolic content of thoughts to the process of thinking, and from the symbolic meaning of dreams to the process of dreaming.

(Ogden, 2007, p. 576)

Further clarifying the meaning of dreaming for Ogden as a reader of Bion:

> For Bion (1962a), '-function' (an as-yet unknown, and perhaps unknowable, set of mental functions) transforms raw 'sense impressions related to emotional experience' (p. 17) into alpha-elements which can be linked to form affect-laden dream-thoughts. A dream-thought presents an emotional problem with which the individual must struggle (Bion, 1962a, 1962b; Meltzer, 1983), thus supplying the impetus for the development of the capacity for dreaming (which is synonymous with unconscious thinking). '[Dream-]thoughts require an apparatus to cope with them ... Thinking [dreaming] has to be called into existence to cope with [dream-]thoughts' (Bion, 1962b, p. 306). In the absence of -function (either one's own or that provided by another person), one cannot dream and therefore cannot make use of (do unconscious psychological work with) one's lived emotional experience, past and present. Consequently, a person unable to dream is trapped in an endless, unchanging world of what is.

(Ogden, 2007, p. 577)

Experiences which are impossible to be thought, which are unimaginable, can come from a trauma – unbearably painful emotional experience – and can also arise from an "intrapsychic trauma", that is, the oppression of conscious or unconscious fantasies. These can be the result of a mother's failure to sustain the baby and contain its primitive anxieties, or it can also be related to a constitutional psychic fragility. The undreamed dreams – the unimaginable experience – whether it comes from external or intrapsychic forces – presents itself "in such forms as psychosomatic illness, split-off psychosis, 'dis-affected' states (McDougall, 1984), pockets of autism (Tustin, 1981), severe perversions (De M'Uzan, 2003) and addictions" (Ogden, 2007, p. 577).

Finally, Ogden writes about his conception of the therapeutic process:

> It is this conception of dreaming and of not being able to dream that underlies my own thinking regarding psychoanalysis as a therapeutic process. As I have previously discussed (Ogden, 2004, 2005), I view psychoanalysis as an experience in which patient and analyst engage in an experiment within the analytic frame that is designed to create conditions in which the analysand (with the analyst's participation) may be able to dream formerly undreamable emotional experience (his 'undreamt dreams'). I view talking-as-dreaming as an improvisation in the form of loosely structured conversation (concerning virtually any subject) in which the analyst participates in the patient's dreaming previously undreamt

dreams. In so doing, the analyst facilitates the patient's dreaming himself more fully into existence.

(Ogden, 2007, p. 577)

Notes

1 The expression "winged words" is found in several passages of Homer's *Odyssey* (third and second century BC), with numerous published versions. We are using this expression in the sense of words that "wander", words with wings that contain and reveal the emotional truth within an intersubjective analytical situation. We use this expression in the article "Winged words guiding the analytical encounter" (Cesar et al., 2022). Some of the ideas presented in this current text are present in the mentioned article, as well as in the article "The vitalizing function of the analyst and the living word in the analysis room. Reflections from some ideas of Thomas Ogden" (Cesar and Ribeiro, 2022).
2 "[...] Because the way to reduce the isolation that we are within ourselves, surrounded by distances and memories, is by filling words. It's by giving nicknames, telling tall tales. It is, after all, through the wandering words, expanding our limits. [Porque a maneira de reduzir o isolado que somos dentro de nós mesmos, rodeados de distâncias e lembranças, é botando enchimento nas palavras. É botando apelidos, contando lorotas. É, enfim, através das vadias palavras, ir alargando os nossos limites]" (Manoel de Barros, 1985, p. 62); free translation to English.
3 "The analyst's creation of 'metaphorical statements' constituting interpretations must not be an obtrusive event designed to demonstrate the analyst's cleverness with words. F. R. Leavis (1947), in his discussion of Milton, usefully distinguishes between a display of a 'feeling for words' and the capacity to create 'feeling through words' (p. 50)" (Ogden, 1997b, p. 209)
4 "I don't like accustomed words." NT: Free translation of: "Eu não gosto de palavras acostumadas" (Barros, 1996, p. 62)
5 "How I talk with my patients" was published in 2018 as an article, and in 2022 as a chapter in the book *Coming to life in the consulting room*.

References

BARROS, M. (1985). *Livro de pré-coisas: roteiro para uma excursão poética no pantanal*. Rio de Janeiro: Record.

BARROS, M. (1996). *Livro sobre nada*. Rio de Janeiro: Record.

CESAR, F. F. (2009. *Asas presas no sótão: psicanálise dos casos intratáveis*. São Paulo: Ideias & Letras.

CESAR, F. F. (2003). *Dos que moram em móvel-mar: elasticidade da técnica psicanalítica*. São Paulo: Casa do Psicólogo.

CESAR, F. F. (2019). *Do povo do nevoeiro*. São Paulo: Ed. Blucher.

CESAR, F. F.and RIBEIRO, M. F. R. (2022). The vitalizing function of the analyst and the living word in the analysis room. Reflections from some ideas of Thomas Ogden. *Revista de Psicanálise da Sociedade Psicanalítica de Porto Alegre* 25: 18–26, (PPGTP/UFRJ), Revista Ágora).

CESAR, F. F.; RIBEIRO, M. F. R. and FIGUEIREDO, L. C. (2023). *Chuva n'alma. A função vitalizadora do analista*. São Paulo: Ed. Blucher

CESAR, F. F., RIBEIRO, M. F. R. and PERROTTA, C. (2022). *Winged words: Guiding the analytical encounter*. São Paulo: Revista de Psicanálise da SPPA.

CINTRA, E. M. and RIBEIRO, M. F. R. (2018. *Por que Klein?* São Paulo: Ed. Zagodoni.

FIGUEIREDO, L. C., RIBEIRO, M. F. R. and TAMBURRINO, G. (2024, in Press). *Reading Bion's transformation*. London and New York: Routledge.

OGDEN, T. H. (1997a). On the art of psychoanalysis. In: *Reverie and interpretation*. (pp. 21–34). Northvale, NJ and London: Jason Aronson Inc.

OGDEN, T. H. (1997b). On the use of language in psychoanalysis. In: *Reverie and interpretation*. (pp. 183–208). Northvale, NJ and London: Jason Aronson Inc.

OGDEN, T. H. (1997c). Analyzing forms of aliveness and deadness. In: *Reverie and interpretation*. (pp. 35–68). Northvale, NJ and London: Jason Aronson Inc.

OGDEN, T. H. (1997d). *Reverie and interpretation*. Northvale, NJ and London: Jason Aronson Inc.

OGDEN, T. H. (2004). What's true and whose idea was it? In *This art of psychoanalysis: Dreaming undreamt dreams and interrupted cries* (pp. 86–102). London: International Journal of Psychoanalysis.

OGDEN, T. H. (2007). On talking-as-dreaming. *International Journal of Psychoanalysis* 88: 575–589.

OGDEN, T. H. (2012). *Creative readings*. London and New York: Routledge.

OGDEN, T. H. (2014). Fear of breakdown and the unlived life. *International Journal of Psychoanalysis 5*: 205–223.

OGDEN, T. H. (2016). Truth and psychic change: In place of an introduction. In: *Reclaiming unlived life: Experiences in psychoanalysis*. New York: Routledge.

OGDEN, T. H. (2018/2022). How I talk with my patients. In: *Coming to life in the consulting room: Toward a new analytic sensibility*. (pp. 57–71). London and New York: Routledge.

OGDEN, T. H. (2022). On language and truth in psychoanalysis. In: *Coming to life in the consulting room: Toward a new analytic sensibility*. (pp. 141–155) London and New York: Routledge.

RIBEIRO, M. F. R. and CINTRA, E. M. (org.) (2023). *Vastas Emoções e Pensamentos Imperfeitos. Diálogos Bionianos*. São Paulo: Blucher.

WINNICOTT, D. W. (1960–1963). Communicating and not communicating leading to a study of certain opposites. In *The collected works of D. W. Winnicott, Volume 6*. New York: Oxford University Press. Online edition, 2016. Originally published in The maturational processes and the facilitating environment: Studies in the theory of emotional development (pp. 179–192). London: Hogarth, 1965.

WINNICOTT, D. W. (1971). Playing: A theoretical statement. In: *Playing and reality*. (pp. 59–78). London and New York: Tavistock Publications.

WINNICOTT, D. W. (2016) Fear of breakdown. In: The Collected Works of D. W. Winnicott, Volume 6, 1960–1963. Oxford: Oxford University Press.

12 Visitation: When Words Come to Meet Us

Some Thoughts on Thomas H. Ogden's Direct, Tangential, and Non-Sequitur Discourses and the Search for the Unlived Life

*Fátima Flórido Cesar and
Marina F. R. Ribeiro*

Visitation: When words come to meet us

We begin this chapter with parts of Clarice Lispector's work entitled "Annunciation", in which she describes with simplicity and poetry the visitation to the Virgin Mary by the Archangel Gabriel. Certainly, this small poetic prose presents what captures us in this experience of "surprise and anguish" of the Virgin with intoxicating beauty:

> [...] In the painting, the Virgin Mary is seated beside a window and it is clear from her swollen belly that she is pregnant. The archangel at her side is watching her. And the Virgin, as if overwhelmed by the archangel's message, prophesying her destiny and that of future generations, raises her hand to her throat with surprise and anguish.
> [...] This is the most exquisite and harrowing truth the world has to offer.
> All human beings experience annunciation. With pregnant souls we raise our hands to our throats with surprise and anguish. As if each of us had learned at a given moment in life that we have a mission to fulfil.
> That mission is by no means easy: each of us is responsible for the entire world.
>
> (Lispector, 2018, p. 179)[1]

In deep concentration, praying with devotion, Mary is surprised by the visit of the angel announcing the unthinkable: that she is the mother of God's son. She welcomes the message, not without astonishment, which leads us to associate this experience – between sublime and frightening – with so many other human experiences. This is because we are also visited amidst mists of daydreaming by what comes from another place beyond what fits us internally. We are

DOI: 10.4324/9781003423188-12

summoned, announced and possessed by some truth that visits us. How many times are we absorbed, like the Virgin, when we are crossed by a song or a thought, thus captured, gaining a new body, hosting what comes to us as a visit?

Clarice's chronicle offers us an aesthetic experience due to the work's beauty, but also because its reading offers us a visitation, given that *poiesis* is a communication tool that surprises us and brings us a breadth of meanings, although never ultimate.

We witness words of sensitive affectation that occur in the happening of the human encounter and that emerge from unconscious dimensions: this is what we call "visitation" here. They are ways of being, or words, that visit us overwhelmingly, and only then are we captured by states of astonishment that, if we make ourselves available to the condition of hospitality (being hospitable so that the feast of novelty can happen), we will become inhabited, pregnant with infinite possibilities.

We use the metaphorical image of visitation to explain how emotional truth can emerge through the words between the analytic pair, as shown in various clinical reports by Thomas Ogden. We initially chose one of these reports, which are presented in the text "Fear of breakdown and the unlived life" (2014) already presented by us earlier in this volume. We will highlight the transformative strength of the words that points towards what the author indicates as proper to human existence and psychic illness: portions of life that have not been lived and that need to be integrated for the individual to become what they are. We will also present our clinical vignettes, hoping that, from between the lines of the reports, what we call "visitation", as well as the joint search of the pair for the unlived life, can both stand out. We will seek to thread ideas from Ogden that involve language, truth and unlived life, articulating the mentioned text with the chapter "On language and truth in psychoanalysis", from the book *Coming to life in the consulting room: Toward a new analytic sensibility* (Ogden, 2016/2022, our translation), also making use of some ideas and quotes from other texts by the author.

To illustrate the dimension of vitality and devitalization in the analytical process and its relationship with the use of language (we will see three forms of discourses described by Ogden, whose discussion will help in understanding the importance of language), we will begin by presenting a clinical case reported by the author himself in the text "Fear of breakdown and the unlived life" (2014), as quoted.[2]

Mrs. L had suffered severe neglect in childhood, due to her mother's severe depression, and abandonment by her father at the age of two. She would get involved with men who were interested in her, but would later abandon her. She eventually became interested in a car salesman and parked in front of the store every day, watching him, which represented the great motivation of her life and thoughts. Ogden (2014) related Mrs. L's state of helplessness regarding the salesman to her feeling of abandonment by him (Ogden) at the end of the weekend and at the end of the sessions, interruptions that were repudiated with great anger by the patient. The interpretations were stereotyped, lifeless, plasticized. The analytical field was blocked in its psychic creativity and live-liness – the sterility of both parties was what was most real.

But then Ogden tells Mrs. L. that her insistence on seeking the salesman was her healthiest part – it is what leads her to the search for her unlived parts. Mrs. L is surprised by the intervention, thinking that he was mocking her. He replies that he has never been so serious and that she had died in childhood due to the abandonment suffered. She says she thought Ogden had given up on her, attending to her only because he didn't know how to get out of the situation. This was the most truthful and honest thing she had said. Achieving a loving relationship with a person was the part that kept her alive. Stubbornly chasing men meant claiming parts of her unlived life, both in the past and in the present. The struggle to feel alive and real was mutual in the analytical scene: it was by mutually experiencing the lack of vitality in the analysis that they arrived at the only path to truth: that she had "died" in childhood. This was the painfully feared truth, however, sought and made viable through the linguistic exchange of the pair.

Language as visitation

We highlight the idea of "visitation", based on the following statement by Ogden, referring to his experience with Mrs. L: "Only then, were we able to find words – although it felt like the words, such as the word 'shit,' found us – to express what we were experiencing in the present moment" (Ogden, 2014, p. 219). We use this brief mention as a clear example that when we populate fertilized territories, conducive to the emergence of emotional truths, we are often visited by words – that is, they come to meet us – more than we go in pursuit of them.

It is possible to perceive, therefore, in the "visitation", how language can potentiate itself in a transformative role, the analyst reaching and being reached by the patient's words, including what spills from them and what escapes in eloquent silences, or even in those that transmit arid deserts of helplessness. Thomas Ogden in several books and texts brings up his own ideas about language and its central role in carrying forward what he calls "living analysis":

> When the analysis is alive, it unselfconsciously manages for periods of time to be an experiment that has left the well charted waters of prescribed form; it is a discussion fueled by curiosity and by variety of attempt; it is an endeavor that depends upon genuine exchange of views a n d comparison of standpoints. Analysis that has become a routinized form in which "knowledge" is conveyed from analyst to analysand is uninteresting; it is no longer an experiment since the answers, at least in broad outline, are known from the outset.
>
> (Ogden, 1997, p. 8)

For the analysis to be alive, some questions are raised: when do words present themselves as vitalizing and vitalized (considering that vitality and devitalization occur in the analytical pair)? What is the relationship between language and emotional truth? What can be thought of as essential in the therapeutic process? What is the relationship between language and the path to reach the patient, even helping him in the search for his unlived life? These are questions that need to be constantly raised to maintain a mobile position, a renewal of constructions, anchored in the ethical and technical field in dealing with the patient. The predominance of the markers "living analysis/ living language" protect us from falling into paralysis and losing a creative mind of our own.

The role that Ogden gives to language is of great importance, relating it to a vector of vitalization, to the core of what is understood by psychoanalysis, to its intersection with truth and with the search for aspects of unlived life.

Language and truth in the texts of Thomas H. Ogden

The complexity of language gains expansion and depth in the chapter "On language and truth in psychoanalysis" from the book *Coming to life in the consulting room: Toward a new analytic sensibility* (2016/2022), where Ogden discusses three modes of conversation, between analyst and patient, with the intention to arrive at the truth of experience: *direct discourse, tangential discourse, and discourse in non sequiturs.*[3] We will follow these three forms of dialogue, but first we would like to quote a short excerpt that sums up his ideas and initiates what follows:

> Psychoanalysis as a therapeutic process centers much of its energy on helping the patient experience, and give voice to, a truth that has been disturbing him for much of his life, a truth that he has been unable to think or feel because it has been too much to bear. Language plays a pivotal role in bringing to life the emotional truth of previously unbearable experience in the analytic session.
>
> (Ogden, 2016/2022, p. 141)

We will continue with the mentioned text adding some vignettes (one from Ogden and three of our own[4]) to illustrate the three forms of dialogue that allow contact with emotional truth.

But what is the truth?[5] The truth is both sought and feared: and the analyst-patient dialogue will have as a horizon what they experience together: the truth that was impossible to be thought, felt, or put into words. The truth in the session includes aspects of the patient's unlived life and events that the patient was unable to experience. After a therapeutic journey in which the encounter remained devitalized, followed by a change in direction towards vitalization, we witnessed that Ogden and Mrs. L arrived together at the truth that she had died in childhood. A painful truth, but one they could experience together.

We have selected this vignette to illustrate how such a painful truth can be experienced from the joint analyst-patient experience; with the support of the former. Thus, we articulate language and the metaphor of visitation with the search for emotional truth; the latter involving events that the patient has not yet been able to experience, as we saw in Winnicott (1963/1989), thus remaining in the "unlived" (Ogden, 2014).

Reaching the truth with Mrs. L depended on the specific way of dialogue that fit with that patient; therefore, we also need to develop unique ways of speaking with each one of our patients, making it possible to bring to life the truth of what occurs between the participants of the analytic pair. But how is the truth communicated? Not primarily directly, in the reported story, but in the rupture, in the disjunction of the conversation:

> What I have in mind when I refer to the breaks in the discourse are the places where there is disjunction—sometimes a lack of correspondence between the words and their usual meanings, at other times a seemingly incomprehensible gap between what one person says and how the other responds, and at still other times a divide between the feeling or idea that is expected and the one that is actually stated or implied.
>
> (Ogden, 2016/2022, p. 142)

In these ruptures of the discourse, an emotional sense is generated, in which both participants experience the feeling of being lost, but also a sense of wonder in the face of the unknown and the unprecedented. Analyst and analysand can no longer remain in what they thought they knew, because what was previously known is not enough to vigorously contain the elements of the experience that have now emerged. Ogden thus refers to the breaking points of the expected coherence of dialogue – disjunction, gap, breaches – when an experience of awe occurs, transmitting a mixture of fear and wonder.

We now return to Lispector's epigraph, the moment when Mary, at the announcement that she would be the mother of God's son, is gripped by a mix of astonishment and enchantment. In this case, we may also think about the break between the state of prayer, in which Mary was engaged, and the unexpected visit of the angel with his unheard speech.

Just like Mary, who was in devotion, in a state of openness, when something that was not previously known brings her the surprisingly unpredictable, also after the disjunction, in the analytic encounter, something new is inaugurated. What was known before does not encompass sufficiently and significantly what emerges anew in the experience of the pair. From this arises a critical point: either the pair ignores what is happening in the break of discourse, or it opens up and presents itself susceptible to something of the truth of what is happening. This second possibility could be viable, to the extent that:

> The analytic setting—with its unstructured mode of conversation; the maxi-mization of the role of language and sound by means of the patient's use of the couch; the effort to release analyst and patient from the hegemony of secondary process thinking, and in so doing, allowing waking

dreaming (reverie) to become a form of intrasubjective and intersubjective communication—all of this together is designed to help the analytic pair enter into a state of mind in which an experience of the truth, and the truth of the experience, may unfold, both in the form of what is said and what is left out.

(Ogden, 2016/2022, p. 143)

Language needs to be an enabler of openness to the truth, and the analyst's task should be to avoid interposing their acumen, mental agility, or capacity for empathy between the patient and the interpretation.

The literary critic Michael Wood, quoted by Ogden when referring to the place of the writer in his writing, observes: "To write is not to be absent but to become absent; to be someone and then go away, leaving traces" (1994, p. 18, as cited in Ogden, 2005, pp. 68–69). Ogden sees in Wood's words an excellent description of what psychoanalysts seek when making interpretations. Changing the patient would be to create him to the analyst's own image – instead, to offer something that contemplates some truth will allow the patient to carry out a conscious, pre-conscious and unconscious elaboration: "Accompanying any psychological growth achieved in this way, we find not the signature of the analyst (i.e., his presence), nor his absence (which marks his presence in his absence), but traces of him as someone who was present and has become absent, leaving traces." (Ogden, 2005, p. 68). The traces refer to the experience of making use of what the analyst said, did, and was, and not to their identification with him on a personal level. It doesn't matter whose idea it was, where, or from whom the idea that gave rise to the linguistic exchange sprouted, but rather to find words that have a quality that truly corresponds to the lived experience. Experience, truth, presence in the form of traces, living communications are interconnected and speak of the words that circulate between the pairs of the duo. We do not need and cannot reach the "Absolute Truth"; the most important thing, according to Ogden, is to get "very close/to the music of what happens" (Heaney, 1979, p. 173, as cited in Ogden, 2005, p. 69). These are relative truths: "The relative truths arrived at in poetry (and in psychoanalysis) represent 'a clarification of life'—not necessarily a great clarification, such as sects or cults are founded on, but a momentary stay against confusion" (Frost, 1939/1995, p. 777 as cited in Ogden, 2005, p. 69). In the vignettes that will follow, we will seek to glimpse the psychological use of these momentary stays carried out by the analyst together with his patient.

So far, following Ogden, we intend to state how we can think about language – specifically interpretation – in a broad and eloquent way, aided by *poiesis*, by creation. Now, let's move on to the three forms of conversation that can occur in the analytical process.

Before proceeding to the discussion of the three modes of discourse, Ogden emphasizes that when he speaks of patient and analyst "dreaming" together, he will be referring to unconsciously thinking and feeling the truth of a previously unthinkable experience, with the overlap of the dreaming of patient and analyst situated at the heart of the analytical experience. We also highlight his clarification that there are no firm dividing lines between the forms of dialogue: it is not possible to clearly see when one transitions to another.

The forms of dialogue that will be presented allow the patient to experience *with the analyst* the truth that had been impossible to be thought, felt, or put into words: the truth of the session involving events not yet experienced – as shown in the text "Fear of breakdown" by Winnicott (1963b/1989) and his reading by Ogden – these events which, as we have seen, correspond to unlived parts of the patient's life (Ogden, 2012).

There are countless forms of discourse (he also uses the terms "dialogue" and "conversation" in equivalence to the term "discourse"), but we will address three of them: direct discourse, tangential discourse, and *non sequiturs*. Each of them has its own form of language structure, which involves an active interaction between the manifest and the implicit meaning. The form of discourse is not simply the illustration of different conversation formats; it is the unique, proper way for analyst and patient to speak to each other in order to bring to life the truth of what is happening between them.

Direct discourse: What are you thinking about?

This mode of dialogue consists of simple declarative sentences ("What are you feeling?", "Anxiety"), a form of direct discourse, with little use of metaphors, visual images, ironies, etc. However, this type of conversation is capable of conveying a form of truth, which can only make its appearance in this form of dialogue.

Ogden, illustrating the direct exchanges, reports his encounters with a patient, Mrs. V., who described in detail events between her sessions (after reporting what she could remember from the neglect arising from her mother and the isolation in response to the absence of her father – all the story she could remember). We will try to synthetically describe the experience of the pair, seeking to illustrate how the dialogue between the two took place through direct discourse.

After a year of analysis of five sessions per week, from a daydream, Ogden began to ask Mrs. V. to describe what she was feeling during the numerous events she had described. Her responses and Ogden's interventions were not at all received by the patient. Until one day she answered to one of her analyst's questions, stating that she had "felt sad". In reply to such an answer, he asks: "Did you really feel sad?" The patient's final answer was that when he asked what she felt, she really didn't feel anything. Ogden replied to the patient that what she had just said was one of the first true things she had communicated. The patient replied that she thought so, to which the analyst questioned, "Do you really believe that?" (2016/2022, pp. 145–146). She then replied that she didn't know, and the sound of her words seemed sadly true.

From her statement about feeling no emotion, the conversations became more lively and real: the words then carried layers of meaning, where before they had presented a literal meaning, like empty words. On this occasion, she says "My father was somebody, I'm a nobody", stating something that she did not know, until the words came out of her mouth – the double meaning of the word "nobody" (2016/2022, p. 146). In place of the empty words, direct discourse was reactivated with life strength "as it was spoken with feeling that rang true ('I don't know [if I believe what I said]')"), and gestured toward a truth not yet known (what is it for her to be nobody?) (2016/2022, p. 146). The form of discourse continued to present itself through simple declarative sentences, not changing much; what changed was the appearance of a speech without adornments and the perception of how feelings and ideas emerged from her.

We will now try to illustrate, with a vignette from Fátima Flórido,[6] a sample of direct discourse. We will also provide our own examples of other forms of conversation later on.

In the sessions with Mrs. Iza, who is of advanced age, the words composed a vortex (from which we did not move) around statements about the need to die, since she did not want to "be a burden to anyone". She repeatedly insisted that it was time to die and I was sucked in by these direct statements and tempted to say how she was being a burden with her discourse of not wanting to be a burden. It was true that the possibility of imminent death was quite likely, but our sessions swirled around the "being a burden" point. I could not reach her, just as something hidden (an emotional truth) lurked at us in an empty and imprisoning way, like a drowned person entangled with their dead body in a vortex where dark plants did not allow them to be spotted, rescued and mourned.

After a few meetings following this daydream, the name of her late husband emerged in the middle of the session, like a pale flower. He was a very collected person, although prone to occasional outbursts of anger, feeling inferior to all the men in the family, occasionally tormenting Mrs. Iza about her outbursts and sickly ways of living. Pale flower, because the name had emerged delicately, establishing the opening of an unprecedented emotional state between us. A wave of tenderness enveloped us and the words visited me sweetly: "Do you miss him, don't you?" Something new and alive had made its appearance. "There is something unmistakable about the truth when one hears it" says Ogden (2005, p. 75). Mrs. Iza responded in a way as truthful as it was moving: "I miss him so much! He would see me sitting in the room and ask: 'What are you thinking about, my Iza?' – 'About you, my Jozélio,'" she replied. A field of shared sensitivities generated a strongly emotional environment: a genuine truth put into words presented itself. A mild sadness then took me, simultaneously to the truth of the longing that perhaps none of those who knew her suspected she felt that way. It was a living and real encounter freed from the vortex that had been imprisoning us.

Tangential discourse: The cool analyst[7]

In this type of dialogue, metaphor is predominant: "the realm of one feeling or idea or image becoming linked with (transferred to) another, and in so doing, creating new meaning in the space that is created between the two elements being linked to one another" (2016/2022, p. 147): "when two people are engaged in what I am calling tangential discourse, responses on the part of both participants glance off 'the subject' (in both senses of the word) and allude to other subjects, other meanings, other people" (2016/2022, p. 146).

Ogden presents the etymological sense of the word "metaphor": it derives from the Greek *meta* (through or beyond) and *pherein* (to carry or transfer).

In tangential discourse, meanings are transferred from one manifest subject to another. The metaphor creates a space between the two things that are being compared, in which meanings proliferate (but there is not only one possible translation). Dreams also allude to unconscious meaning, but they are not a decoding of meaning. We see that it is an allusion, but not an explanation or translation. It is a visual experience that words are not enough to express. It's as if we were in a formless territory. Dreams and daydreams – and we dream as much sleeping as awake – are metaphors for unconscious thoughts and feelings. Therefore, we are constantly constructing metaphors.

When we dream, we transpose the meaning beyond the visual experience – the visual experience of dreaming the dream – to the verbal experience of understanding the dream. But we cannot speak of understanding in relation to the dream experience. It is a mistake to say that we understand, or know, the unconscious experience; it is inaccessible to consciousness: Ogden claims it is more correct to say that sometimes we are able to experience metaphorical representations of the unconscious: "as is the case with a poem, there are no other words with which to say it, explain it, understand it, translate it, paraphrase it, or the like. A poem is immutably itself, as is a dream" (2016/2022, p. 148).

Now, let's address the tangential discourse in the analytical scenario. For this, we shall present a fragment of analysis of a teenager, Mel. She has been in analysis since childhood. When she came to me, she arrived presenting a gloomy world (in clothes, in music, crying copiously, cutting herself).

I met a desperate girl who felt neglected by her parents, who denied the severity of her emotional condition and devalued subjective life. Soon a bond was formed, her depressive state subsided, giving way to an emotional state of emptiness to be filled by attachment to physical appearance, a compulsive sexual behavior, and brief drug use. Outside of sessions, she would call me when she was desperate for reasons she could not define. A bond of great trust was established, the mentioned symptoms were healed; however, nothing interested her beyond clothes, appearance, frequent sexual relations, and what seemed to attract her most was the partner's gaze. My gaze was valuable to her, from the answer to the questions: "Am I thin? Am I beautiful?", all the way to my efforts to see in her particles of subjective life with some potential to blossom.

I have the habit of using the word "cool". Whenever I say that something is cool, Mel finds it funny, saying that such a word is no longer used. Recently, when she said this, I remembered many years ago when I worked in a daycare. Many children spent the whole day there and I was enchanted with some of them. Two of them called me "mother" from time to time. Following this daydream of mine, Mel stated that it was cool to say cool and we laughed together. This form of dialogue fit at that moment, it referred only to us. The speech – in this case, the word "cool" – could only be used by Mel because it was said in terms that apply to her, at that moment, while remaining true with respect to human nature in general, as Ogden emphasizes when articulating what approaches both universal and personal truth.

What is the truth that we touch? What emerged from the metaphorical communication? The word "cool", which "is no longer used", points to the difference in generations and to the fact that I am old enough to be her mother. Perhaps I represented a cool mother, compared to the abandonment experienced with the mother, who may not be so cool. Therefore, we lightly approach a painful truth.

Non-sequitur discourse: "Speaking one's mind"

The discourse in the form of *non sequitur* presents itself as an extreme mode of tangential discourse: sometimes the comprehensibility of the connection between two thoughts or feelings escapes us; nevertheless, or precisely because of this, thoughts and feelings previously unexpressed can be communicated. What is incomprehensible is the gap between the two statements from a conscious point of view, although to some extent intelligible from an unconscious point of view.

The psychic truth expressed in the form of *non sequitur* is, therefore, apprehended unconsciously, and yet it remains disturbing for both. The truths had not been recognized until then because they were very painful and difficult to bear.

As mentioned, this form of communication, like the other two, never occurs in a pure form. Here, an apparent disconnection hides a deeply intimate conversation and requires that both pairs of the discourse do a lot of unconscious psychological work, as they are dealing with the apparently disconnected elements of the *non sequitur*. It is essential to highlight that unconscious thoughts and feelings are "inexplicable" to the extent that they do not correspond to the secondary process. From the point of view of the secondary process, they would be untranslatable. The *non sequitur* discourse stands out in relation to other discourses in the sense that it closely communicates the unconscious experience. We continue with a vignette (by Fátima Flórido) that seems to express the *non sequitur* discourse in the analytical scenario.

I speak of Tomás, with whom I developed a unique form of dialogue, as were the unique ways of conversation with Mrs. Iza and Mel. With him, I am led to present myself spontaneously, with liveliness, lending my body-mind; the free gestures contrary to rigid body, offers not just words, but living words, populated with affection, my voice in a diversity of intonations, interpretations that modulate more as creative reasons/epistemes and less as an invitation to an intellectualized understanding. I experience a form of freedom that reaches the body, words, voice, various intonations, free gestures, in short, a living presence and in possession of my sensitivity and affections. Such a way of being with Tomás happens like a choreography sprouted solely from the meeting of the two of us.

It was in this atmosphere of "speaking one's mind" – word-body-affections – that we were walking. Tomás seemed to need me to fight for him (in the sense of helping him stay in the analysis); our beginning was of great importance to weave a field of reliability and hope: we circulated in whirls between the arduous and tender cries of beginnings. Flashes of faith emerged amid anguish, as well as moments when he lamented "getting nowhere" around repeated complaints. On one occasion when he was complaining, as if walking in a muddy sludge – this image came to my mind – when further ahead a beach could be within his reach, I moved in the armchair and with vigorous gestures and tone of voice I told him: "Will you stop, girl?!"

I got scared! I was very embarrassed – "you say too much." What nonsense was that? Then came the worst part: I "got lost", I started to theorize (oh! The theory that shelters us by making us homeless), total disaster! Tomás said nothing. At the end of the session, I was still watchful, I thought I had hurt him in his homosexuality. How would he react? Would he come back?

In the following session, nothing was said. In another, in the middle of something that we were talking about, Tomás remained silent, I gave it some time, enough for something to be gestated. I called him: "What are you thinking?" It was Tomás' turn to speak his mind:

It's just that when you called me a girl, I really liked it. When I was in college, we treated each other like this: Toni, for example, was Antonia. Here at home I need to be careful with gestures, I really wanted to have this freedom to use the feminine or be called that way.

(I remembered that he had already told me that he liked to dress himself "in drag",[8] something said a long time ago and that now entered again in the field of the encounter, something that had stayed in the "cloud" and that we built together when I "spoke my mind".)

I said: "I recall that you like to dress yourself 'in drag'".

"Since we're together, I'm going to show you something," Tomás told me. It was a photo of him in drag, proud of how beautiful he looked in that way.

I reacted with a vibrant voice: "How beautiful, girl!", and we continued commenting on the perfect wig, the makeup and how I would like to know how to do the beautiful and well-drawn mouth.

Hospitality and visitation

We now return to the metaphor of visitation and the annunciation of the Virgin Mary. Mary needed to be in a condition of hospitality: the body in a concave position, with the exposure of her bare skin, making available the vulnerability of a skin with sensitivity offered to caress, but also open to outrage and injury, as she had received in surprise and fright the mission, such is the surrender to the designs of her God. Such a disposition to host in her body the son of God, in the form of a mission, was a condition to both being visited and to receive the annunciation that – behold the unthinkable unusual – although virgin, she would give birth.

We also need to inhabit an ethic of hospitality for us to be visited, although it is essential to remember that the visit of the unexpected arrives for the analytic pair; both in a concave condition for the reception of what Ogden calls "disjunction". The author of an understanding (relative truth) was not one, nor the other, and if there was an author, it was the third unconscious subject of the analysis, who is everyone and no one; in the words of Ogden:

> (…) I view the analyst's reverie experience as a creation of an unconscious intersubjectivity that I call "the analytic third," a third subject of analysis, which is jointly, but asymmetrically, created by analyst and patient.
>
> (Ogden, 2005, pp. 75–76)

And clarifying even more:

> (…) I view the co-created unconscious analytic third as standing in dialectical tension with the unconscious of the analysand and of the analyst as separate people, each with his or her own personal history, personality organization, qualities of self-consciousness, bodily experience and so on.
>
> (Ogden, 2005, p. 128)

> (…) If there was an author, it was the unconscious third subject of analysis who is everyone and no one – a subject who was both Mr. V and I, and neither of us.
>
> (Ogden, 2005, p. 76)

The words that manifest themselves through the three discourses are not sought, as Ogden says. They come to us, they visit us. The three forms of dialogue can change from one to the other, in this search to live what has not yet been lived, and can refer to the emotional truth of the patient. The four vignettes presented in the three types of conversation expanded the emotional truth related to aspects of the unlived life. Many of our patients "died in childhood" – a painful and feared truth, as in the case of Mrs. L, by Ogden, or Mel (our vignette).

By linking "the unlived life" to the three discourses (none of these modes of conversation with greater intimacy than the other and, simultaneously, each one presenting itself as oscillating vertices), we reaffirm the relationship of language with truth. Articulating Ogden's reading of Winnicott's text "Fear of breakdown" (1963/1989) with the search for truth, which is both feared and desired, we also link language as a means to favor the integration of aspects of the unlived life, the urgent search to find them to complete oneself, for the individual to become whole through the integration of as much as possible of his unlived life, so that he may become what he is.

Each analytic pair is engaged from the beginning in the task of creating a way of speaking together that is appropriate, to give expression both to the patient's fear and to the patient's need to know the truth of their experience.

As analysts, we should preserve an ethic in which one gives up a "signature" of the therapeutic process: being present and then absent, leaving "traces". Thus, we hope that our patients are left only with the traces, wishing that, in the work of the pair, we have managed to achieve a "momentary stay against confusion".

In conclusion, language and truth are intertwined: the truth that presents itself as a difficult one to be experienced in the analytic setting, is the truth of experiences that were unbearable in the past which continue to be unbearable and referred to aspects of the unlived life.

We shall finish this chapter with the winged words of Thomas Ogden:

> It seems that paradoxically what is true is timeless, placeless and larger than any individual; and yet alive only for an instant and unique to the set of circumstances constituting that moment of lived experienced by one person. In other words, in an analysis, what is universally true is also exquisitely personal and unique to each patient and to each analyst. An analytic interpretation, in order to be utilizable by the patient, must speak in terms that could only apply to that patient at that moment while at the same time holding true to human nature in general.
>
> (Ogden, 2005, p. 68)

The annunciation of winged words leaves traces in us that constitute our being with every analytical experience, lived and dreamed.

Notes

1 Anunciação (...) Nele, Maria está sentada perto de uma janela e vê-se pelo volume de seu ventre que está rávida. O arcanjo, de pé ao seu lado, olha-a. E ela, como se mal suportasse o que lhe fora anunciado como destino seu e destino para a humanidade futura através dela, Maria aperta a garganta com a mão, em surpresa e angústia (...) É a mais bela e cruciante verdade do mundo. Cada ser humano recebe a anunciação: e, grávido de alma, leva a mão à garganta em susto e angústia. Como se houvesse para cada um, em algum momento da vida, a anunciação de que

há uma missão a cumprir. A missão não é leve: cada homem é responsável pelo mundo inteiro (Lispector, 2018, p. 179). The reader also can find this fragment on https://simipress.com/cronicas/.

2 Some ideas about this case are also present in the book *Do povo do nevoeiro: psicanálise dos casos difíceis*. Cesar, F. F. São Paulo: Blucher, 2019. Free translation of the book's title: *People from the fog: Psychoanalysis of difficult cases*.

3 Meaning non-sequential, when there is a more radical break.

4 We are using the plural, as the text is ours; however, the vignettes are from Fátima Flórido Cesar's clinic.

5 The answer to this question cannot be "finalized"; we will discuss it throughout the text.

6 The description of the vignette is in the first person.

7 Although the Portuguese word "bacana" has been translated as "cool", it's important to understand that "bacana" is considered somewhat outdated in Brazilian Portuguese. It's often used by people who maintain the vocabulary of past times. Therefore, while "cool" is an approximate translation, it may not fully convey the cultural and historical context of the word "bacana". In this particular case, the patient finds the analyst's use of this word strange and old-fashioned.

8 Translator's note: the expression "in drag" is the term used to refer to a person, commonly a man, dressed as the opposite sex.

References

CINTRA, E. M., & RIBEIRO, M. F. R. (2018). *Por que Klein?* São Paulo: Ed. Zagodoni.

FIGUEIREDO, L. C., RIBEIRO, M. F. R., & Tamburrino, G. (2024, in Press). Reading Bion's transformation. London and New York: Routledge.

FROST, R. (1939/1995). The figure a poem makes. In: R. Poirier, M. Richardson (eds.). *Robert Frost: Collected poems, prose and plays* (pp. 776–778). New York: Library of America.

HEANEY, S. S. (1979). In: *Opened ground: Selected poems*. New York: Farrar, Straus and Giroux.

LISPECTOR, C. (2018). *Todas as crônicas*. Rio de Janeiro: Rocco.

OGDEN, T. H. (1997). On the art of psychoanalysis. In: *Reverie and interpretation. Reverie e interpretation* (pp. 1–20). Northvale, NJ and London: Jason Aronson Inc.

OGDEN, T. H. (2005). What's true and whose idea was it? In idem, *This art of psychoanalysis: Dreaming undreamt dreams and interrupted cries* (pp. 61–76). London and New York: Routledge.

OGDEN, T. H. (2007). *On talking-as-dreaming* (pp. 575–589). London: International Journal of Psychoanalysis.

OGDEN, T. H. (2012). *Creative readings*. London and New York: Routledge.

OGDEN, T. H. (2014). Fear of breakdown and the unlived life. *International Journal of Psychoanalysis* 95(2): 205–224. Republished in T. H. Ogden (2016), *Reclaiming Unlived Life: Experiences in Psychoanalysis*. London: Routledge.

OGDEN, T. H. (2016/2022). On language and truth in psychoanalysis. In: *Coming to life in the consulting room: Toward a new analytic sensibility* (pp. 141–155). London and New York: Routledge.

OGDEN, T. H. (2018/2022). How I talk with my patients. In: *Coming to life in the consulting room: Toward a new analytic sensibility* (pp. 55–71). London and New York: Routledge.

RIBEIRO, M. F. R., & CINTRA, E. M. (org.) (2023). *Vastas Emoções e Pensamentos Imperfeitos. Diálogos Bionianos*. São Paulo: Blucher.

WINNICOTT, D. W. (1963/1989). Fear of breakdown. In: *Psycho-analytic explorations*. (pp. 70–76). Cambridge, MA: Harvard University Press.

WOOD, M. (1994). *The magician's doubts: Nabokov and the risks of fiction*. Princeton, NJ: Princeton University Press.

Appendix
Thomas H. Ogden: Timeline

Alberto Rocha Barros

1946: Thomas Henry Ogden is born in Manhattan, New York.

1962: He reads Freud for the first time, at the age of 16: *A General Introduction to Psychoanalysis*, an experience that convinces him to become an analyst.

1968: He earns his *Magna cum laude* degree in English Language and Literature from Amherst College, Massachusetts, and becomes a member of Phi Beta Kappa.

1972: He graduates from Yale School of Medicine, New Haven, Connecticut.

1972: He begins his residency in psychiatry at Yale School of Medicine.

1974: He publishes his first scientific work: "A psychoanalytic psychotherapy of a patient with cerebral palsy: The relation of aggression to self- and body-representations". *International Journal of Psychoanalytic Psychotherapy*, 3: 419–433, 1974 [Not translated into Portuguese].

1975: He completes his residency in psychiatry (Yale School of Medicine).

1975–1976: He moves to London, where he begins his training at the British Psychoanalytic Society and is hired as an associate psychiatrist at the Tavistock Clinic.

1976: He joins Mount Zion Hospital, in San Francisco, California as a psychiatrist. He holds this position from 1976 to 1979.

1976: He publishes the article "Unevenness of psychological functioning in the academically successful student". *International Journal of Psychoanalytic Psychotherapy*, 5: 437–448, 1976. [Not translated into Portuguese].

1976–1977: He returns to the United States and settles in San Francisco, California.

1978: He publishes the article: "A developmental view of identifications resulting from maternal impingements". *International Journal of Psychoanalytic Psychotherapy*, 7: 486–507, 1978. [Not translated into Portuguese].

1978: He publishes the article: "A reply to Dr. Ornston's discussion of 'Identifications Resulting from Maternal Impingements.'" *International Journal of Psychoanalytic Psychotherapy*, 7: 528–532, 1978.

1979: He begins his psychoanalytic training at the San Francisco Psychoanalytic Institute.

1979: He publishes the article: "On projective identification." *International Journal of Psychoanalysis*, 60 (3): 357–373 [Not translated into Portuguese].

1979: He becomes training director of psychiatric residents at Herrick Hospital and Medical Center, Berkeley, California, where he remains from 1979 to 1983.

1980: He is hired as a consultant psychiatrist at the Charila Foundation (a women's psychiatric hospital that has been deactivated), where he works from 1980 to 1983, when the hospital closes its doors.

1980: He publishes the article: "On the nature of schizophrenic conflict". *International Journal of Psychoanalysis*, 61 (4): 513–533. Republished in the book: Thomas H. Ogden, *Projective identification and psychotherapeutic technique*. New York: Jason Aronson, Inc., 1982/London: Karnac, 1992. [Not translated into Portuguese].

1981: He publishes the article: "Projective identification in psychiatric hospital treatment". *Bulletin of the Menninger Clinic*, 45: 319–333, 1981. Republished in the book: Thomas H. Ogden, *Projective identification and psychotherapeutic technique*. New York: Jason Aronson, Inc., 1982/London: Karnac, 1992. [Not translated into Portuguese].

1982: He publishes an article as a book chapter: "Treatment of the schizophrenic state of non-experience". In *Technical aspects of treating the disturbed patient*, L. B. Boyer and P. L. Giovacchini (eds.). New York: Jason Aronson, 1982. Republished in the book: Thomas H. Ogden, *Projective identification and psychotherapeutic technique*. New York: Jason Aronson, Inc., 1982/London: Karnac, 1992. [Not translated into Portuguese].

1982: He publishes his first book: *Projective identification and psychotherapeutic technique*. New York: Jason Aronson, Inc., 1982/London: Karnac, 1992. [Not translated into Portuguese].

1982: He becomes director of the Center for the Advanced Study of the Psychoses, San Francisco, California.

1983: He publishes the article: "The concept of internal object relations". *International Journal of Psychoanalysis*, 64 (2): 227–241. [Not translated into Portuguese].

1984: He publishes the article: "Instinct, phantasy, and psychological deep structure". *Contemporary Psychoanalysis*, 20 (4): 500–525. [Translated into Portuguese as: "Instinto, fantasia e estrutura psicológica profunda no trabalho de Melanie Klein". In: Thomas H. Ogden, *A Matriz da Mente*. São Paulo: Blucher, 2017: 19–49].

1985: He publishes the article: "Instinct, structure, and personal meaning". *Yearbook of Psychoanalysis and Psychotherapy*, 1: 327–334. [Not translated into Portuguese].

1985: He publishes: "On potential space". *International Journal of Psychoanalysis*, 66 (2): 129–141. [Translated into Portuguese as: "O espaço potencial". In: Thomas H. Ogden, *A matriz da mente*. São Paulo: Blucher, 2017: 207–235].

1985: He publishes the article: "The mother, the infant, and the matrix: Interpretations of aspects of the work of Donald Winnicott". *Contemporary Psychoanalysis*, 21 (3): 346–371, 1985. (Also published in *Donald Winnicott today*, J. Abram, ed. [New Library of Psychoanalysis] London and New York: Routledge, 2013). [Translated into Portuguese and included in the book: *A matriz da mente*. São Paulo: Blucher, 2017].

1986: He publishes the book: *The matrix of the mind: Object relations and the psychoanalytic dialogue*. Northvale, NJ: Jason Aronson, 1986/ London: Karnac, 1992. [In Portuguese: *A matriz da mente: Relações objetais e o diálogo psicanalítico*. São Paulo: Editora Blucher, 2017].

1986: He graduates as psychoanalyst from the San Francisco Psychoanalytic Institute and becomes a full member of the American Psychoanalytic Association and the International Psychoanalytic Association.

1987: He publishes the article: "The transitional Oedipal relationship in female development". *International Journal of Psychoanalysis*, 68 (94): 485–498. Republished in: *The primitive edge of experience* (1989). Also republished in: *In one's bones: The clinical genius of Winnicott*, D. Goldman, ed. Northvale, NJ: Jason Aronson, 1993, pp. 223–240.). [Not translated into Portuguese].

1987: He becomes assistant chief of the Psychiatry Department at Mount Zion Hospital and Medical Center, where he remains from 1987 to 1996.

1988: He publishes the article: "On the dialectical structure of experience". *Contemporary Psychoanalysis*, 24: 27–45, 1988. Republished in: *Master clinicians on treating the regressed patient*, L. B. Boyer and P. L. Giovacchini, eds. Northvale, NJ: Jason Aronson, 1990.) Republished with the title "The structure of experience" in *The primitive edge of experience* (1989). [Not translated into Portuguese].

1988: He publishes the article: "Misrecognitions and the fear of not knowing". *The Psychoanalytic Quarterly*, 57 (4): 643–666, 1988. Republished in: *The place of reality in psychoanalytic theory and technique*, S. Abend, J. Arlow, D. Boesky and O. Renik, eds. Northvale: NJ: Jason Aronson, 1996.). Republished in: *The primitive edge of experience* (1989). [Not translated into Portuguese].

1989: He publishes the article: "The threshold of the male Oedipus complex". *Bulletin of the Menninger Clinic*, 53: 394–413, 1989. Republished in: *The primitive edge of experience* (1989). [Not translated into Portuguese].

1989: He publishes an article as a book chapter: "Playing, dreaming and interpreting experience". In *The facilitating environment*, M. Fromm and B. Smith, eds. Madison, CT: International Universities Press, 1989. [Not translated into Portuguese].

1989: He starts teaching as a faculty member at the San Francisco Psychoanalytic Institute (1989–2015).

1989: He becomes a teaching psychoanalyst at the San Francisco Psychoanalytic Institute (1989–2015).

1989: He publishes the article: "On the concept of an autistic-contiguous position". *International Journal of Psychoanalysis*, 70 (1): 127–140. [Translated into Portuguese: "Sobre o conceito de uma posição Autística contígua". *Revista Brasileira de Psicanálise*, Vol. XXX (2) (1996): 341–364]. Republished in the book: *The primitive edge of experience*. Northvale, NJ: Jason Aronson,1989/London: Karnac, 1992

1989: He publishes the book: *The primitive edge of experience*. Northvale, NJ: Jason Aronson,1989/London: Karnac, 1992. [Not translated into Portuguese].

1991: He gives his first interview, which is published: Ogden, T. H. (1991). "An interview with Thomas Ogden". *Psychoanalytic Dialogues*, 1 (3): 361–376. [Not translated into Portuguese].

1991: He publishes the article: "Analyzing the matrix of transference". *International Journal of Psychoanalysis*, 72 (4): 593–605. [Republished and translated into Portuguese in *Os sujeitos da psicanálise* (1994), Chapter 8].

1991: He publishes the article: "Some theoretical comments on personal isolation". *Psychoanalytic Dialogues*, 1 (3): 377–390, 1991. Republished in: *Encounters with autistic states*, T. and J. Mitrani, eds. Northvale, NJ: Jason Aronson, pp. 179–194, 1997.) [Republished and translated into Portuguese in *Os sujeitos da psicanálise* (1994), Chapter 9].

1992: He publishes the article: "Comments on transference and counter-transference in the initial analytic meeting". *Psychoanalytic Inquiry*, 12 (2): 225–247. [Not translated into Portuguese].

1992: He publishes the article: "The dialectically constituted/decentered subject of psychoanalysis. I: The Freudian subject". *International Journal of Psychoanalysis*, 73 (3): 517–526. [Republished with modifications and translated into Portuguese as Chapter 2 of *Os sujeitos da psicanálise* (1994)].

1992: He publishes the article: "The dialectically constituted/decentered subject of psychoanalysis. II: The contributions of Klein and Winnicott". *International Journal of Psychoanalysis*, 73 (4): 613–626. [Republished with modifications and translated into Portuguese as Chapters 3 and 4 of *Os sujeitos da psicanálise* (1994)].

1993: He publishes an article as a book chapter: "The analytic management and interpretation of projective identification". In *Countertransference: Theory, technique, teaching*, A. Alexandris and G. Vaslamatzis, eds. London: Karnac, 1993, pp. 21–46. [Not translated into Portuguese].

1994: He publishes the article: "The concept of interpretive action". *The Psychoanalytic Quarterly*, 63 (2): 219–245. [Republished and translated into Portuguese in *Os sujeitos da psicanálise* (1994), Chapter 7].

1994: He publishes the article: "The analytic third – Working with intersubjective clinical facts". *International Journal of Psychoanalysis*, 75 (1): 3–20. [Republished and translated into Portuguese in *Os Sujeitos da Psicanálise*

(1994), Chapter 5]. Republished in: Lewis Aron and Stephen A. Mitchell, eds., *Relational psychoanalysis: The emergence of a tradition.* London and New York: Routledge, 1999.

1994: He publishes the book: *Subjects of analysis.* Northvale, NJ: Jason Aronson, 1994/London: Karnac, 1994. [Published in Brazil as: *Os sujeitos da psicanálise.* São Paulo: Casa do Psicólogo, 1996].

1994: He writes a book review for *The Taming of Solitude: Separation Anxiety in Psychoanalysis,* by J. M. Quinodoz. In *International Journal of Psycho-Analysis,* 75: 163–165, 1994

1995: He publishes the article: "Analyzing forms of aliveness and deadness of the transference-countertransference". *International Journal of Psychoanalysis,* 76 (4): 695–709. [Published in Brazil as: "Analisando formas de vitalidade e de mortificação da transferência-contratransferência". *Revista de Psicanálise,* Porto Alegre, 3 (2): 465–488. Republished with new translation in: Thomas H. Ogden, *Reverie e interpretação.* São Paulo: Editora Escuta, 2013).

1996: He publishes the article: "The perverse subject of analysis". *Journal of the American Psychoanalytic Association (JAPA),* 44 (4): 1121–1146. [Published in Brazil as: "O sujeito perverso da análise". *Revista de Psicanálise* (Sociedade Brasileira de Psicanálise de Porto Alegre, SBPPA), 4 (3): 487–509. Also published in: Thomas H. Ogden. *Rêverie e Interpretação: Captando algo humano.* São Paulo: Editora Escuta, 2013].

1996: He publishes the article: "Reconsidering three aspects of psychoanalytic technique". *International Journal of Psychoanalysis,* 77 (5): 883–899. [Published in Brazil as: "Reconsiderando três aspectos da técnica psicanalítica". *Revista de Psicanálise da SPPA* (Porto Alegre), 3 (3), 1996: 421–444].

1997: He publishes the article: "Listening: Three Frost poems". *Psychoanalytic Dialogues,* 7 (5): 619–639. [Republished and translated into Portuguese as "Escuta: três poemas de Frost" in: Thomas H. Ogden, *Rêverie e interpretação: captando algo humano.* São Paulo: Editora Escuta, 2013, Chapter 8].

1997: He publishes the article: "Some thoughts on the use of language in psychoanalysis". *Psychoanalytic Dialogues,* 7 (1): 1–22, 1997. [Published in Portuguese as: "Algumas considerações sobre o uso da linguagem em psicanálise". *Revista Brasileira de Psicanálise,* 31 (3), 1997: 771–788. Republished in: Thomas H. Ogden, *Rêverie e interpretação: captando algo humano.* São Paulo: Editora Escuta, 2013, Chapter 7].

1997: He publishes: "Reverie and interpretation". *The Psychoanalytic Quarterly,* 66: 567–595. [Published in Brazil in *Revista Brasileira de Psicanálise,* vol. 32, 1998; and in *Revista de Psicanálise,* Fortaleza, vol. 1 (1), 2007, in a special issue dedicated to the theme of reverie. Also published as "Rêverie e interpretação" in: Thomas H. Ogden. *Rêverie e* *interpretação: Captando algo humano.* São Paulo: Editora Escuta, 2013, Chapter 6].

1997: He publishes the book: *Reverie and interpretation: Sensing something human.* Northvale, NJ: Jason Aronson, 1997/London: Karnac, 1999. [Published in Brazil as: *Rêverie e Interpretação: Captando algo humano.* São Paulo: Editora Escuta, 2013].

1997: He publishes the article: "Reverie and metaphor: Some thoughts on how I work as a psychoanalyst". *International Journal of Psychoanalysis,* 78 (4): 719–732. Republished in *Conversations at the frontier of dreaming* (2001). [Published in Brazil as: "Rêverie e metáfora: Algumas reflexões sobre como eu trabalho como analista". *Pulsional,* 11 (110), 1998: 56–75].

1998: He publishes the article: "A question of voice in poetry and psychoanalysis". *The Psychoanalytic Quarterly,* 67 (3): 426–448. Republished in: Thomas H. Ogden, *Conversations at the frontier of dreaming* (2001). [Published in Brazil as: "Uma questão de voz na poesia e na psicanálise". *Revista Brasileira de Psicanálise,* 32 (3): 585–604.]

1999: He publishes the article: "The analytic third: An overview". *Fort Da,* 5 (1). (Also published in *Relational Psychoanalysis: The Emergence of a Tradition,* eds. S. Mitchell and L. Aron. Hillsdale, NJ: Analytic Press, pp. 487–492, 1999.) [Not translated into Portuguese].

1999: He publishes the article: "'The music what happens' in poetry and psychoanalysis". *International Journal of Psychoanalysis,* 80 (5): 979–994, 1999. (Also published in *Key papers in literature and psychoanalysis,* P. Williams and G. Gabbard, eds. London: Karnac, pp. 49–76, 2007.). Republished in: Thomas H. Ogden, *Conversations at the frontier of dreaming* (2001). [Not translated into Portuguese].

2000: He publishes the chapter: "Questions de théorie et de pratique analytiques". In *Sur Les Controverses Américaines dans la Psychanalyse,* eds. M.-C. Durieux and A. Fine, Paris: Presses Universitaires de Paris, 2000, pp. 153–168.

2000: He publishes the chapter: "Foreword". *Intimacy and Alienation,* Russell Meares. London: Routledge, 2000.

2000: He publishes a clinical commentary: "A picture of mourning: Commentary on paper by Jeanne Wolff Bernstein". *Psychoanalytic Dialogues* 10 (3): 371–375. [Not translated into Portuguese].

2000: He publishes the article: "Borges and the art of mourning". *Psychoanalytic Dialogues,* 10 (1): 65–88. Republished in: Thomas H. Ogden, *Conversations at the frontier of dreaming* (2001). [Not translated into Portuguese].

2000: He publishes the poem: "Stumbling upon a Borges poem". *Fort Da,* 6 (1): 101–102.

2001: He publishes: "Re-minding the body". *American Journal of Psychotherapy,* 55 (1): 92–104. [Published in Brazil with the title "Trabalhando com a contratransferência: relembrando o corpo". In: Jacó Zaslavsky and Manuel J. P. dos Santos, eds. *Contratransferência e Prática Clínica.* Porto Alegre: Artmed, 2006].

2001: He publishes the article in French: "Travailler la frontière du rêve". *Revue Française de Psychanalyse*, 65: 133–142. The article is re-edited as the first chapter of the book: Thomas H. Ogden, *Conversations at the frontier of dreaming* (2001). [Not translated into Portuguese].

2001: He publishes the article: "An Elegy, a Love Song and a Lullaby". *Psychoanalytic Dialogues*, 11(2): 293–311. Republished in: Thomas H. Ogden, *Conversations at the frontier of dreaming* (2001). [Not translated into Portuguese].

2001: He publishes the book: *Conversations at the frontier of dreaming*. Northvale, NJ: Jason Aronson, 2001/London: Karnac, 2002. [Not translated into Portuguese].

2001: He publishes the article: "Reading Winnicott". *Psychoanalytic Quarterly*, 70 (2): 299–323, 2001. Republished in: *Donald Winnicott today*, J. Abram, ed. [New Library of Psychoanalysis] London and New York: Routledge, 2013). [Translated into Portuguese as "'Desenvolvimento emocional primitivo', of Winnicott. In: Thomas H. Ogden, *Leituras criativas: Ensaios sobre obras analíticas seminais*. São Paulo: Editora Escuta, 2014, Chapter 5].

2001: A new interview with Thomas Ogden is published: Ogden, T. H. (2001). "Interview with Thomas Ogden on *Conversations at the frontier of dreaming*". *Fort Da*, 7 (2): 15–18.

2002: He publishes a clinical commentary: "The analyst at work: Commentary on Tomas Bohm's 'Sara in her fourth analytic year'". *International Journal of Psychoanalysis*, 83 (5): 1008–1012, 2002. [Published in Portuguese in *Livro Anual de Psicanalise*, 18 (2006): 205–208].

2002: He publishes the article: "A new reading of the origins of object relations theory". *International Journal of Psychoanalysis*, 83 (4): 767–782. Published as a chapter in: *On Freud's "Mourning and melancholia"*.L. Fiorini, T Bokanowski and S. Lewkowicz, eds.. London: International Psychoanalytical Assn. Press, 2007, pp. 123–144). [Published in Brazil as: "Uma nova leitura das origens da teoria das relações objetais". *Livro Anual de Psicanálise*, 18: 85–98, 2004. Also republished in: Thomas H. Ogden, *Leituras criativas: Ensaios sobre obras analíticas seminais*. São Paulo: Editora Escuta, 2014, Chapter 2].

2003: He publishes the article: "What's true and whose idea was it?" *International Journal of Psychoanalysis*, 84 (3):593–606. [Published in Brazil as: "O que é verdadeiro e de quem foi a ideia?" *Psicanálise* (Porto Alegre), 5 (2): 393–419, 2003. Republished in: Thomas H. Ogden, *Esta arte da psicanálise: Sonhando sonhos não sonhados e gritos interrompidos*. Porto Alegre: Artmed, 2010, Chapter 5].

2003: He publishes the article: "On not being able to dream". *International Journal of Psychoanalysis*, 84 (1):17–30 [Published in Brazil as "Sobre não ser capaz de sonhar". In: Thomas H. Ogden, *Esta arte da psicanálise: Sonhando sonhos não sonhados e gritos interrompidos*. Porto Alegre: Artmed, 2010, Chapter 4].

2003: He writes a book review for *Can Love Last? The Fate of Romance Over Time*, by Stephen A. Mitchell. In *Psychoanalytic Dialogues: A Journal of Relational Perspectives*, Vol. 13, 2003.

2004: He publishes the article: "The analytic third: Implications for theory and technique". *Psychoanalytic Quarterly*, 73 (1):167–195. Republished with author's comments in: *Contemporary psychoanalysis in America: Leading analysts present their work*, A. M. Cooper, ed. Washington, DC: American Psychiatric Press, 2006, pp. 419–444. [Not translated into Portuguese].

2004: He publishes the article: "An Introduction to the Reading of Bion". *International Journal of Psychoanalysis*, 85 (2): 285–300. [Published in Brazil as: Thomas H. Ogden, *Leituras criativas: Ensaios sobre obras analíticas seminais*. São Paulo: Editora Escuta, 2014, Chapter 6].

2004: He publishes the article: "This art of psychoanalysis: Dreaming undreamt dreams and interrupted cries". *International Journal of Psychoanalysis*, 85 (4): 857–878. [Published in Brazil as: Thomas H. Ogden, *Esta arte da psicanálise: Sonhando sonhos não sonhados e gritos interrompidos*. Porto Alegre: Artmed, 2010, Chapter 1].

2004: He publishes the article: "On holding and containing, being and dreaming". *International Journal of Psychoanalysis*, 85 (6): 1349–1364. Republished in: *Winnicott and the psychoanalytic tradition*, L. Caldwell, ed. London: Karnac, 2008, pp. 76–96). [Published in Brazil as "Sobre sustentar e conter, ser e sonhar". In: Thomas H. Ogden, *Esta arte da psicanálise: Sonhando sonhos não sonhados e gritos interrompidos*. Porto Alegre: Artmed, 2010, Chaper 7].

2004: He publishes the poem: "Crumbs (a poem)". *Psychoanalytic Perspectives*, 2 (1): 88.

2005: He publishes the chapter: "Foreword". *Seeds of Illness, Seeds of Recovery: The Genesis of Suffering and the Role of Psychoanalysis*, Antonino Ferro, New York: Brunner-Routledge, 2005.

2005: He publishes the article: "On psychoanalytic writing". *International Journal of Psychoanalysis*, 86 (1): 15–29. [Published in Brazil as "Sobre a escrita psicanalítica". In: Thomas H. Ogden, *Esta arte da psicanálise: Sonhando sonhos não sonhados e gritos interrompidos*. Porto Alegre: Artmed, 2010, chapter 8].

2005: He publishes the article: "What I would not part with". *Fort Da*, 11: 8–17. [Published in Brazil as: "Do que eu não abriria mão". *Revista de Psicanálise da SPPA*, 12: 403–415, 2005. Republished in: Thomas H. Ogden, *Esta arte da psicanálise: Sonhando sonhos não sonhados e gritos interrompidos*. Porto Alegre: Artmed, 2010, Chapter 2].

2005: He publishes the book: *This art of psychoanalysis: Dreaming undreamt dreams and interrupted cries*. London and New York: Routledge. [Published in Brazil as: *Esta arte da psicanálise: Sonhando sonhos não sonhados e gritos interrompidos*. Porto Alegre: Artmed, 2010].

2005: He publishes the article: "On psychoanalytic supervision". *International Journal of Psychoanalysis*, 86 (5): 1265–1280. Republished in the book: *Rediscovering psychoanalysis: Thinking and dreaming, learning and forgetting* (2009). [Not translated into Portuguese].

2006: He publishes the chapter: "Foreword". *The Soul, the Mind, and the Psychoanalyst: The Creation of the Psychoanalytic Setting in Patients with Psychotic Aspects*, David Rosenfeld. Karnac, London, 2006.

2006: He publishes the article: "Reading Loewald: Oedipus reconceived". *International Journal of Psychoanalysis*, 87 (3): 651–666. [Published in Brazil as "Lendo Loewald: Édipo reformulado. In: Thomas H. Ogden, *Leituras criativas: Ensaios sobre obras analíticas seminais*. São Paulo: Editora Escuta, 2014, chapter 8].

2006: He publishes the article: "On teaching psychoanalysis". *International Journal of Psychoanalysis*, 87 (4): 1069–1085. Republished in the book: Thomas H. Ogden, *Rediscovering psychoanalysis: Thinking and dreaming, learning and forgetting* (2009). [Not translated into Portuguese].

2007: He publishes the article: "Reading Harold Searles". *International Journal of Psychoanalysis*, 88 (2): 353–369. [Published in Portuguese as: 'Amor edípico na contratransferência' e 'Identificação inconsciente', de Harold Searles". In: Thomas H. Ogden, *Leituras criativas: Ensaios sobre obras analíticas seminais*. São Paulo: Editora Escuta, 2014, Chapter 9].

2007: He publishes the article: "On talking-As-dreaming". *International Journal of Psychoanalysis*, 88 (3): 575–589. Republished in the book: Thomas H. Ogden, *Rediscovering psychoanalysis: Thinking and dreaming, learning and forgetting* (2009). Republished in: *Of things invisible to mortal sight: Celebrating the work of James Grotstein*. London: Karnac, 2017). [Not translated into Portuguese].

2007: He publishes the article: "Elements of analytic style: Bion's clinical seminars". *International Journal of Psychoanalysis*, 88 (5): 1185–1200. [Published in Portuguese as: "Elementos de estilo analítico: Seminários clínicos de Bion". In: Thomas H. Ogden, *Leituras criativas: Ensaios sobre obras analíticas seminais*. São Paulo: Editora Escuta, 2014, Chapter 7].

2007: He publishes the chapter: "Foreword". *The Language of Winnicott*, 2nd edition, Jan Abram. London: Karnac, 2007.

2008: He publishes the article: "Bion's four principles of mental functioning". *Fort Da* 14: 11–35. [Published in Brazil as: "Os quatro princípios do funcionamento mental segundo Bion" in *Diálogos psicanalíticos contemporâneos: Bion e Laplanche – do afeto ao pensamento*, Talya S. Candi, ed. São Paulo: Editora Escuta, 2019].

2008: He publishes an article as a book chapter: "Working analytically with autistic-contiguous aspects of experience" in *Autism in childhood and autistic features in adults*, K. Barrows, ed. London: Karnac, 2008, pp. 223–242. [Not translated into Portuguese].

2009: He publishes the book: *Rediscovering psychoanalysis: Thinking and dreaming, learning and forgetting*. London and New York: Routledge. [Not translated into Portuguese].

2009: He publishes the article: "On becoming a psychoanalyst" (co-authored with G. O. Gabbard). *International Journal of Psychoanalysis*, 90: 311–327. Republished in: *Relational psychoanalysis, Vol. 5: Evolution of process*. New York: Routledge, 2011.). [Not translated into Portuguese].

2009: He publishes the article: "Kafka, Borges and the creation of consciousness. Part I. Kafka: Dark ironies of the 'gift' of consciousness". *Psychoanalytic Quarterly*, 78 (2): 343–367 [Not translated into Portuguese].

2009: He publishes the article, as a continuation of the previous one: "Kafka, Borges and the creation of consciousness. Part II. Borges: A life of letters encompassing everything and nothing". *Psychoanalytic Quarterly*, 78 (2): 369–396. [Not translated into Portuguese].

2010: He publishes the article: "The lure of the symptom in psychoanalytic treatment" (co-authored with G. O. Gabbard). *Journal of the American Psychoanalytic Association*, 58 (3): 533–544. [Not translated into Portuguese].

2010: He publishes the article: "Why read Fairbairn?" *International Journal of Psychoanalysis*, 91 (1): 101–118, 20. [Published in Brazil in *Livro Annual de Psicanálise*, Vol. 26, 2012. Republished as: "Por que ler Fairbairn?" in: Thomas H. Ogden, *Leituras criativas: Ensaios sobre obras analíticas seminais*. São Paulo: Editora Escuta, 2014, Chapter 4].

2010: He publishes the article: "On three types of thinking: Magical thinking, dream thinking and transformative thinking". *Psychoanalytic Quarterly* 79 (2): 314–347. Republished in: *Reclaiming unlived life: Experiences in psychoanalysis* (2016). [Published in Brazil as: "Sobre três formas de pensar: O pensamento mágico, o pensamento onírico e o pensamento transformativo". *Revista Brasileira de Psicanálise*, 46 (2): 193–214.]

2010: He is awarded the Haskell Norman Prize for his contributions to psychoanalysis.

2011: He publishes the article: "Reading Susan Isaacs: Toward a radically revised theory of thinking". *International Journal of Psychoanalysis*, 92 (4): 925–942. [Published in Brazil as: "Lendo Susan Isaacs: Para uma revisão radical da teoria do pensar". In: Thomas H. Ogden, *Leituras criativas: Ensaios sobre obras analíticas seminais*. São Paulo: Editora Escuta, 2014, Chapter 3].

2012: He publishes the book: *Creative readings: Essays on seminal analytic works*. London and New York: Routledge. [Published in Brazil as: *Leituras criativas: Ensaios sobre obras analíticas seminais*. São Paulo: Editora Escuta, 2014].

2012: He publishes a commentary on a paper by Rachael Peltz: "Psychoanalysis as a pocket of resistance against inhumanity: Commentary on a paper by Rachael Peltz". *Psychoanalytic Dialogues* 22 (3): 291–295. [Not translated into Portuguese].

2012: With his son, Benjamin H. Ogden, he publishes the article: "How the analyst thinks as clinician and literary reader". *Psychoanalytic Perspectives* 9 (2): 243–273. [Published in Brazil as: "Como pensa o analista enquanto clínico e leitor de literatura". In: Thomas H. Ogden and Benjamin H. Ogden, *O ouvido do analista e o olho do crítico: Repensando psicanálise e literatura*. São Paulo: Editora Escuta, 2014, Chapter 2].

2012: He is awarded the Sigourney Award for his contributions to psychoanalysis.

2013: He publishes a book on psychoanalysis and literary criticism, written together with his son, Benjamin H. Ogden, a literary critic: *The analyst's ear and the critic's eye: Rethinking psychoanalysis and literature*. London and New York: Routledge. [Published in Brazil as: *O ouvido do analista e o olho do crítico: Repensando psicanálise e literatura*. São Paulo: Editora Escuta, 2014].

2013: With his son, Benjamin H. Ogden, he publishes the article: "What is psychoanalytic literary criticism?" *Fort Da*, 19: 8–28. [Not translated into Portuguese].

2013: In Italy, he gives an interview to Luca Di Donna: T. H. Ogden and L. Di Donna. "Thomas Ogden em conversa com Luca Di Donna". *Revista de Psicanálise da SPPA*, 23 (3) (December 2013): 429–446.

2013: He publishes the short story that will later become his first novel: "The parts left out". *Fort Da*, 19: 63–82. [Not translated into Portuguese].

2014: He publishes his first novel: *The parts left out*. London: Karnac. [Published in Brazil as: *Meias verdades*. São Paulo: Editora Blucher, 2017].

2014: He gives an interview to Maureen Kurpinsky about his first novel: T. H. Ogden and M. Kurpinsky. "Conversations with clinicians: Thomas Ogden in conversation with Maureen Kurpinsky". *Fort Da*, 20 (2) (2014): 81–95.

2014: He is awarded the Hans Loewald Award for his contributions to psychoanalysis.

2014: He publishes the article: "Fear of breakdown and the unlived life". *International Journal of Psychoanalysis* 95 (2): 205–224. Republished in the book: Thomas H. Ogden, *Reclaiming unlived life: Experiences in psychoanalysis* (2016). [Published in Brazil as: "O medo do colapso e a vida não vivida". *Livro Anual de Psicanálise*, 30 (1), 2016: 77–93].

2015: He publishes the article: "Intuiting the truth of what's happening: On Bion's 'Notes on memory and desire'". *Psychoanalytic Quarterly* 84 (2): 285–306. Republished in the book: Thomas H. Ogden, *Reclaiming unlived life: Experiences in psychoanalysis* (2016). [Not translated into Portuguese].

2016: He publishes the book: *Reclaiming unlived life: Experiences in psychoanalysis*. London and New York: Routledge. [Translated into Portuguese: Thomas H. Ogden, *Recupernado a vida não vivida: Experiências em psicanálise*. São Paulo: Editora Escuta, 2023].

2016: He publishes his second novel: *The hands of gravity and chance*. London: Karnac. [Not translated into Portuguese].

2016: He publishes the article in Italy: "Thoughts on the essence of psychoanalysis". *Psychotherapy and the Human Sciences (Psicoterapia e Scienze Umane)* 50: 560–561. [Not translated into Portuguese].

2016: He publishes the article: "Some thoughts on practicing psychoanalysis". *Fort Da* 22: 21–36. Republished in: *Psychoanalytic credo: Personal and professional journeys of psychoanalysts*, J. Salberg, ed. London: Routledge, 2022). [Not translated into Portuguese].

2016: He publishes the article: "Destruction reconceived: On Winnicott's 'Use of an object and relating through identifications'". *International Journal of Psychoanalysis*, 97 (5): 1243–1262. Republished in the book: Thomas. H. Ogden, *Coming to life in the consulting room* (2021). [Published in Brazil: "A destruição repensada em 'O uso do objeto e relações por meio de identificações' de Winnicott". *Livro Anual de Psicanálise*, São Paulo, 32 (2) (2018): 321–339].

2016: He publishes the article: "On language and truth in psychoanalysis." *Psychoanalytic Quarterly* 85 (2): 411–426. [Not translated into Portuguese].

2017: He publishes the article: "Dreaming the analytic session: A clinical essay". *Psychoanalytic Quarterly*, 86 (1): 1–20. Republished in the book: Thomas H. Ogden, *Coming to life in the consulting room* (2021). [Not translated into Portuguese].

2017: He gives an interview to Noya Kohavi about his activity as a novel writer: T. H. Ogden and N. Kohavi. "An interview with Thomas Ogden by Noya Kohavi: How psychoanalyst Thomas Ogden found his true self in fiction". *Haaretz*, March 29, 2017.

2018: He publishes the article: "The feeling of real: On Winnicott's 'Communicating and not communicating leading to a study of certain opposites'". *International Journal of Psychoanalysis* 99 (6): 1288–1304. [Translated into Portuguese: "O sentimento do real: Acerca de 'Comunicação e falta de comunicação levando ao estudo de certos opostos' de Winnicott". *Livro Anual de Psicanálise*, São Paulo, 34 (2) (2020): 319–337].

2018: He publishes the article: "How I talk with my patients". *Psychoanalytic Quarterly* 87 (3): 399–413. Republished in the book: Thomas H. Ogden, *Coming to life in the consulting room* (2021). [Translated into Portuguese: "Como falo com meus pacientes", *Revista Multiverso* (Recife), 5 (2022): 140–157].

2018: He publishes a conversation with Ricardo Lombardi: T. H. Ogden and R. Lombardi. "Infinity, The conscious and unconscious mind: A conversation between Thomas Ogden and Riccardo Lombardi". *The Psychoanalytic Quarterly*, 87 (2018): 757–766.

2019: He publishes the article: "Ontological psychoanalysis or 'What do you want to be when you grow up?'" *Psychoanalytic Quarterly*, 88 (4): 661–684. Republished in the book: Thomas H. Ogden, *Coming to life in the consulting room* (2021). [Translated into Portuguese: "Psicanálise ontológica ou 'O que você quer ser quando crescer?'". *Revista Brasileira de Psicanálise*, 54 (1) (2020): 23–45.]

2020: He publishes the article: "Toward a revised form of analytic thinking and practice: The evolution of the analytic theory of mind". *Psychoanalytic Quarterly*, 89 (2): 219–243. Republished in the book: Thomas

H. Ogden, *Coming to life in the consulting room* (2021). [Available in Portuguese: "Rumo a uma forma revisada de pensamento e prática psicanalíticos: A evolução da teoria analítica da mente". *Revista Brasileira de Psicanálise*, 54 (4) (2020): 23–46.

2020: He publishes the article: "Experiencing the poetry of Robert Frost and Emily Dickinson". *Psychoanalytic Perspective*, 17 (2): 183–188. Republished in the book: Thomas H. Ogden, *Coming to life in the consulting room* (2021). [Not translated into Portuguese].

2020: He publishes the article: "Notes on being and becoming". *Fort Da*, 26 (2): 13–20. Republished in the book: Thomas H. Ogden, *Coming to life in the consulting room* (2021). [Not translated into Portuguese].

2021: He publishes his third novel: *This will do … .* London: Sphinx Books. [Not translated into Portuguese].

2021: He publishes the short story: "After the fire: A short story". *Fort Da*, 27: 53–59. [Not translated into Portuguese].

2021: He publishes the poem: "328 West 110th, 11F". *Critica: Newsletter of the Psychoanalytic Institute of Northern California*, September 2021.

2021: He publishes the article: "Analytic writing as a form of fiction". *Journal of the American Psychoanalytic Association (JAPA)*, 69 (1): 221–223. Republished in the book: Thomas H. Ogden, *Coming to life in the consulting room* (2021). [Not translated into Portuguese].

2021: He gives an interview to Nicolas Gougoulis and Katrynn Driffield: N. Gougoulis and K. Driffield. "Interview with Thomas Ogden". *International Forum of Psychoanalysis*, 30 (4) (2021): 223–233. [Not translated into Portuguese].

2021: He publishes the article: "What alive means: On Winnicott's 'Transitional objects and transitional phenomena'". *International Journal of Psychoanalysis*, 102 (5): 837–856. [To be published in Portuguese in *Livro Annual de Psicanálise*, 2023].

2022: He publishes the book: *Coming to life in the consulting room: Toward a new analytic sensibility*. London and New York: Routledge. [Not translated into Portuguese].

2023: He publishes the article: "Like the belly of a bird breathing: On Winnicott's 'Mind and its relation to the psyche-soma'". *International Journal of Psychoanalysis*, 104 (1): 7–22. [Not yet translated into Portuguese].

2024: "Rethinking the concepts of the unconscious and analytic time". *International Journal of Psychoanalysis* 105: 275–291.

2024: "Ontological psychoanalysis in clinical practice". *Psychoanalytic Quarterly* 93: 13–31.

2024: "A morning with Maria Kodama". *Fort Da*, 2024.

2024: "Transformations at the dawn of verbal language". *Journal of the American Psychoanalytic Association*.

2024: "Giving back what the patient brings: On Winnicott's 'mirror-role of mother and family in child development'". *Psychoanalytic Quarterly* 93.

2024: "A letter to a young writer". *Parapraxis,* Summer, 2024.
2024: Will publish the book, *What alive means: Psychoanalytic explorations.* London and New York: Routledge, in press.
2024: Will publish a short-story collection, *Aunt Birdie and other stories.* London: Sphinx Publishers, in press.

Index

For Product Safety Concerns and Information please contact our EU
representative GPSR@taylorandfrancis.com
Taylor & Francis Verlag GmbH, Kaufingerstraße 24, 80331 München, Germany

www.ingramcontent.com/pod-product-compliance
Lightning Source LLC
Chambersburg PA
CBHW050639280326
41932CB00015B/2705

* 9 7 8 1 0 3 2 7 2 9 4 6 6 *